Happy Shopping!

The $erious $hopper's Guide To Vancouver... and Beyond

Serious Publishing
Vancouver

Canadian Cataloguing in Publication Data

Garber, Anne
The serious shopper's guide to Vancouver

Includes index.

1. Shopping--British Columbia--Vancouver--Guidebooks. 2. Shopping--British Columbia--Lower Mainland--Guidebooks. I. Gannon, Lorraine, 1952- II. Title.
TX337.C22V353 1992 381'.45'0002571133
C92-091552-3

Please note: Prices, hours and even proprietors of the stores and shopping areas mentioned herein are subject to change, and therefore specific details cannot be guaranteed. Please call ahead to assure you will not be disappointed! Inclusion in this book is not to be considered an endorsement of goods, stores or shopping areas by the authors or publisher. No remuneration, goods or services have been tendered to or accepted by the authors or publisher in return for inclusion or favourable comment in this book.

Serious Publishing Co.
7249 Waverley Ave.
Burnaby, B.C. V5J 4A7
fax: (604) 875-0007

ISBN 0-9695187-0-6

Anne Garber

The $erious $hopper's Guide To Vancouver... and Beyond

With Lorraine Gannon

Serious Publishing
Vancouver

This book is lovingly dedicated as follows:

To Becky and Kit, who once again were willing to put their needs aside (sort of) and wait patiently while I checked out "just one more place". A.G.

For my family, with love -- especially David and Graham who had to deal with a shopping mother, and Robert, who had to cope with the bills.
L.G.

Another Mercerized edition: Cover design and finished art by Bob Mercer

Furthermore, the text has been Harrised (or would that be 'harrassed'?): We owe an enormous debt of thanks to Doc Harris for desktop publishing this entire sheaf of material and making it come out looking like a book!

Printed and bound in the U.S.A. by
Patterson Printing, Benton Harbor, Michigan

Additional research and assistance by Suzanne Fennell and Becky Johnson.

Additional computer support by Robert Gannon, Peter Macdonald and Doc Harris.

First printing: September 1992, Serious Publishing

Distributed in Canada by Raincoast Book Distribution Ltd.,
112 East 3rd Avenue, Vancouver, B.C. V5T 1C8
(604) 873-6581; fax: (604) 874-2711

Distributed in the United States by Pacific Pipeline,
8030 S. 228th, Kent, WA 98032
(206) 872-5523

Additional distribution (by agreement with): Pacific Press, c/o Promotion Desk,
2250 Granville St. Vancouver, B.C. V6H 3G2
(604) 732-2304

Single copies available directly from Serious Publishing Co. See last page for ordering information.

■Table of Contents■

■ Introduction ■

The genesis of this project actually came not so much from explorations in and around Vancouver, but from travels to foreign cities. For example, we both had separately shopped in Hong Kong and had had similar experiences: while that city (and Kowloon, just across the water) has a small, concentrated downtown, it was quite possible for us to make the trek to one tiny factory outlet at the end of the MTR (subway) only to discover upon returning to our hotel that another place in which we'd loved to have shopped was just around the corner all the time -- and we'd have found it if only we had known about it before we set out.

We learned that even shopping on our home turf in the lower mainland can provide similar disappointments. Without a tipster familiar with a particular area, we were lost. When Anne first began journeying out to the far reaches of Langley and Cloverdale she was like a babe in the woods. Lorraine often worked in Langley, and Anne's girlfriend Lynne had come from Cloverdale, so she could always ring them up in advance for tips on where to go and where to stop for a cup of tea while "out there". But no reference material or guide book was available to address the problem. Local papers -- while often featuring interesting classified ads and tips about sales events -- were no substitute for a handy-dandy, concise guide to the where, the what, and the how much, in areas off our particular beaten track. So we wrote this book.

The Serious Shopper's Guide to Vancouver was written as a companion volume to Anne's earlier -- and very successful -- Vancouver Super Shopper. We hope a long-awaited new edition of the latter book will appear in bookstores in the Summer of 1993.

We wrote each section as a guide to any reader -- whether an in-the-know local, or a just-arrived tourist -- because that's the kind of guidebook we would use.

We know only too well that prices (and even management) change, so where we've referred to the specifics of cost, stock or staff, it is meant merely as a guideline to help you separate the major bargains from the lesser deals, or to sort the truly unique from the mundane.

Our criteria for including a business in this volume were very subjective. We looked for bargains, to be sure, but we also wanted to highlight unusual, hand-made or one-of-a-kind items, and eccentric, amusing ones. Some shops are strictly high-end, but their goods are so remarkable and wonderful, we know you would want us to share them with you!

We also realize that we may have left out your very favourite shopping haunts, so we'd love to hear from you if we've overlooked a special place or area. Please write and let us know why we should consider including it -- and we promise to give it our full consideration for next time. Please write to us at Serious Publishing, 7249 Waverley Ave., Burnaby V5J 4A7, or fax details to 875-0007.

Payment at most stores is acceptable with Visa or Mastercard, and many places will take personal cheques (as long as the cheques are not drawn on an out-of-town bank). The large department stores (and many mall shops) usually accept American Express, but we discovered that London Drugs -- a fairly large chain -- does NOT accept Amex, so plan accordingly. We've tried to note stores that do business on a cash-only basis, but please call ahead to check with a few of the places that sound most interesting to you, if you're going to travel far for a tour and have only credit cards and no money with you!

At the beginning of each tour, we've outlined our best 'guesstimate' length of the tour if you stop at every single place mentioned. We remind you to wear comfortable, appropriate attire and shoes, and to haul rain gear around in the car "just in case". Travel with a friend to save gas (and for a second opinion on impulse purchases) and remember to take this book with you everywhere, so you can take advantage of the restaurant discounts woven into the text. Please note that each restaurant offer IS IN EFFECT ONLY UNTIL DECEMBER 31, 1993.

How to use this book:

With the Serious Shopper's Guide to Vancouver you can choose from quick shopping jaunts, all-day excursions, mall stops, or adventures in new territory. Tours are described by region or municipality.

Comprehensive directions from common departure points (including locations in the U.S.) will bring you quickly to the tour area. For most tours, we have given specifics about how to get to the tour starting point by public transit. Maps which focus tightly on the tour area are interspersed with text, so you can quickly and easily pinpoint the stops that interest you.

We have tried to arrange shopping tours in a natural progression. For example, where the tour is several blocks long (on the same street), the description will usually take you down one side of the street and back on the other.

Those unfamiliar with certain areas will benefit from these hints: Vancouver avenues run east and west (numbering starts at 1st Ave. to the north and avenue numbers get higher as you move southward). Streets run north and south.

Because there are 15 "name" avenues to the north before the numbered avenues begin, in order to find the avenue crossroad by the number on a STREET, subtract 15 from the "hundred" block. So the crossroad for the 3300 block of Dunbar St. would be 18th Ave. The crossroad for the 5800 block of Fraser St. is 43rd Ave., and so on. This greatly simplifies finding your way around.

It's also important to know that the major east-west avenues are 4th Ave. (which at some points becomes 2nd and 6th Avenues); Broadway (the equivalent of 9th Avenue); Grandview Highway which becomes 12th Avenue, which later flows into West 10th Ave. at MacDonald St.; 16th Ave.; King Edward (also known as 25th Ave.); 33rd Ave; 41st Ave; 49th Ave.; and 57th Ave.

Major roads which connect Vancouver to other areas are Kingsway and Marine Drive.

Ontario St. is the central north-south street in Vancouver. Avenues to the east are "East 8th" and those to the west are "West 8th". Numbering ascends 100 numbers per block outward from Ontario St.

In West Van, avenues cleverly ascend the mountain in roughly alphabetical order: Argyle, Bellevue, Clyde, Duchess, Esquimalt, Fulton, Gordon, Haywood, Inglewood, Jefferson and so on. We'll bet most Vancouverites don't know that secret!

Most motorists from outside of the lower mainland are unfamiliar with uncontrolled intersections, which means just because *you* don't have a stopsign, doesn't mean motorists crossing your path will automatically have one. And a flashing green light is not an "advanced green". It indicates a pedestrian-controlled traffic light which may change quickly. Pedestrians have the right of way at ALL intersections, even if the crossing is not marked with a formal crosswalk! Seatbelts are compulsory in B.C.

Back to our book: Read carefully through the table of contents at the front, and simplify your choices. You'll also find it useful to browse through the index at the back of this book -- it's full of essential items you didn't even realize you needed!

We have tried to note hours of operation, so you will not waste time by showing up on Lonsdale at 9 am, only to discover that nothing opens until 10:30. Some areas traditionally close on a weekday (often Monday or Wednesday), and others close for Sunday, so try to read the operating time descriptions carefully, to avoid a trip-for-nothing.

During long forays to research this book, we discovered that the 'work' of shopping really saps our energy, so if you have the same reaction, you'll appreciate a little rest stop en route. Our remedy was to approach a number of restaurants and cafes along the big stretches, to ask them if they could give our readers some kind of perk, discount or freebie, IF READERS BROUGHT IN A COPY OF THE SERIOUS SHOPPER'S GUIDE when they stopped by. What resulted was a bonus for Serious Shoppers: Bring in this book, show it to the server in any of the designated dining establishments, and you'll receive the benefit described in the text for the tour. For instance, the refreshment stop on our West Broadway tour is Benny's Bagels. Their offer to our readers is a free hot beverage with any meal. If you're shopping with two friends and bring along your copy of the book, you'll EACH get free coffee with your sandwiches -- but remember to bring and show your book before ordering. Restaurant offers will be honoured up to and including December 31, 1993.

Now, what are you sitting here reading for? Grab your coat and your Serious Shopper's Guide and get shopping!

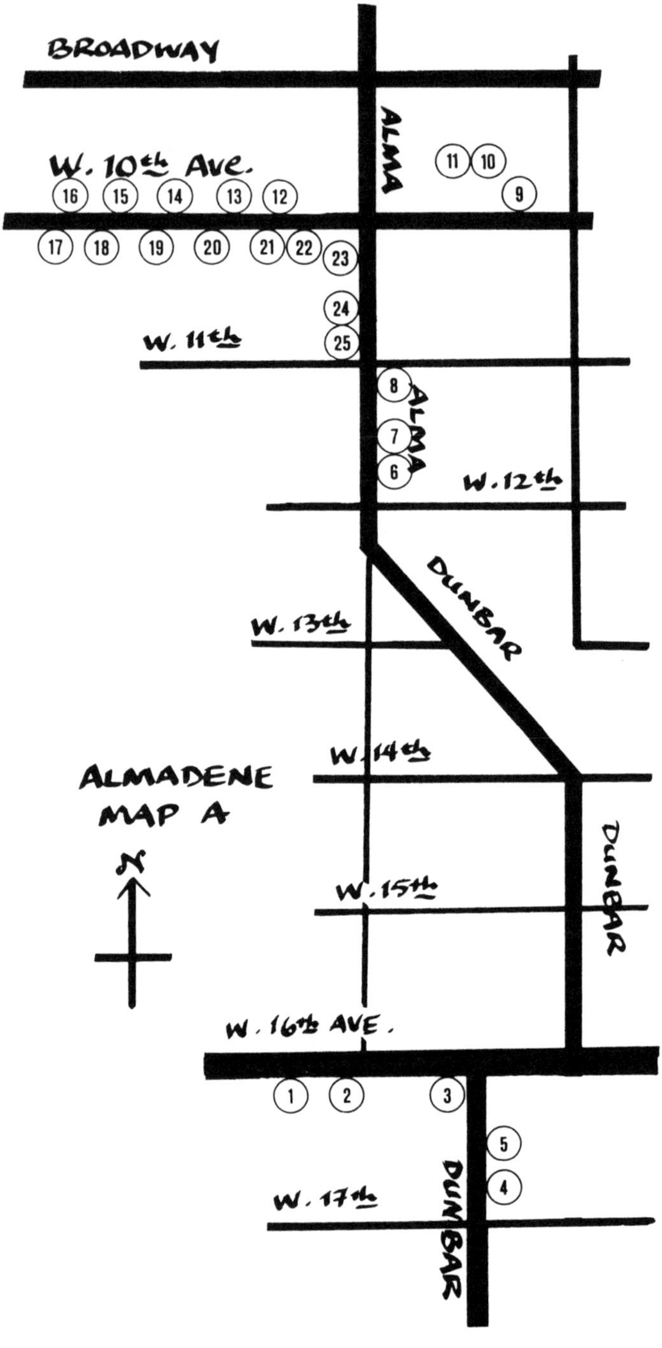
BROADWAY
ALMA
W. 10th AVE.
W. 11th
ALMA
W. 12th
DUNBAR
W. 13th
W. 14th
ALMADENE
MAP A
N
W. 15th
DUNBAR
W. 16th AVE.
DUNBAR
W. 17th
1
2
3
4
5
6
7
8
9
10
11
12
13
14
15
16
17
18
19
20
21
22
23
24
25

Almadene

Eclectic: Something for every taste

This is an ancilliary tour, which can be appended to Pt. Grey, Broadway, West 4th Ave. or even the Kerrisdale tour. You can visit all stops in under one hour.

Technically, the area locals refer to as 'Almadene' is pretty much just the area on Broadway and West 10th one block on either side of Alma, but in order to include some other good shopping finds, we've added a few places in the 'North Dunbar' area, near West 16th and Dunbar. As Dunbar approaches West 16th Ave., the road curves sharply eastward -- and when you drive out of that curve, you discover you're then on Alma. North of West 14th Ave., in fact, Dunbar is a tiny residential street, not at all resembling the bustling commercial street it is just to the south.

Street parking is easy to find and it's free. As well, a small lot serves patrons of the few shops in the tiny strip mall anchored by The Captain.

To get to the area, follow directions given for our Pt. Grey tour and head south on Alma, past the curve at 16th. Our tour starts at 16th and Dunbar.

<u>Cheapskates:</u> 3644 West 16th (222-1125). This is the original location of the consignment sporting goods store which is so wonderful that it has virtually dominated the market in its chosen field. This branch stocks skis, hockey equipment and skates in winter; baseball gear, tennis, squash and badminton racquets, camping items and hiking boots in summer. Everything in the store is sold on consignment, with prices reduced every couple of weeks until someone buys it. After the store takes off its modest commission, the balance is sent to the seller by cheque, which is very convenient for all concerned. Hours are Monday to Thursday 11 to 6; Friday 11 to 8; Saturday 10 to 6; and Sunday 11 to 5. Map A circle 1.

<u>Bizarre Bazaar:</u> 3626 West 16th Ave. (224-6212). This shop buys and sells collectible sports cards, comics, illustration magazines and books and other memorabilia. Hours are Monday to Thursday 10 to 5:30; Friday noon to 6; Saturday noon to 7; and Sunday noon to 5. Map A circle 2.

<u>D & R Secondhand Store:</u> 3211 Dunbar St. (222-0122). Self- described as an antique store, actually this is mostly full of used stereos, TVs, VCRs and some other appliances. There are a few antiques, as well.

Hours are Monday to Saturday 10 to 6; and Sunday 10 to 5. Map A circle 3.

Cheapskates Too: 3228 Dunbar (734-1191). Just around the corner from the original you'll find another shop (owner Barry Gilpin says instead of going up the escalator in the department store, you walk down the sidewalk to the next department -- kind of a horizontal department store). This one sells bicycles, bike parts, golf equipment, and windsurfing, waterskiing and scuba stuff. Hours identical to Cheapskates. Map A circle 4.

Cheapskates-3?: 3208 Dunbar (739-1125). The next 'department' is two doors down. This one carries consigned sports clothing and a selection of new samples, seconds, ends-of-lines, etc. for cyclists. Same hours as the other two stores. Map A circle 5.

Navigate your way around the curve (to the right, then to the left) to continue the tour.

Prussin Music: 2780 Alma (736-3036). Here is one of Vancouver's finest sources for brass, woodwinds and expert service for these and other instruments. Open Monday to Friday 10 to 6; and Saturday 10 to 5. Map A circle 6.

The Doyen Violin Shop: 2760 Alma (731-7422). This place, with its hand-hewn wooden sign, is another top source: this time as violin (viola, 'cello) dealers and restorers. Hours: Monday to Friday 1:30 to 5:30; and Saturday 10:30 to 5:30. Map A circle 7.

Ernie's Austria Bakery & Delicatessen: 2660 Alma (731-3010). These folks keep trying to retire, but the legions of fans of their German-style breads won't let them! Many claim their sourdough rye is the best in town. Open Tuesday to Thursday 10 to 7; Friday 9 to 8; Saturday 9 to 6; and closed Sunday and Monday. Map A circle 8.

The Captain's Antiques & Furniture: 3645 West 10th (222-2775). Featured here are electronics, musical instruments, a few lovely pieces of antique furniture, clocks, wardrobes and even some used bikes out front. Hours are Monday to Saturday 10 to 8; and Sunday noon to 6. Map A circle 9.

Patisserie Bordeaux: 3675 West 10th (731-6551). A genuine Franch bake shop, this one features croque'm'bouche, Paris Brest, St. Honore, pit'hiviers, mousses, savarin, tourtieres, quiches, pastries, gateaux, breads, home-made multi-grain crackers, and a brilliant assortment of other petits-fours. Custom orders and catering are available. Open

Tuesday to Friday 8 to 7; weekends 8 to 6; closed Mondays. Map A circle 10.

Georgie's: 3675 West 10th (739-8121). Formerly Jericho Coffee & Tea, this place has relocated right next door to Patisserie Bordeaux on the site of Hasta be Pasta in the little strip mall anchored by "the Captain". The place includes a cappuccino bar, some tables, and serves muffins, light sandwiches and of course, coffee. They also sell coffee and tea accessories, imported lines of those beverages, collectors' tea pots, small cappuccino machines for home-use and stove-top espresso machines. Georgie's is our official rest-stop for the Almadene tour, so if you bring your copy of the Serious Shopper's Guide with you when you stop in for a bite, you *(and anyone shopping with you)* will receive a discount of 20 percent off any food and drink you order. Map A circle 11.

Jim Shockey Folkart Antiques: 3715 West 10th (228-1011). This wonderful and unique store houses a collection of nice pine furniture, but everywhere - in every nook and cranny, and even right underfoot -- is the most incredible folk art you'll ever see! Most of the art pieces were done "by an old guy who lives on Vancouver Island" (said the store manager), a talented and whimsical fellow named Don Thompson. There's a wooden sleeping dog on a hearth mat. There are lots of cows, cows dressed as waitresses, cow skulls, cowboys, cactus, mounties, dogs and cats. There are birds and fish. Many of these one-of-a-kind carved and painted beauties have been rented out to dress film sets. They're not cheap, but they are terrific. Hours are Monday to Saturday 10 to 6; and Sunday noon to 4. Map A circle 12.

Siliconnections: 3727 West 10th (222-2221). This place specializes (as you might have guessed) in magazines, business books, special orders and everything imaginable for the computer whiz -- or novice. Hours are Monday to Friday 9 to 7; and Saturday 10 to 6. Map A circle 13.

Forest Hills Antiques: 3733 West 10th (222-4992). A new antique store to the area, this one carries quality items of several vintages, and specializes in early Canadian pine and accessories from Eastern Canada. Hours are Tuesday to Saturday 11 to 6 and sometimes change seasonally, so call ahead. Map A circle 14.

Oven-Fresh Bakery: 3735 West 10th (228-8438). Longjohns and glazed doughnuts beckon from the window. They also sell the most ginormous cottage cheese buns dusted with icing sugar (cheap at 89 cents apiece) and big, healthy cookies for just 70 cents. Hours are Monday to Thursday 9 to 6; Friday 9 to 7; and Saturday 9 to 6:30. Map A circle 15.

West Point Cycles: 3771 West 10th (224-3536). Here the focus is on mountain bikes, helmets, tires, bike magazines and racing pants. Hours are Monday to Saturday 9:30 to 6; and Sunday 11 to 5. Map A circle 16.

A Piece of Cake: 3788 West 10th (228-9816). Take out a cappuccino or slice of (or entire) delicious cake. Hours are Monday to Saturday 7 a.m. to midnight; and Sunday 9 a.m. to 10 p.m. Map A circle 17.

Ashley's Books: 3754 West 10th (228-1180). This place offers a big selection of nicely-presented, good quality used books, both hardvoer and paperbacks. Hours are Monday to Friday noon to 8; Saturday noon to 5; and Sunday 11 to 5. Map A circle 18.

Hopeful Market: 3742 West 10th (228-0173). You could easily overlook this place (it looks like any old corner grocery) -- but don't: They offer great prices on potted bulbs and cut flowers, such as mini-daffs in a clay pot for just 99 cents; African violets for $1.45; and a bunch of cut tulips for 99 cents! As well, if you need centrepieces, for example, there's a discount on any five purchases of 10 percent; and buying 10 items reduces your cost by 20 percent. Open seven days 9 to 7. Map A circle 19.

Ted Mould Upholstery Service: 3730 West 10th (228-8820). Excellent (and reasonable) upholsterers, they work only by appointment. Parking available in the back. Map A circle 20.

Old Country Antiques: 3720 West 10th (224-8660). Here you'll find pine furniture - cupboards, tables, chests, blanket boxes, benches, marble-topped washstands, shelves and so on, all immaculately hand-finished. In fact, they sell their own 'old antique pine wax' in jars that look just like my preserves! They also carry a fine assortment of potpourri and decor accents, but by far the most unique items are the statues and garden benches made in England from reconstituted stone and sand. There are cherubs ($245), a whimsical pig in bas-relief ($195.) and a serenading cat ($245), to name but a few. Hours are Monday to Saturday 10 to 6; and Sunday noon to 5. Map A circle 21.

Garcia Flowers: 3714 West 10th (222-0202). This quality flower shop sells dried and fresh flowers in arrangements in baskets, pots or tubs, all ready for giving. They also carry silk flowers, potpourri, piñatas and even chocolates by Tout Sweet. Hours are Monday to Saturday 9 to 6. Map A circle 22.

Nipper's Tog'n Toy: 3712 West 10th (222-4035). Moved for some time from its earlier location in south Dunbar, the store still carries the same selection of good-quality children's consignment clothing, toys and other goods (like the vintage wooden high chairs in the window). Hours are Monday and Saturday 10 to 5; Tuesday to Friday 9:30 to 4:30; and closed Sunday. Map A circle 23.

Crystal Gift Shop: 2615 Alma (228-9460). A subtle reminder that we do indeed live on the Westcoast, this little shop sells (and repairs) custom jewellery, incense, tarot cards, cards, posters, crystals, chakra kits and chakra oils, and offers psychic readings, tarot readings and palmistry. Open Monday to Saturday 11 to 6:30; closed Sunday. Map A circle 24.

Rufus Guitar Shop: 2621 Alma (222-1717). Fine instruments and repairs are the focus here, with guitars, banjos, sitars, electric instruments, and even a musical saw for sale. Hours: Monday to Friday 10 to 6; Saturday 10 to 5; closed Sunday. Map A circle 25.

Further up the Dunbar hill (and not technically in Almadene) are these two shops so unique that we just had to include them:

Puddleduck Lane: 4288 Dunbar (736-2240). This new kids' consignment shop at 27th and Dunbar is operated by Janet Dodson and Nancy Leard who have scouted the area for talented home-sewers. Items of every kind are attractively displayed in the store. Anything you like can be custom-ordered to your specifications. They also stock some new samples and are keeping a display board for people who want to buy or sell large items like cribs and prams. Hours are Monday to Saturday 10 to 5.

Fourteen Plus: 4235 Dunbar (222-1895). This is the newest incarnation of "Fancy a New Look?" but it still carries the same fine consignment stock for queen sized women. Hours are Monday to Friday 10 to 6; and Saturday 9:30 to 6.

NOTES:

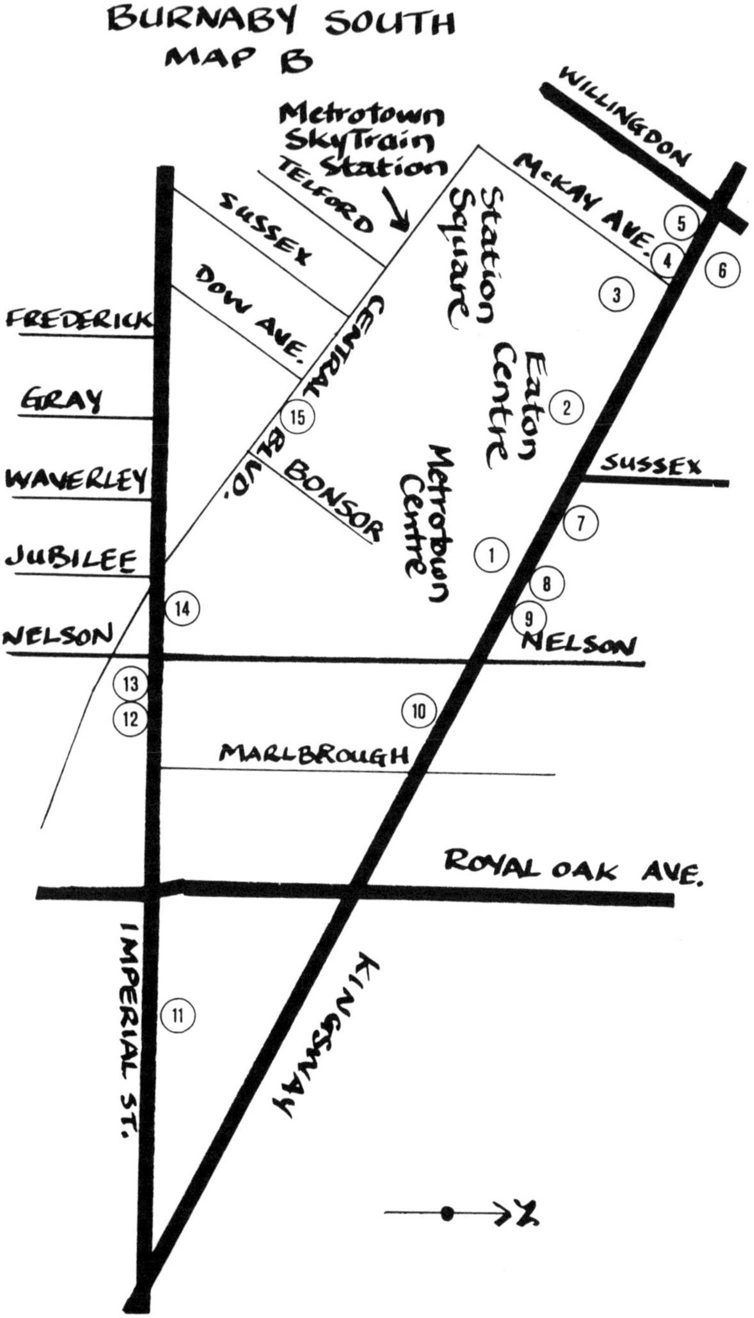
BURNABY SOUTH
MAP B
WILLINGDON
Metrotown
SkyTrain
Station
TELFORD
McKAY AVE.
SUSSEX
Station
Square
DOW AVE.
FREDERICK
CENTRAL BLVD.
Eaton
Centre
GRAY
BONSOR
Metrotown
Centre
SUSSEX
WAVERLEY
JUBILEE
NELSON
NELSON
MARLBROUGH
ROYAL OAK AVE.
IMPERIAL ST.
KINGSWAY
1
2
3
4
5
6
7
8
9
10
11
12
13
14
15

Burnaby (South), for Bargains

This is a major tour for which you should budget three to four hours, if you plan to stop at each place.

The area we refer to as South Burnaby runs pretty much from Willingdon to Royal Oak Ave., in a big triangle between Imperial and Kingsway.

The area can be reached from Kingsway (the original 'main' street connecting Vancouver, Burnaby, New West and Surrey). You can also get there via Imperial, which is an eastern extension (in Burnaby) of 49th Ave. in Vancouver. Transit patrons can take the SkyTrain right to Metrotown station, which will place you in the approximate epicentre of some of the lower mainland's best bargains.

Parking is sometimes difficult on Kingsway (avoid rush hour!), but Metrotown and its sister shopping malls offer scads of free parking undercover, at street level, and rooftop. Many of our tour stops are within walking distance of the mall. We've noted which places are actually IN one of the malls, to save you time and confusion. Except where noted in text for specific stores, most shops follow Metrotown and Eaton Centre mall hours, which are Monday and Tuesday 10 to 6; Wednesday to Friday 10 to 9; Saturday 9:30 to 6; and Sunday noon to 5.

Fun Under $5 (Metrotown): 338, 4820 Kingsway (439-7468). Nothing here costs more than $5 and most of the items are less. Choose from housewares, toys, gift items, seasonal things and our favorite (cheap) shareware computer programs for IBM. Find the shop on the top floor, near the Bay. Map B circle 1.

Classic Rattan & Wicker (Metrotown): 318, 4820 Kingsway (431-8677). Though they don't bill themselves as discounters, we find the prices so good that we had to include them in this tour. They sell wicker and rattan furniture and accessories. Find them on the top floor of the Bay connector. Map B circle 1.

The Clothing Mart (Metrotown): 202, 4820 Kingsway (431-1822). This is a good discount source for jeans, jackets, T-shirts and casual clothing in men's and women's sizes. Find them on the ground floor level in the Bay connector. Map B circle 1.

Frugal Feet (Metrotown): 216, 4820 Kingsway (436-5817). Here we found discount runners and some sports clothing, also bargain-priced. The store is located on the ground floor of the Bay connector. Map B circle 1.

Book Warehouse (Metrotown): 258, 4820 Kingsway (434-5711). This is one of the best deals in town: 'remaindered' soft and hard-cover books, posters, calendars and even some candles and greeting cards - all at deeply discounted prices. Even current best-sellers are 20 percent off! We have two secrets to share: one is to shop Book Warehouse "generically", which means look for books in a category, rather than by specific title. So if your friend Barb would appreciate a book on barbecuing, just go to the cookbook section and browse -- you're sure to find something perfect; the other is that stock-code numbers on their price tags that begin with "35" are usually one of a kind bargains that won't be there next time if you hesitate to buy it now. No risk is involved, because -- provided you do not remove the price-tag and you keep your receipt -- all books may be cheerfully refunded for a full credit if you've made a mistake. Find the store fronting on Kingsway and on the ground floor of the Bay connector. Map B circle 1.

Braemar Clearance (Metrotown): 288, 4800 Kingsway (430-1719). Quality designer clothing is cleared at up to 70 percent off at this clearance centre located on the ground level near Sears. There is always a rack of even further-reduced items at the store's entrance. Map B circle 1.

Sears Clearance Centre (Metrotown): 4750 Kingsway (433-3211). Huge savings on family clothing, housewares and some furniture (usually scratch'n'dent) may be had here for the patient shopper willing to sift the wheat from the chaff. It's located in the basement of Sears. Map B circle 1.

Willson's Stationery Annex (Metrotown): 199, 4800 Kingsway (435-0205). This is the clearance centre for the chain of Willson Stationers, where everyday office supplies and stationery, as well as seasonal items are significantly reduced. We found great stocking stuffers and small gift items, too. It's located on the basement level across from the regular Willson store, near Sears. Map B circle 1.

Field's (Metrotown): 165, 4800 Kingsway (434-4416). The lower-end source is well known for family clothing, footwear and some household goods. The also have a large 'Plus Size' section for the larger woman. Find it at the basement level, near Woodward's. Map B circle 1.

Woodwynn (Metrotown): 4800 Kingsway (433-1222). This is Woodward's own discount family clothing and footwear store, located at the basement level of the Woodward's store. We've often found good buys in bedding and towels here. Map B circle 1.

The Bread Garden: 4575 Central Blvd. (435-5177). This is the designated rest stop for South Burnaby. Owner and entrepreneur Linda Meinhardt puts her personal stamp on everything she does, and this location of her now-famous Bread Gardens is no different. The advantage for devotees of this book is that this particular Bread Garden offers the person carrying the Serious Shoppers Guide -- and a guest -- a free cup of coffee with their order if they show this book to their server prior to ordering. The offer, like others in this book, is in effect until December 31, 1993. Open seven days, 24 hours. Map B circle 15.

Flash (Eaton Centre): 1136A, 4700 Kingsway (439-9444). Costume jewellery, earrings and hair accessories are all sold at marked-down prices. Earrings are conveniently arranged by colour and non-pierced styles are indicated by a dot on their display card. Find it on the ground floor near McDonald's and across from Bentley's. Map B circle 2.

Bentley (Eaton Centre): 1165, 4700 Kingsway (432-9229). Across from Flash (and on the ground floor near McDonald's) you'll find this discount source for handbags, wallets, costume jewellery and hats. Map B circle 2.

The Real Canadian Superstore (Eaton Centre): 4700 Kingsway (439-4400). Much as we hate to admit it, the concept of the low-frills mega store seems to make economic sense to families watching their budgets. And this particular edition of Superstore is pretty much our personal favourite: we save at least 30 percent on our groceries by shopping here. On the downside, choices are sometimes limited and if you don't shop for specials early in the sale period (starting each Sunday), you will often find they're out of stock -- and NO rainchecks are given.

In addition to groceries, there's family clothing (with mark-down clothing racks at the back of that section), bulk foods and a case lot section. Occasional items are discounted at the back of the housewares department, too. Bring your own bags (and prepare to pack them yourself, too). Hours here are 9 a.m. to 10 p.m., seven days. Map B circle 2.

Save-on Foods & Drugs (Station Square): 6100 McKay (433-2774). While the mega stores duke it out, consumers can save -- bigtime! Here, there's a special case lot department, tidy bulk foods, fresh seafood, and in-store bakery and discounted books and magazines (standard discount is 10 percent -- sometimes they have special deals and the savings are even greater). Hours are 8 a.m. to midnight, seven days. Map B circle 3.

Consumers Distributing (Station Square): 128, 6200 McKay (432-1124). Again, they're often out of something you want, but their prices are usually unbeatable. Still we remember to "caveat emptor" here. Map B circle 3.

Egghead Discount Software (Station Square): 140, 6200 McKay Ave. (432-6633). This is one place to visit after you've price-checked elsewhere, because they are not always the cheapest -- yet they'll price-match all competitors. They have a sale catalogue they'll send to you if you add your name to their list. They also offer their free "cue" card deal for 5 percent off -- inquire about how it works. AND, there's a table of mark-down software. Map B circle 3.

Future Shop (Station Square): 144, 6200 McKay (435-5111). Sometimes criticized for its high-pressure tactics, this place is still worth including in your hunt for low prices for stereos, phones, barbecues and TVs. Loss-leaders are usually great deals and their seasonal sales are legendary. Map B circle 3.

Discount Shoes & Boots (Station Square): 6207 McKay Ave. (438-0317). Now moved to a new, more visible location in the mall, they sell western boots and men's and women's shoes at low prices. Open Monday, Tuesday and Saturday 11 to 6; Wednesday 11 to 7; and Thursday and Friday 11 to 8. Map B circle 3.

A & B Sound: 4568 Kingsway (439-0223). This place offers sales of one kind or another year-round and their Boxing Day blowout sale makes crowds queue around the block. Some of the best prices we've found are here, on stereos and compact discs, and they offer their "30 day price protection" policy, insuring you that they offer the cheapest prices. Open Monday, Tuesday and Saturday 9 to 6; Wednesday to Friday 9 to 9; and Sunday 11 to 5. Map B circle 4.

Save-on-thrift Store: 4530 Kingsway (439-1912). This place buys and sells used books, furniture, china, clothing and jewellery. Open Monday to Saturday 11 to 5. Map B circle 5.

Sport Mart: 4533 Kingsway (430-1999). Their stated pledge is: "Canada's guaranteed lowest prices! We will beat any price in Canada by 25 percent of the difference, or it's your free". Of course they will -- what's 25 percent of the DIFFERENCE, anyway? But this does help insure their prices are low. Choose from discount sports equipment and clothing. The bulk of their stock changes seasonally (ie. in winter lots of ski stuff). Hours are Monday to Thursday and Saturday 9 to 6; Friday 9 to 9; and Sunday 11 to 5. Map B circle 6.

Finders Keepers: 4785 Kingsway (437-5530). This one sells antiques, collectibles, used housewares, beer company neon signs, jewellery and old license plates, etc. Open Monday to Thursday and Saturday 10 to 5:30; Friday 10 to 8. Map B circle 7.

Shoe Strings: 4853 Kingsway (435-6504). Advertising "Brand name apparel & footwear", this store does not have all sizes in all styles, but you'll find great buys if they do have what you want in your size. Open Monday to Wednesday 10 to 5:30; Thursday and Friday 10 to 9; Saturday 9:30 to 5; and Sunday noon to 5. Map B circle 8.

Dave's Surplus: 4865 Kingsway (431-6232). This new military surplus store sports both the Canadian and American flags on its sign. There is a great deal of military clothing -- and that's just what it is: A great deal! There are boots, uniforms (including authentic Desert Storm camouflage items) and everything else from ammo-boxes to mess-trays (which are surprisingly practical for picnics!). They also carry new and used camping equipment. Open Monday to Saturday 9:30 to 5:30. Map B circle 9.

London Drugs: 4870 Kingsway (520-9006). This is not the largest of their branches, but London Drugs is such a good bargain-hunter's standby that we had to include it. There's always a 10 percent discount on books and magazines, an excellent camera department, and usually some featured buys in cameras, housewares, electronics, small electricals, candy and video or audio tape. Open Monday to Saturday 9 a.m. to 10 p.m.; Sunday 10 to 8. Map B circle 10.

Metrotown New & Used Liquidators: 5329 Imperial (438-6629). Something of a misnomer, because they're actually southeast of Metrotown, this place sells used office furniture, antiques and collectibles, store close-outs, etc. We found them not overly cheap in the used furniture area, but the close-outs offer some unexpected deals -- certainly worth a look on your tour. Open Monday to Friday 9:30 to 5. Map B circle 11.

Tri Software Inc: 4926 Imperial (431-7978). Here you can buy a lifetime membership for $25. Among other things, this entitles you to get a 2-day 'evaluation' of a software program (ie time to copy it) and you can also bring in your own software and trade 'evaluation' time with them -- sort of like video rentals for computers. Open Monday to Friday 5 to 10; and Saturday noon to 5. Map B circle 12.

Imperial Books: 4924 Imperial (432-9940). They advertise "new and used", but we've only ever seen used paperback and magazines here. The store is partitioned: one half is adult only and the other emphasizes spy, western, science fiction and other adventure novels, with a few romances salted in for balance. There are bargain boxes and a table of under-$2 values. Open Monday to Friday 10 to 8; Saturday 10 to 6; and Sunday noon to 6. Map B circle 13.

The Compact Disc Exchange: 4853 Imperial (439-7666). A favourite stop of ours ever since we got our CD deck, this one carries used compact discs on a buy, sell and exchange basis. They'll buy yours for up to $6 and most of their discs for sale go for about $9. Hours are Monday to Thursday 11 to 6; Friday 11 to 9; Saturday 10 to 5; and Sunday noon to 5. Map B circle 14.

NOTES:

Burnaby-Coquitlam

This is a mini-tour which should take under two hours.

You can reach this area easily via either the Lougheed Highway or TransCanada 1. Watch for the North Road exit.

If travelling from the U.S., cross at Blaine (Peace Arch), follow Hwy 99 north and cross the Pattullo Bridge into New West. You'll see signs immediately for "North Road, Coquitlam" which will lead you there. Parking is easy in this area.

The simplest transit route is to take the SkyTrain to Columbia Station and transfer to the #147 or #148 bus.

Unique Gallery: 101, 4501 North Road. (421-3996). Their signage says "quality furniture with the extra touch of elegance but without the high price tag" and that kind of covers the subject. We found wicker furniture, rattan rockers, baskets and accent pieces all at good prices. We especially liked the palm frond covered pottery jars. Open Monday to Saturday 10 to 5. Map C circle 1.

Dots Discount Ladies' Wear: 103, 4501 North Road (421-1050). They make the gutsy claim "lowest prices in Canada or its yours free". This location is a little more "jumbley" than the others, but they do have their share of Esprit, Marc A'Alcy, Naf Naf, Daymor and some large size lines like Leslie Faye. They even carry some children's sizes here. Open Monday to Friday 10 to 9; Saturday 10 to 5:30; and Sunday 11 to 5. Map C circle 2.

Canadian Tire: 106, 4501 North Road (421-9390). The usual sporting goods, camping supplies, car accessories and housewares you expect to find at Canadian Tire are here, and they have good sales, too (with a good stock of the sale items). Open Mon, Tuesday and Saturday 9 to 6; Wednesday to Friday 9 to 9; and Sunday 10 to 6. Map C circle 3.

Fanny's Fabrics: 110, 4501 North Road (420-5016). Fabric Club members get special deals here. There's a clearance wall and a good selection of fabric and craft supplies, as well as frequent spotlight sales. Open Monday and Tuesday 9:30 to 6; Wednesday to Friday 9:30 to 9; Saturday 9:30 to 5; and Sunday 11 to 5. Map C circle 4.

Once Again Rose: 207, 4501 North Road (420-0912). This nice assortment of consignment clothing and shoes is further enhanced by new jewellery and the promise of even greater bargains in the back room, where the discount is 25 percent. Open Tuesday to Saturday 10 to 5. Map C circle 5.

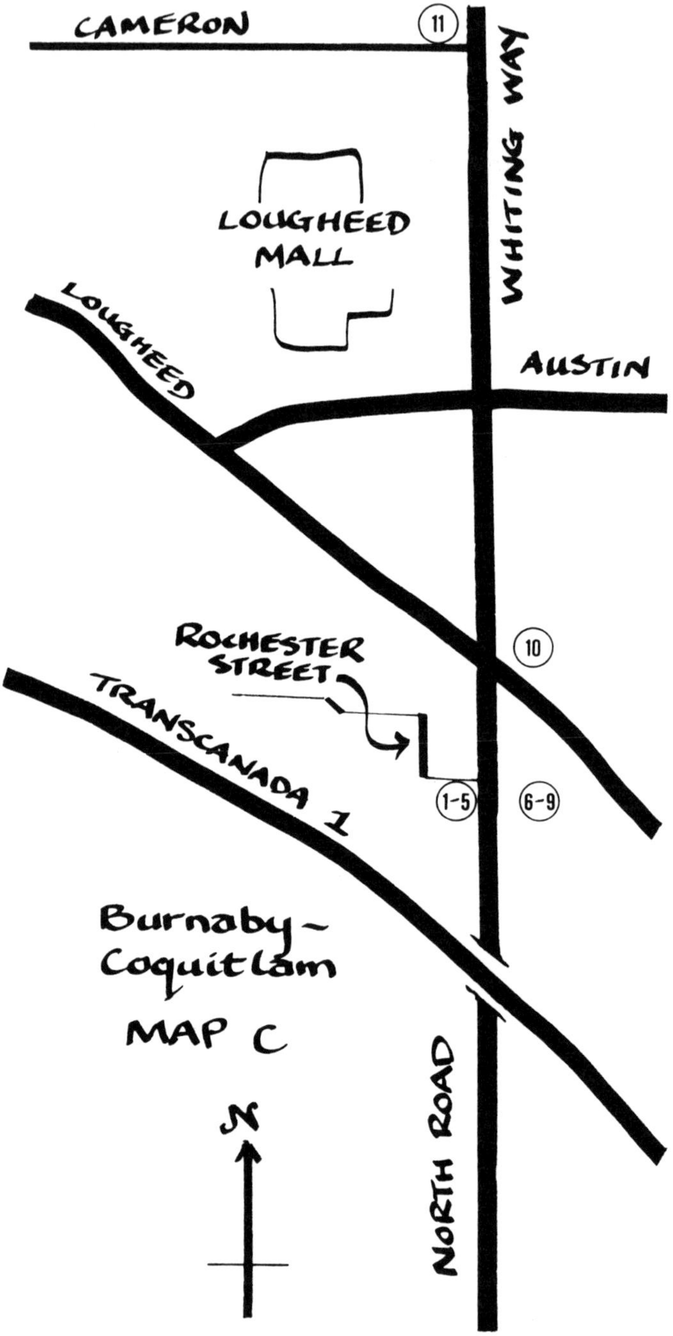
CAMERON
11
WHITING WAY
LOUGHEED
MALL
LOUGHEED
AUSTIN
ROCHESTER
STREET
10
TRANSCANADA 1
1-5
6-9
Burnaby-
Coquitlam
MAP C
N
NORTH ROAD

London Drugs: 100, 329 North Road (520-9025). Another London Drugs outlet with housewares, excellent (fast) photofinishing and 10 percent off all books. Open Monday to Saturday 9 a.m. to 10 p.m.; and Sunday 10 to 8. Map C circle 6.

McGavin's Bread Basket: 260, 329 North Road (936-2112). We've been known to fill our freezers with the 10-loaf special (you can mix varieties of bread) and even their "normal" bread is discounted. Seniors get an extra 10 percent off on Wednesday and Sunday and Tuesday everyone gets 10 percent off. They also sell crackers, buns and packaged cookies. Open Monday to Saturday 9:30 to 5:30; and Sunday noon to 5. Map C circle 7.

Field's: 600, 329 North Road (939-6555). Family clothing and footwear is the feature here. This particular store has a large children's section and it's more upbeat, neat and tidy than most. They have a small "Plus Size" department for larger sizes. Open Monday to Thursday and Saturday 9:30 to 5:30; Friday 9:30 to 9; and Sunday noon to 5. Map C circle 8.

Ed's Linen Warehouse: 530, 329 North Road (936-2722). This discount store sells sheets, towels, placemats and bathroom items and offers a made-to-order service as well. Open Monday to Wednesday and Saturday 9:30 to 5:30; Thursday and Friday 9:30 to 9; and Sunday noon to 5. Map C circle 9.

Las Vegas Discount Golf & Tennis: 207, 403 North Road (939-0101). This large store sells clubs, racquets, clothing and sport supplies at a discount and there's even a mini-putting green so you can practise your "short game". Open Monday to Thursday and Saturday 10 to 6; Friday 10 to 9; and Sunday 11 to 5. Map C circle 10.

Pennington's Wearhouse Store: 150, 3355 North Road (420-0118). Specializing in large size clothing has paid off for this store, shall we say through thick and thin? This is the clearance centre for all the regional retail stores, and they also purchase some lower priced items just to sell at this location. There are petite (short) sizes as well as regular lengths. Open Monday, Tuesday and Saturday 9:30 to 5:30; Wednesday to Friday 9:30 to 9; and Sunday noon to 5. Map C circle 11.

NOTES:

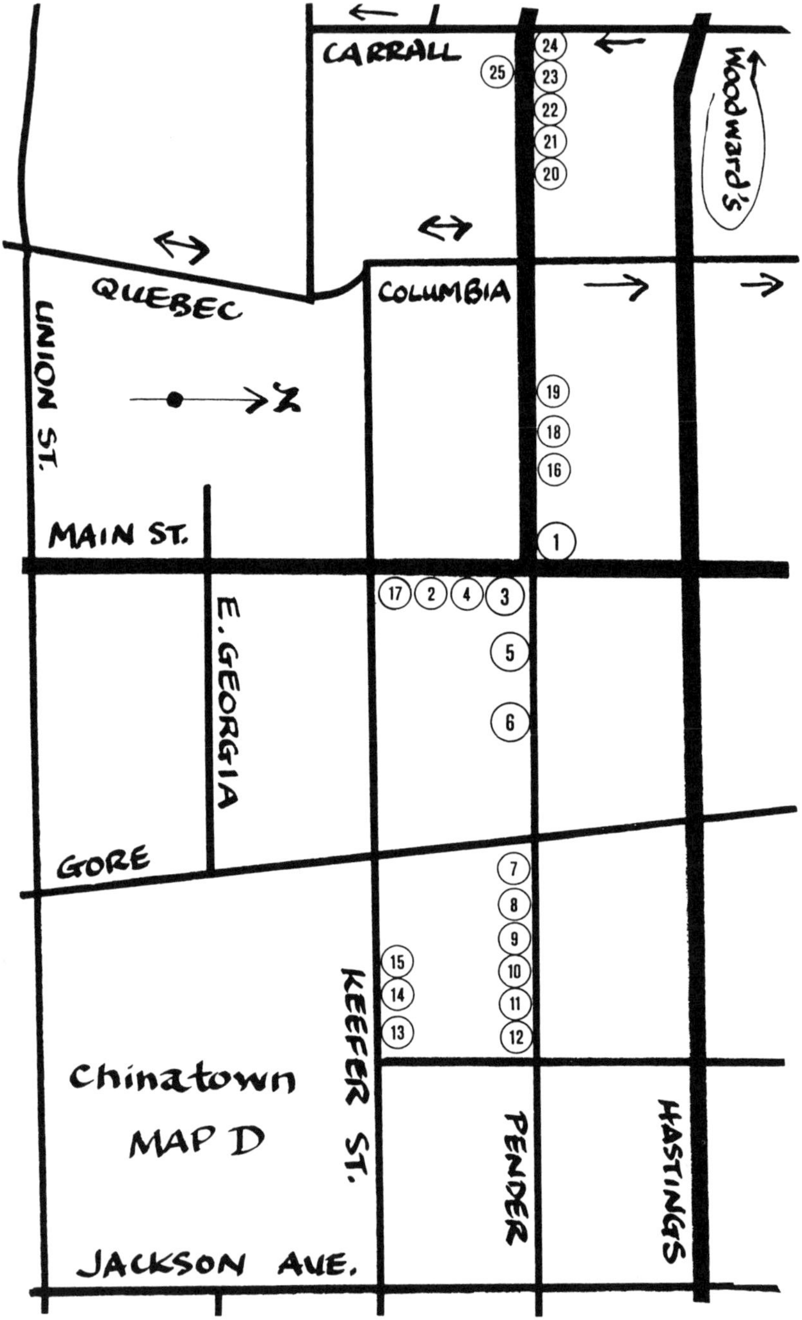
CARRALL
QUEBEC
COLUMBIA
UNION ST.
MAIN ST.
E. GEORGIA
GORE
KEEFER ST.
PENDER
HASTINGS
Woodward's
JACKSON AVE.
Chinatown
MAP D
1
2
3
4
5
6
7
8
9
10
11
12
13
14
15
16
17
18
19
20
21
22
23
24
25

Chinatown

Another world

This is a medium-sized tour which should take one to two hours. If you dawdle or get stalled at a tea ceremony, plan to spend longer.

Vancouver's Chinatown is the largest in Canada, and in North America it's second in size only to San Francisco's! Don't miss the world's thinnest building (Guinness Book of Records) -- the Sam Kee Building at 8 West Pender, which today houses the offices of well-known businessman Jack Chow. The Sun Yat Sen Gardens are worth a visit, too (fabulous gift shop) at 578 Carrall St. If you're looking for baskets, we like Cathay Imports, but it's wise to shop door-to-door for prices and styles you like. We've found dollars of difference from one shop to another in the same block.

The area, bordering on the residential section of Chinatown known as Strathcona, is found in the vicinity of Main and Pender Streets. To reach the area by public transit, take the #22 bus south on Burrard or the #19 bus east on Pender.

Parking is scarce as hen's teeth (though come to think of it, you can probably BUY hen's teeth in Chinatown -- they've got everything else!), so our best tip is to park at the DPC lot at Keefer and Columbia where hourly rates are cheap. Choose a clear day because this is a tour which is definitely better on foot.

Chung Kiu Chinese Products Emporium: 495 Main St. (682-7990). This place looks exactly like the Chinese Arts & Crafts shops in Hong kong, with everything from jade carvings and silk imports to silk-covered boxes, fans, rosewood chopsticks and more. Open seven days 10 to 6. Map D circle 1.

Park Lock Seafood Restaurant: 544 Main St. (688-1581). This is a local favourite for dim sum, offering a simplified dim sum guide for the uninitiated. Open seven days 10 to 3; and Tuesday to Sunday 5 to 10. Map D circle 2.

Hing Wah Limited: 506 Main (683-3838). This shop is filled with herbal remedies, dried seahorses, dried snakes, lizards, jinseng and more than 20 varieties of tea. We found black seaweed imported from China (the long strands, like the vermicelli they also sell, represent wishes for the long life of family and guests).

This is also the location of the practise of the famous Dr. Wu, an herbalist so renowned that people come from a number of U.S. states as well as all over B.C. to queue up for hours for a consultation. It's first come, first served (take a number on arrival) and prescribed herbs are then chopped up and dispensed on site. Open seven days 9 to 6. Map D circle 3.

Hing Lung Foods: 512 Main (688-3300). Here's a good source for bright and inexpensive gift wrap. Open seven days 9 to 6. Map D circle 4.

Cathay Importers: 104 East Pender (684-2632). This is Anne's favourite Chinatown source for baskets. Open Monday to Saturday 9 to 6; and Sunday 11 to 6. Map D circle 5.

Oriental Dragon: 154 East Pender (681-0030). This is a nice gift shop with a variety of unusual items. Open seven days 10:30 to 6:15. Map D circle 6.

Man Sing Meat Centre: 224 East Pender (681-4491, 687-5252). Nearly 20 butchers (including a woman, wielding a cleaver) are hard at work in neat white caps here serving throngs of customers. Theirs is considered the best roast pork in town. They also sell barbecue pork and roast duck among other succulent delicacies. Open seven days 8 to 6:30. Map D circle 7.

Soon Cheong Trading Centre: 236 East Pender (683-3333). This bustling grocery store sells persimmons, lotus seeds coated with sugar, coconut strips, red pumpkin seeds, lotus root, candied watermelon rind and candied kumquats, among other traditional food items. Open seven days 9 to 6. Map D circle 8.

Yuen Fong: 242 East Pender (683-6858). Novelty food items and specialty condiments are found here, plus housewares, steamers, cleavers and some gifts. Open Monday to Saturday 9 to 6; and Sunday 9:30 to 5:30. Map D circle 9.

Le Kiu Poultry and Grocery: 254 East Pender (683-7451). This is a poultry outlet with chicken and other birds dressed and ready for cooking. Open Monday to Saturday 8 to 6. Map D circle 10.

Le Kiu Grocery: 262 East Pender (683-7451). The other half of this operation is the main grocery action: Salted duck eggs, spices and ingredients from all over South East Asia, Thailand, Indonesia and Japan. We found some spicy "Jufran Banana Sauce" we'd never seen before. Open Monday to Saturday 8 to 6; and Sunday 8 to 5:30. Map D circle 11.

Dollar Meat Store: 266 East Pender (681-1052, 681-8442, 681-0536). This sister operation to Man Sing Meats is owned by the same family, that of King Wong, a prominent businessman. Open seven days 8 to 6. Map D circle 12.

Kiu Shun Trading: 261 Keefer (682-2621). Another herbal remedy place, this one sells ginseng, deer's horn and health herbs. Open seven days 9 to 6. Map D circle 13.

Maxim's Bakery & Restaurant: 257 Keefer (688-6281). Here you can refresh yourselves with Hong Kong style coffee (half coffee and tea), hot almond powder drink, Horlicks, Ovaltine with egg, and hot lemon coke! In the shop we found purse-shaped dumplings filled with blackbean or coconut, which are usually available for luck near Chinese New Year. The fillings symbolize money, diamonds and wealth. Open seven days 8 to 7. Map D circle 14.

Loong Foong: 247 Keefer (688-0837). Anne's favourite restaurant-bakery for "dessert buns", has been under renovation lately ("seems like years", says Anne). Open Monday to Saturday 7:30 to 6; and Sunday 8 to 6. Map D circle 15.

Mitzie's Restaurant: 179 East Pender (683-6662, 683-6670). Very typical of the restaurants you find in Hong Kong itself, this one is renowned for its Hainan style chicken (rice cooked in the chicken broth and flavoured with ginger; chicken boiled and served with ginger and chili sauce; and the soup -- a thick chicken broth with vegetables. Open Monday to Friday 8 to 11; and weekends 10 to 11. Map D circle 16.

Ten Ren Tea & Jinseng Co.: 550 Main (684-1566). We've actually been to this place's sister operation in Hong Kong, and this one is every bit as authentic. If they have time, they will honour you with a Chinese tea ceremony. At the very least, attentive staff rush to you with tiny samples cups of tea -- and the tea is irresistable, so don't enter if you haven't come to buy! Open seven days 9:30 to 6. Map D circle 17.

Hong Kong Cafe: 149 East Pender (684-4629). Here's the source for the best apple tarts in town, but if you don't shop early in the day, they're all gone! Arrive at 1 p.m. and the tarts are fresh out of the oven. Open Monday to Saturday 6:30 to 5:30; and closed Sunday. Map D circle 18.

Artland: 111 East Pender (688-0383). We'd heard you could buy chops in town and finally discovered this place - and they cost about the same as you'd pay in Hong Kong. Chops are chunks of granite or marble, often topped with a carving of the zodiac animal for the recipient's birth-year. It takes about three days to have the carving done into the bottom so it can be used as a stamp, or you can buy some common words pre-carved into samples on the spot. With ink, case and carving, prices start under $30. Open Monday to Saturday noon to 5; and Sunday by appointment. Map D circle 19.

Universal Arts: 49 East Pender (681-2939). This place also sells chops or "stone stamps" as they call them. Hours vary, so please call ahead. Map D circle 20.

China West: 41 East Pender (681-9665). A great source for cheap toys for children (wooden snakes, colourful kites, travel games, novelties). Open seven days 10 to 6. Map D circle 21.

Chinese Linen & Silk: 27 East Pender (681-1820). A gorgeous array of silk shantung, charmeuse, brocades, jacquards and prints, and various weights of pure linen are sold here at very competitive prices. Open Monday to Saturday 10:30 to 6; and Sunday 1 to 4. Map D circle 22.

Ming Wo: 23 East Pender (683-7268). Vancouver's first and best kitchenware shop, this is the place to find the hard-to-find. Still owned by the prominent Wong family, they've spread their wares in shops far and wide across the lower mainland, but this is the original, dating back to 1919. Open Monday to Saturday 9 to 6; and Sunday 11 to 5. Map D circle 23.

Hung Lin Wig Shop: 17 East Pender (684-2917). This is Anne's favourite party wig shop, with what she calls "the best prices in town -- I've checked!". They also sell hairpieces and hair weaves from a huge stock. Open Monday, Tuesday and Thursday to Saturday 9:30 to 5; and closed Wednesday and Sunday. Map D circle 24.

C.C. Arts Centre: 20 East Pender (669-2601). This place has been in Chinatown forever, it seems. Mr. Lam, the owner has an incredible collection of Chinese opera masks and unique art pieces from Mainland China that you won't find anywhere else in Canada! Mr. Lam also provides framing and matting services for your fine art at very low prices. Open Monday to Saturday 10 to 6. Map D circle 25.

NOTES:

Clark & Venables

Bargains galore!

This tour should last about two hours, because the stops are close together and similar in nature. Parking is easy (and free) in the area. *Clark is east of Main and Venables is north of 1st Ave.* Most of the wholesalers accept cash payment only.

Clark & Venables used to be just about our favourite shopping area because (a) no one seemed to know about it; and (b) there were so many great bargain shops to visit. Today, Moss Designs (a cottage industry baby products outlet) is gone, as is the once-famous Hutch Apparel. Still, there are great discounts to be had in the remaining places:

Livingston Eggs: 1725 Venables (254-1641). Here you'll find large eggs, Avalon milk in bottles, bulk food (including liquid types like ketchup) and a fine soup and sandwich combo if you start out hungry. There are also Jamaican patties for 99 cents each. Hours are Monday to Friday 8 to 4:30; and Saturday 9 to 4:30. Map E circle 1.

Uprising Breads Bakery: 1697 Venables (254-5635). For special diets, there's 100 percent rice bread here, vegetarian salads from $1.50 to $1.75 (daily specials), yummy-looking whole-wheat noodle deli salads, homemade soups and a vast assortment of wholesome homemade breads. Open Monday to Saturday 8:30 to 5:30. Map E circle 2.

Exclusive Espresso Centre: 1505 Venables (254-3340). This interesting stop sells institutional-style, used food equipment, and provides sales, service and rentals on coffee machines. They also sell bargain-priced cappuccino-to-go at only $1.25. Coffee beans are sold in up to 5-pound lots at good prices from a wide variety of blends. Hours are Monday to Friday 9 to 5; and Saturday 9:30 to 4:30. Map E circle 3.

Profile Business Supplies Ltd.: 1461 Venables (251-4343). Here's a good spot for office supplies and new and used furniture. You'll also find school supplies here at discount prices. Hours are Monday to Friday 8 to 5. Map E circle 4.

Busy Kitchen Coffee Shop: 1345 Venables (255-6893). Ah - one of our favourite stops. Their omelettes are huge and satisfying in this classic trucker-style cafe. The breakfast special (2 eggs, meat, hashbrowns, toast and coffee/tea is $2.75 from 6:45 to 11 a.m. Otherwise, hours are Monday to Friday 6:45 to 4:30; and Saturday 9 to 2:30. Map E circle 5.

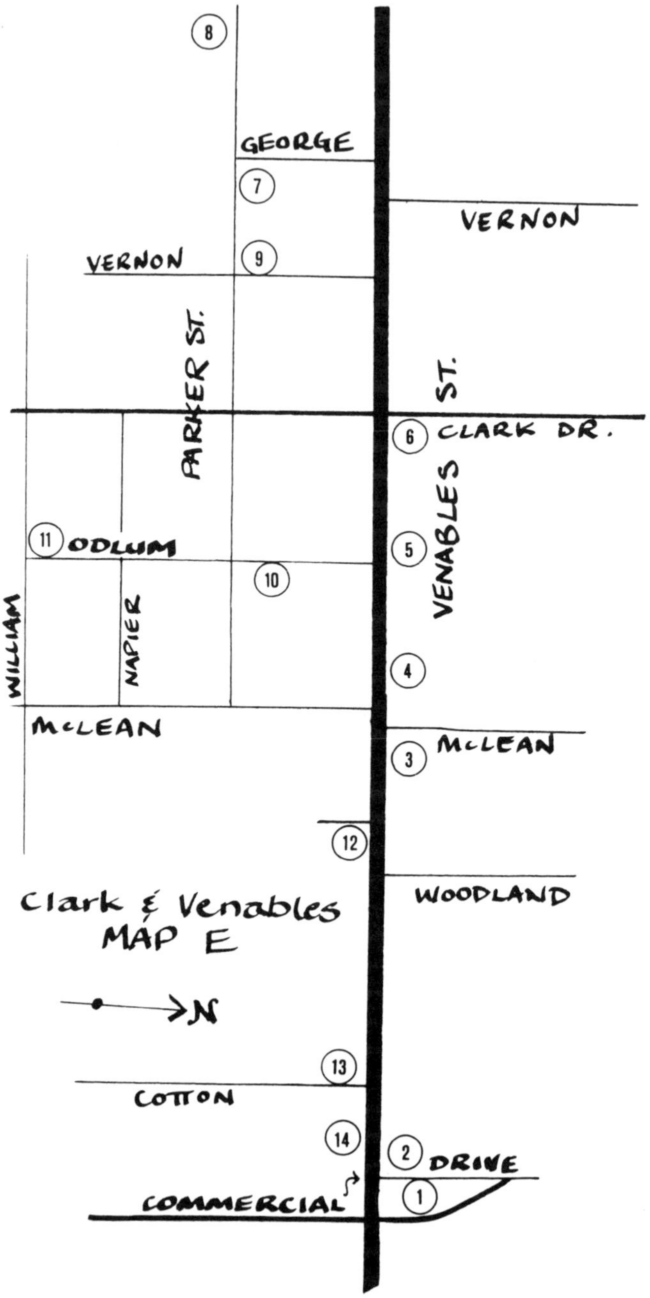
GEORGE
VERNON
VERNON
PARKER ST.
VENABLES ST.
CLARK DR.
ODLUM
WILLIAM
NAPIER
McLEAN
McLEAN
WOODLAND
Clark & Venables
MAP E
N
COTTON
DRIVE
COMMERCIAL
1
2
3
4
5
6
7
8
9
10
11
12
13
14

Mr. Mattress: 1315 Venables (255-2113). They claim to offer the "largest mattress selection in B.C." and their prices are certainly good. This discounter sells famous-name mattresses and also offers free delivery to seniors. Open Monday to Thursday and Saturday 9:30 to 5; Fridays 9:30 to 8; and Sunday noon to 4. Map E circle 6.

Vancouver Fancy Meats: 1169 Parker St. (254-3522). You could drive within a block of this place daily for years and never know it was there, but this trip, you'll find it. The sandwichboard on Venables refers to it as a "Factory Outlet Deli", which pretty much sums it up. They sell lean beef, Lyoner, mortadella, summer sausage and take-out (custom-made) sandwiches Monday to Friday from 9:30 to 4:15; and Saturday 9 to 2:45. Map E circle 7.

Domingos Fashion Group: 2nd floor, 1000 Parker St. (251-5054, 251-1190). Ana Domingos is the designer behind Anabelts - designer-quality men's and women's belts, purses, fashionable printed tights and other gorgeous accessories. Though they are true wholesalers and therefore not open to the public everyday, they do hold period sales (notably early in the summer and before Christmas). To get your name on their mailing list, call ahead. Sale times are usually 11 to 5 or 6 on a weekend. Map E circle 8.

Maywest Manufacturing: 975 Vernon (251-1756). This place used to open to the public only for its once-a-year sale in the spring, but as of September 1992, it operates a genuine factory outlet. Available are samples of their skiwear, casual and sports clothing for men, women and youths, plus excess stock in full size-ranges. Open Monday to Friday 10 to 5. Map E circle 9.

Bonsure du Canada Garment Manufacturing Ltd.: 908 Odlum (251-6771). Here you'll find jeans, shirts and casuals at clear-out prices. Last time in we saw nylon team jackets, too. Note: It's not always staffed -- sometimes there is a sign telling you to ring a bell for entry and then someone comes downstairs to open the door. Hours are Wednesday to Saturday 10 to 5. Map E circle 10.

Pure Silk Fashion Clearance Centre: 1391 William (254-8332). Right on the corner of Odlum and William, this new fashion silk outlet has opened up. There's easy street parking, by the way, or a free lot at the back of the building. Inside you'll find a huge warehouse operation selling washable silk solids and prints in yard goods, men's and women's designs (some European designer labels) in a full range of colors and sizes at manufacturers' clearance prices. There are also accessories like purses, scarves and belts. Open Monday to Saturday 10 to 6; and Sunday noon to 6. Map E circle 11.

B & E Liquidators: 900 Woodland Dr. (253-3727). We've always liked the name, but they've been in business so long, we're now certain the initials don't stand for "break and enter". They sell wall units, bedroom suites, sofas, lamps and tables in an updated showroom. Hours are Monday to Thursday and Saturday 10 to 6; Friday 10 to 8; and Sunday noon to 5. Map E circle 12.

Delane Handbag Fashion: 915 Cotton (254-2279). This shop is not open for regular business, but does have periodic sales of eelskin purses, wallets, briefcases and shoes at factory prices. We must mention that eelskin wallets could be the reason for de-magnetizing your credit cards, so be forewarned. If the place is open, you can add your name to their mailing list, but generally we find it wise to scan the Province for sales notices especially before Christmas. Map E circle 13.

Pico Garment Factory Ltd.: 1636 Venables (253-2819). Pico seems to have outlasted them all -- a denim discounter with massive stock including cut-label items from other manufacturers, plus tops, shorts, casual items and sportswear -- men's, women's and some children's sizes. Another real factory outlet, so you'll see the sewing machines at work at the back. They're back in their original small store and open 10 to 5:30, Monday to Saturday. Map E circle 14.

NOTES:

Cloverdale

Antiques and Collectibles

This is a two-hour mini-tour, focussed almost exclusively on antiques and bric-a-brac. You can easily walk this route in fair weather.

Location: There are three major routes to follow to get to Cloverdale from Vancouver: (1) from South Vancouver, take the Knight Street Bridge southbound into Richmond, and follow the road right onto Hwy. 99 south, as if you were going into the U.S. Once you get past the Deas Tunnel, however, you will want to change to Hwy. 10 east, which will take you right into 'downtown' Cloverdale; (2) from East Van, Burnaby or New West, cross over the Alex Fraser Bridge (southbound), following Hwy. 91 south until it intersects with Hwy. 10 east; or (3) if taking either the Pattulo Bridge (Hwy 1A / Fraser Hwy.) or the Port Mann Bridge (TransCanada 1), take the 176th Street exit south into Cloverdale. From the Pattulo Bridge, you can also follow King George Hwy. (99A) south through Surrey until it intersects with Hwy. 10 and turn east on Hwy. 10 just past the Surrey Public Market.

If you're travelling from the U.S., the major border point is the Douglas border crossing at Peace Portal (Blaine) which puts you on Hwy. 99 north, intersecting with Hwy. 10 past Colebrook Road. Turn east on Hwy 10 and continue on until 176th Street, which leads into Cloverdale.

You can also cross at the Pacific Hwy. border point, which places you slightly east of Douglas. From there, you can travel straight up Hwy 15 (north) into Cloverdale.

From the Aldergrove (Sumas) crossing, take Hwy. 13 north to Hwy. 1A (Fraser Hwy.), turn west on 1A and proceed to Langley City. In Langley, you change to Hwy 10 west, which takes you right into Cloverdale.

Residents of Cloverdale think of it as "the antique capital of B.C.", and they could be right. When the town celebrated its 100th birthday in 1991 it was recognized as one of the oldest communities in the Fraser Valley.

The 'main drag' of Cloverdale is 176th St. With the exception of *Maynard's Valley Tack Shop* (17735 56th Ave., 574-3133), *The Equerry Equestrian Co. Tack Shop* (Hwy 10 & 176th, 576-2363), and *The Cloverdale Thrift Shop* (which has lots of used books at 5622 177B St., 574-0703), most shops sell antiques and collectibles and are right on 176th.

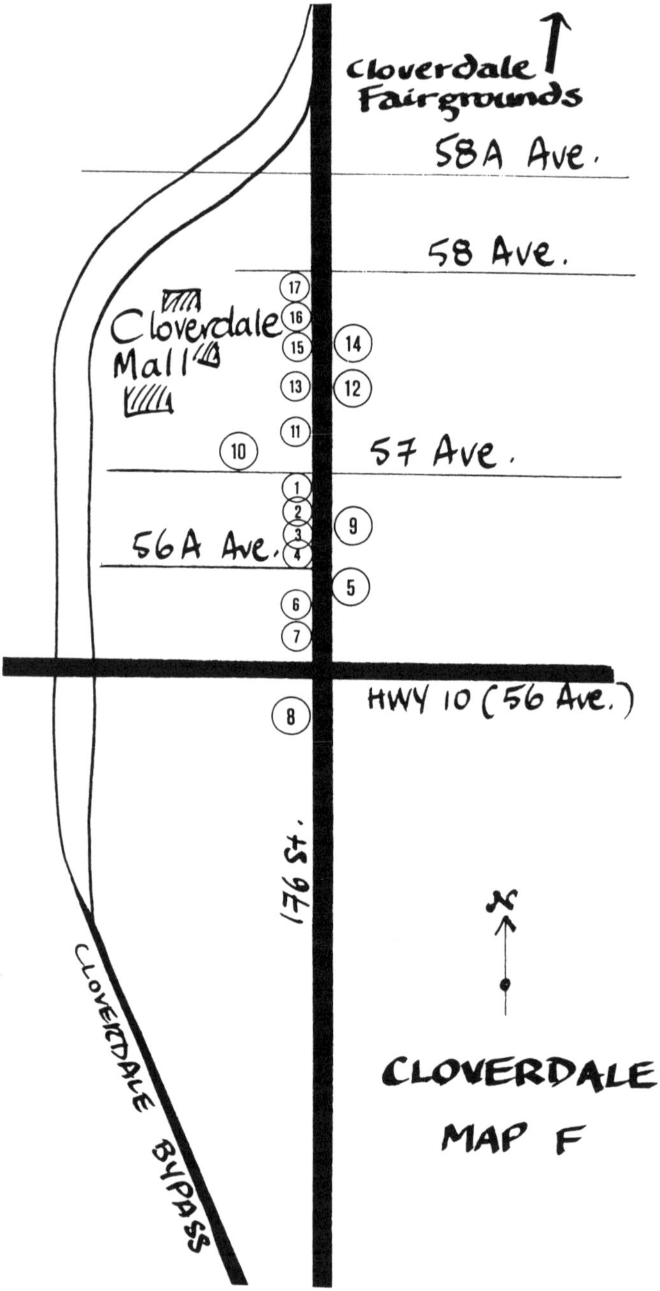
Cloverdale Fairgrounds
58A Ave.
58 Ave.
Cloverdale Mall
57 Ave.
56A Ave.
HWY 10 (56 Ave.)
176 St.
CLOVERDALE BYPASS
N
CLOVERDALE
MAP F
1
2
3
4
5
6
7
8
9
10
11
12
13
14
15
16
17

Rosemary's Antiques: 5693 176th St. (576-2377, 574-0466). It sells lots of dolls, old lace and heritage costuming. Hours are Tuesday, Thursday and Friday 10:30 to 4:30; Saturday 11 to 4:30; and Sunday 11 to 3; closed Monday and Wednesday. Map F circle 1.

Cerebral Palsy Assn. Thrift Shop: 5685 176th St. (576-6400) This little thrift shop is open Monday to Saturday 10 to 4. Map F circle 2.

Ye Olde Piggy Bank: 5683 176th St. (574-3223). This shop is situated in a building which was formerly a Bank of Montreal dating back to 1912. They sell china and bric-a-brac, and also do custom costumes (and costume rentals). Hours are Monday noon to 5; and Tuesday to Sunday 10:30 to 5. Map F circle 3.

Mellowood Antiques: 5679 176th St. (530-0066, 579-3221). They have a good selection of kitchen trine (old-fashioned implements), old tins from 'way back when, and furniture. Open seven days 10:30 to 4:30. Map F circle 4.

The Salvation Army Thrift Store: 5654 176th St. (576-6217). They do a bustling business plus they offer a 10 percent discount to seniors everyday. Open Monday to Saturday 9 to 5. Map F circle 5.

Robert Martin Jewellers: 5629 176th St. (574-7312). Martin sells antiques, antique jewellery and Royal Doulton china at good prices. His repairs are so inexpensive and competent, that a number of devout readers wrote to Anne over the years at The Province to sing his praises. Hours are Wednesday to Saturday 10 to 3. Map F circle 6.

The Emporium Antiques: 5625 176th St. (576-6477) has a great wooden bear (full-size) out front, and sells both antiques (such as French provincial) and jewellery. Open seven days 11 to 5. Map F circle 7.

Red Barn I: 5553 176th St. (576-8737). This original location of Red Barn is south of Hwy 10. A third outlet is at 12251 #1 Road in Steveston (see Steveston tour for details). At this Cloverdale location, they offer a staggering array of antiques, stained glass, collectors' scales and more. Hours are Monday to Saturday 9:30 to 5; and Sunday 11 to 5. Map F circle 8.

Little Antique House: 5674 176th St. (576-9222). Also going by the name "Antiques Just Great", Jake Van Staalduinen specializes in silver and other goodies. Open Monday to Saturday 10 to 5. Map F circle 9.

The Old Stove Works: 17585 57th Ave. (574-2092). This one around the corner, is also run by really nice people. They sell old stoves and old kitchen utensils. Open Monday to Saturday 9 to 5. Map F circle 10.

Red Barn Antiques: 5723 176th St. (576-2228). This is "Barn II", among they "three barns full" of "fine imported antiques and Canadiana" in their ads. This one is the smallest of their three operations carries lots of oak furniture, all high quality. Hours there are Monday to Saturday 10 to 5; and Sunday 11 to 5. Map F circle 11.

Antique World: 5738 176th St. (573-1775). Here you'll find fine silver and beautiful furniture from really friendly folks. Open Monday to Saturday 10 to 6; and Sunday 11 to 5. Map F circle 12.

Paddock Cafe: 5737 176th St. (576-6777). Your rest stop on this tour is a nice, clean cafe. Owner Anne Sharkey will treat you and anyone with whom you're shopping to a free dessert with your meal. Be sure to show your server your copy of The Serious Shopper's Guide to qualify for your freebie. Open Tuesday to Saturday 9:30 to 3. Map F circle 13.

Ken Baker Antiques and Collectables: 5754 176th St. (574-5699). Here they sell furniture, medals, spoons and jewellery. Open seven days 1 to 5. Map F circle 14.

Hometown Antiques: 5757 176th St. (576-0088). This place also sells "smalls" -- glassware and the like. Open 10:30 to 4:30 Tuesday to Thursday; 10:30 to 4 Friday and Saturday; noon to 5 Sunday; and closed Monday. Map F circle 15.

Grannie's Cupboard: 5759 176th St. (574-4514). Bob and Bette Keeper own this sweet little shop for antiques, collectibles, dolls and china -- or as their card says "knick knacks to paddy wacks". They are friendly folks who sell scads of crystal and antique "smalls". Last time in, Anne coveted a wonderful antique dental cabinet with its original milk-glass trays -- straight out of its original home in Assinaboia, Saskatchewan, circa 1920-25 and priced at just $400! Hours are Wednesday to Saturday 10 to 4:30; Sunday noon to 4; and closed Monday and Tuesday. Map F circle 16.

Neilson's Furniture Shoppe: 5775 176th St. (574-4955). You'll find antiques and pine-with-white furniture here, as well as custom oak furniture (you can shop from their catalogue, too) made for them in Abbotsford. Hours are Monday to Thursday 10 to 5; Friday 10 to 6; Saturday 10 to 5:30; and closed Sunday. Map F circle 17.

Commercial Drive

New-age, funky/hip clothing, fruit & veggies

This is a medium-sized tour which you could accomplish in two hours without a break if you move steadily from place to place.

To reach the area from the east, follow Grandview Highway to 12th Avenue. From outside of Vancouver, take TransCanada 1 to the Grandview exit and continue westward.

From the U.S., take King George Hwy. (99A) or 264th St. (depending on your crossing) to TransCanada 1 and travel east on Hwy 1 until you exit at Grandview Highway. Watch the signs carefully so you don't overshoot that exit, or you'll end up in North Van!

By public transit, take the SkyTrain to Broadway Station (Broadway and Commercial), or bus #20 from downtown.

Commercial Drive (or simply "The Drive", as locals call it) was also called Little Italy for years. Nowadays it's rich with ethnic food, culture and spirit from places as diverse as the West Indies, Central America, Japan, Portugal, Holland and Asia, as well as its original backbone of Italian restaurants, stores and services. And it has gone "uptown", with Mercedes as much in evidence as the politically-correct Birkenstock sandals and Guatemalan ponchos.

Parking is catch-as-catch-can, and you may have to resort to side streets.

We start our tour a little off the main drag, at 12th and Commercial.

Tea and Silk: 2767 Commercial (872-1688). This excellent restaurant specializes in eight different Asian cuisines and what we've come to know as "fusion". They also feature an innovative wine list, ever-changing and reasonable. Open Monday to Saturday 11:30 to 2; Monday to Thursday and Sunday 5:30 to 9; and Friday and Saturday 5:30 to 10. Map G circle 1.

The Dutch Cheese Market: 2621 Commercial (876-7331). They sell - what else? -- Dutch cheese. Open Monday to Thursday and Saturday 9:30 to 6; Friday 9:30 to 7; and Sunday 9:30 to noon. Map G circle 2.

Allium Fine Foods: 1885 Commercial (253-4224). This wonderful firm caters to films, caters to your whims and offers fine dine-in and take-out foods of the highest calibre. They also produce a line of take-away

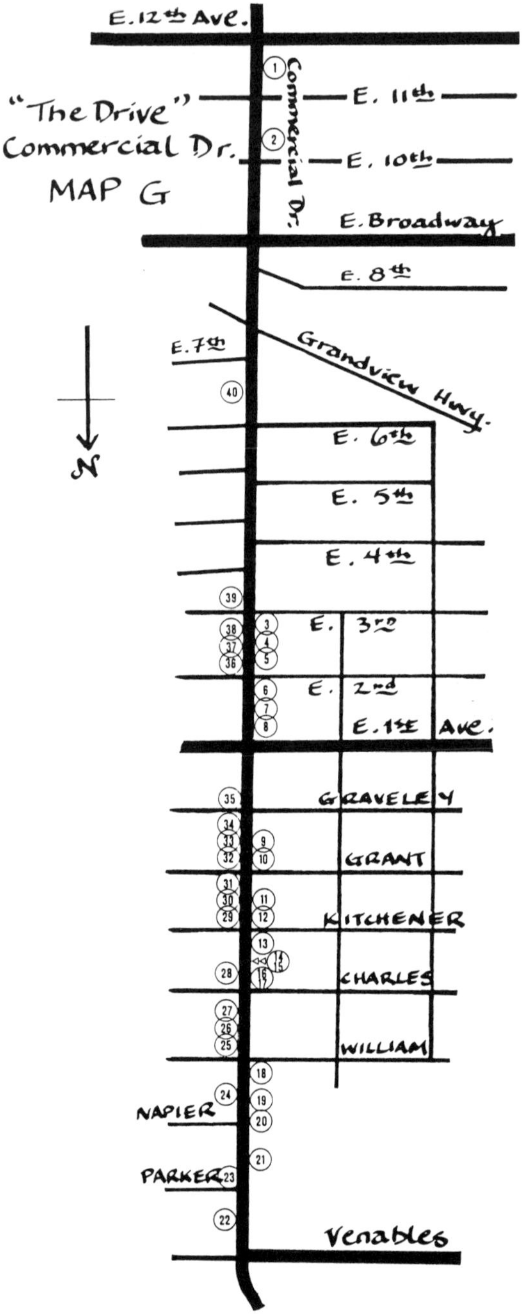
E. 12th Ave.
"The Drive"
Commercial Dr.
MAP G
Commercial Dr.
E. 11th
E. 10th
E. Broadway
E. 8th
E. 7th
Grandview Hwy.
N
E. 6th
E. 5th
E. 4th
E. 3rd
E. 2nd
E. 1st Ave.
GRAVELEY
GRANT
KITCHENER
CHARLES
WILLIAM
NAPIER
PARKER
Venables
1
2
3
4
5
6
7
8
9
10
11
12
13
14
15
16
17
18
19
20
21
22
23
24
25
26
27
28
29
30
31
32
33
34
35
36
37
38
39
40

condiments of superior quality. Open Monday to Saturday 10 to 5. Map G circle 3.

Nuff Niceness Jamaican Deli: 1861 Commercial (255-4211). This atmospheric shop naturally focusses on West Indies deli items. Open Tuesday 12:30 to 8; Wednesday to Saturday 11 to 8; and Sunday 1 to 6. Map G circle 4.

Barrett Electronics: 1859 Commercial (254-4232). This shop offers repairs and electronics sales, plus West Indies records and tapes (reggae, calypso and African). Open Monday to Thursday and Saturday 10 to 6; Friday 10 to 8; and Sundays in August. Map G circle 5.

Renato's Fine Italian Baking and Pastry: 1795 Commercial (255-8921). Not much to add after you read the title of the shop. Open Monday to Saturday 9 to 5. Map G circle 6.

La Grotta del Formaggio: 1791 Commercial (255-3911). Not only do they sell deli meats and cheeses, but they also carry videos and cassettes! Open Monday to Thursday and Saturday 9 to 6; Friday 9 to 8; and Sunday 9:30 to 5. Map G circle 7.

Cafe Calabria: 1745 Commercial (253-7017). Many claim this is the finest coffee bar in Vancouver and who are we to argue? Open seven days, 8:30 a.m. to midnight. Map G circle 8.

St. Tropez Boutique: 1509 Commercial (254-8168). This is a great men's and women's clothing store with hot fashions, reasonable prices. Open Monday to Thursday 10 to 6; and Friday 10:30 to 9; and Saturday 10:30 to 6. Map G circle 9.

Rasta Wares: 1505 Commercial (255-3600). Here they sell funky knit caps, pouches, hangings, jewellery, candles and the like -- worth a visit if just to soak up the atmosphere and music. Open Monday to Saturday 11 to 7; and Sunday noon to 5. Map G circle 10.

Cricket Clothing: 1417 Commercial (251-7130). Here you'll find good styles (mostly women's; some men's) in casual togs. Open Monday to Saturday 11 to 6. Map G circle 11.

The Dr. Vigari Gallery: 1407 Commercial (255-9513). This is the inspired brain-child of designer and entrepreneur Bill Gotts, whose Bill Shirt Company does T-shirts and sweats for everyone from the folk festival to rock bands. Bill's latest venture is to move his Victoria Drive sometime-art gallery onto The Drive, as a context from which to sell some of the most creative and innovative furniture and art you'll ever find in Vancouver! On the walls are constantly-changing shows of local fine art paintings, but the gallery's main focus is on local furniture designers, featuring the gifted designs of Arnt Arntzen. Open Tuesday to Sunday 11 to 6. Map G circle 12.

Carmelo's Pasticceria: 1399 Commercial (254-7024). Look for the caramel-coloured awning -- it's a great place for fancy cakes, especially wedding cakes and pastries. Open Monday to Saturday 9 to 5. Map G circle 13.

Ace Gallery: 1319 Commercial (253-6441). This art gallery is avant garde, so rightly located on The Drive. Among the featured talents are those of twig-furniture maker Lloyd Arntzen. Hours: Wednesday to Saturday 11:30 to 5:30; and Sunday 1 to 5. Map G circle 14.

Highlife Records & Music: 1317 Commercial (251-6964). This is a lifestyle focal-point on The Drive, for tapes, records, CDs -- the works. Open seven days 11 to 6. Map G circle 15.

Latin Quarter Restaurant: 1305 Commercial (251-1144). Doug Bennett (of the world-famous Doug and the Slugs) and his wife Nancy Hare love this spot with its Greek-Italian influenced menu. Try the radical clams steamed in wine and herbs. Free jazz on certain evenings. Open Monday to Saturday 5 p.m. to 1:30 a.m.; and Sunday 5 p.m. to 1 a.m. Map G circle 16.

San Marcos Bakery: 1303 Commercial (255-9145). Here's the only local source we've found for Salvadoran baked goods, plus a tasty pizza. Open seven days 8 a.m. to 9 p.m. Map G circle 17.

Santos Tapas: 1191 Commercial (253-0444). If you like your tapas Portuguese-style, this is for you. Open Tuesday to Sunday 5:30 p.m. to 1 a.m. Map G circle 18.

La Quena Coffee House: 1111 Commercial (251-6626). Here's authentic Latin food and many vegetarian specialties served by co-op members. There's free entertainment sometimes, too. Open Monday 11 to 6; and Tuesday to Sunday 11 to 11. Map G circle 19.

Sweet Cherubim Natural Foods: 1105 Commercial (253-0969). The last stronghold of hippie counter-culture, here's a genuine health food store in a form virtually unchanged since the '60s. Open Monday to Saturday 10 to 8; and Sunday 11 to 7. Map G circle 20.

Circling Dawn Organic Foods: 1045 Commercial (255-2326). A great place for unsprayed produce, grains, nuts and other bulk foods at good prices, plus the people are charming, knowledgeable and helpful without being preachy. Open Monday 10 a.m. to 11 p.m.; Wednesday, Thursday and Sunday 10 to 9; Tuesday 10 to 8; and Friday and Saturday 10 to 11. Map G circle 21.

Cross the street now, and head south again.

Attic Treasures: 944 Commercial (254-0220). An area resident says "and they ARE treasures". Good quality antiques. Nice people, too. Hours vary. Map G circle 22.

The Peg General Store & Antiquities: 1003 Commercial (255-3844). More old stuff than actual antiques, this place is an interesting browse. Open Monday to Saturday 10 to 6. Map G circle 23.

Octopus Books East: 1146 Commercial (253-0913). There was once an Octopus West, but now there's just this one fine store selling new and used books. Open seven days 10 to 6. Map G circle 24.

Mecca: 1204 Commercial (251-7390). This is a really stylish men's and women's consignment store with great window displays and ever-changing stock. Open Monday to Friday noon to 6; Saturday noon to 5:30; and Sunday 1 to 5. Map G circle 25.

Hot Pepper Cafe: 1206 Commercial (251-2999). A local favourite, this cafe lives up to its name. Open seven days 7:30 a.m. to 3 p.m. Map G circle 26.

Ace Novelties: 1212 Commercial (255-2661). A great find for jokes, novelties, party favours, decorations and costumes, this place seems to have been on this spot forever. Open Monday to Saturday 9 to 5. Map G circle 27.

Beckwoman's: 1314 Commercial (254-8056). No visit to The Drive would be complete without a stop at this source of rings, pendants, cards, art and chatchkas. Open Monday to Saturday 10 to 6; Sunday 11 to 5. Map G circle 28.

Nazare Barbecue Chicken: 1408 Commercial (251-1844). One of the highlights of The Drive for many, this is tops in our book for take-out chicken -- it's fabulous! "The chickens await you." If you like spicy food, remember to ask for yours "with medicine". Open seven days 11 to 7:30. Map G circle 29.

Dream Futon: 1420 Commercial (254-5012). Irma McGuiness has created a solid reputation for her sage design advice, fabulous imported fabrics (bargain-priced, too), well-made futons (she's the Canadian board member of an international organization for futons) and brilliantly-inspired window designs. Her window once held an actual woman who lived, lounged, read and slept there for a week just to see what it was like! A must-see. Open Monday to Thursday 10 to 6; Friday 10 to 7; Saturday 10:30 to 5; and Sunday 1 to 5. Map G circle 30.

<u>Divine Decadence:</u> 1432 Commercial (251-7833). Here's the local source for well-priced Doc Marten's and the hippest women's clothing. They also sell men's jeans, rayon shirts, blazers and some great vests. Open Monday to Friday 11 to 7; Saturday 10 to 6; and Sunday noon to 6. Map G circle 31.

<u>Caffe Roma:</u> 1510 Commercial (251-7084). A great spot for Italian ice cream, espresso and take-out pizza. Open seven days 8 a.m. to 1 a.m.; closes at midnight when it's slow. Map G circle 32.

<u>Kalena Shoes:</u> 1526 Commercial (255-3727). In the same location for nearly three decades, this place makes and imports the finest Italian shoes imaginable, sure to give a comfortable fit to any foot. People travel from all over the province to visit Kalena. Open Monday to Thursday 10 to 6; Friday 10 to 8; and Saturday 9:30 to 5:30. Map G circle 33.

<u>Columbus 5 Men's Wear:</u> 1566 Commercial (253-0745). Another store that's been on The Drive for ages, this one sells tailored men's clothes for the "over-forty preppie crowd" as one local wit put it. Open Monday to Thursday and Saturday 9:30 to 5:30; and Friday 9:30 to 8. Map G circle 34.

<u>Norman's Fruit & Salad:</u> 1604 Commercial (251-5159). What a flashback to the early '70s! This place is virtually unchanged from its previous incarnation as the Salad Market (which moved years ago up to 1st Ave. in Il Mercado). It's a great source for inexpensive produce and canned goods, with displays spilling well out onto the sidewalk under the awning next to the green and white diagonal stripes on the building. Open Monday to Wednesday and Saturday 9 to 8; Thursday and Friday 9 to 9; and Sunday 9 to 7. Map G circle 35.

<u>Continental Coffee:</u> 1806 Commercial (255-0712). Here you'll find fabulous roasted coffee beans, cappuccino and authentic Italian ice cream. Open Monday to Thursday and Saturday 9:30 to 5:30; and Friday 9:30 to 6. Map G circle 36.

<u>Falcone Bros. Meat Market:</u> 1810 Commercial (253-6131). In business in the same spot since 1967, this place sells fresh and cured meats,

sausages, whole rounds of cheese and those distinctive Italian cheeses like the giant ones hanging in the window. Open Monday to Thursday and Saturday 9 to 5:45; and Friday 9 to 7. Map G circle 37.

Hangups Thrift Boutique: 1832 Commercial (251-9779). What we like so much about this charity thrift shop (its sister operation is in our West Broadway tour) is that all of the proceeds go directly to the mentally handicapped, for whom the charity operates. Staff is entirely volunteer. They have a good stock of household items, clothing and bric-a-brac -- cheap as dirt! Open Monday to Saturday 10 to 5. Map G circle 38.

Olivieri's Ravioli Store: 1900 Commercial (255-8844). Another flash from the past, we love the way they greet us with "Ciao, bella!" and the smell of cured meats and fragrant spices. It's worth a visit just to look at the exquisite cans of extra virgin olive oil and marinated artichoke hearts. Open Monday to Thursday and Saturday 9 to 6; Friday 9 to 7; and Sunday 10 to 4. Map G circle 39.

Torrefazione Coliera: 2206 Commercial (254-3723). Partial translation: The House of Coffee. The scent of fresh-ground and roasted coffee positively seduces you in the door! It's both a tiny cafe and a great source for whole coffee beans and custom-ground coffees. Open Monday to Friday 9:30 to 6; and Saturday 9:30 to 5:30. Map G circle 40.

NOTES:

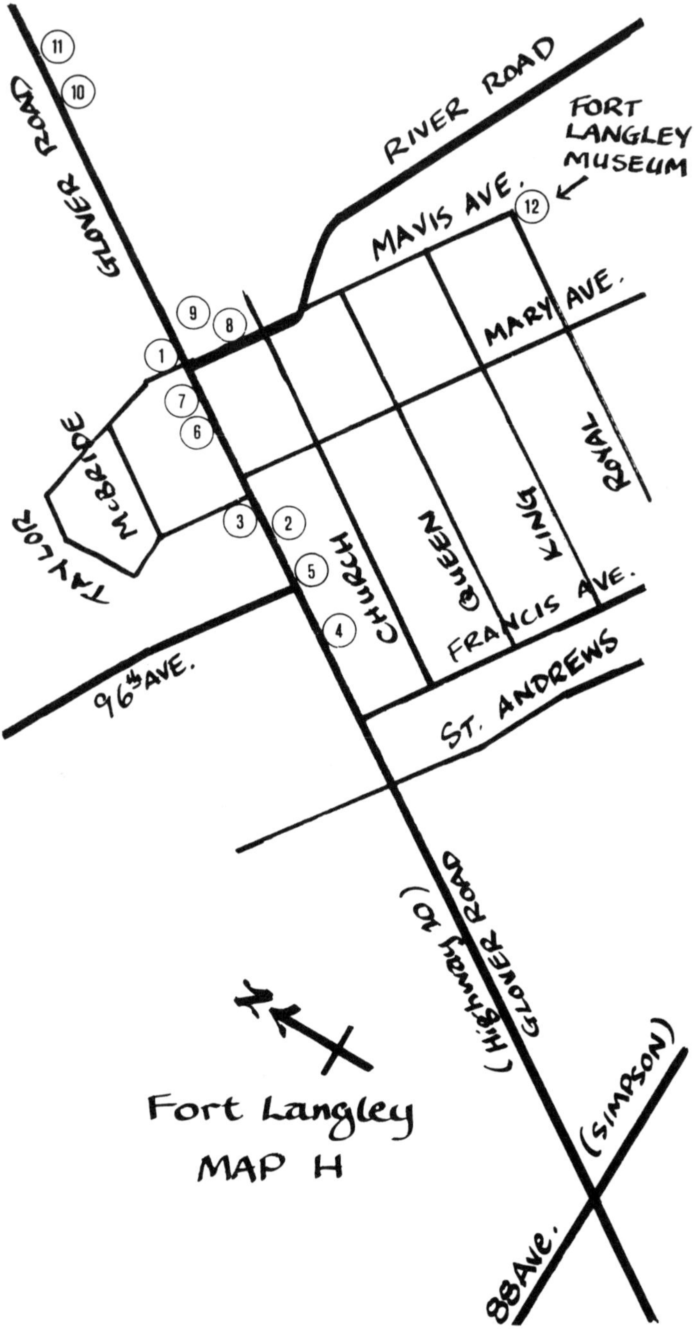

Fort Langley
MAP H

Fort Langley

This is a mini-tour which can be accomplished in one hour, or you can tack it on to Langley City for a fuller shopping experience.

The most direct way to reach Fort Langley is to take TransCanada 1 east to Highway 10 and take Highway 10 east until it becomes Glover Road, which transects Fort Langley, the "birthplace of B.C." A longer route (but still picturesque) involves taking Highway 10 all the way from Richmond, Delta or Surrey eastward.

Alternately, those on the north side of the North Arm of the Fraser have the option of taking the Albion Ferry (a free, 10-minute crossing, car and all) from Albion which is on the Lougheed Highway past Maple Ridge. The ferry lands at the foot of Glover Road and there's a great fish and chip shop there that also sells smoked salmon.

U.S. Visitors should take Highway 15 (176th St.) north to Highway 10, and then take 10 to Fort Langley.

If you do take Highway 10 to Fort Langley, watch for Milner Food Market at 6830 216th Ave (530-3622) near the junction of Hwy. 10 and Glover Road. It's an old-fashioned general store including a rural post office - just like something out of the '50s.

We won't even attempt to include public transit instructions because the trip would take so long, you'd have no time left to shop! If you're set on bus travel, however, call 261-5100 for details.

We have not included hours for most of these shops, but most are open Monday to Thursday 10 to 6; Friday 10 to 6 (or 8); Saturday 10:30 to 5:30; and several open Sunday noon to 5. Call ahead to check hours if one stop is of particular interest. For this tour, there are several restaurants included, because they themselves are an important part of the historical fabric of the town.

<u>Lampliter Garden Cafe:</u> 9213 Glover Road (888-2808). This cosy eatery is done in dusty rose and cafe curtains. Map H circle 1.

<u>Fort Langley European Deli & Meats:</u> 9110 Glover Road (888-0153). Tucked into the Fort Mall is a classic deli which sells bratwurst, beer sausage and Lyoner sausage, as well as other German meat specialties. Map H circle 2.

<u>The Fox & the Ferryman Cafe:</u> 9145 Glover Road (888-3137). Another charming cottage, this one is finished in grey trim and teal, with an equally appealing menu. Map H circle 3.

The Fort Gallery: 9048 Glover Road (888-3994). This fine arts and craft shop sells unique and wonderful stoneware -- BUT -- it's only open Friday through Sunday. Look for the yellow shiplap exterior. Map H circle 4.

The Marr House: 9090 Glover Road (888-6455). Historical, yes. Bargains? That, too. Great antiques. Closed Tuesdays. Map H circle 5.

Trove Cottage: 9205 Glover (888-2337). Another fine local giftshop, open seven days. Map H circle 6.

Susan Galick Fashion Design: 9207 Glover Road (888-7034). Here's real couturiere quality at reasonable prices in a sweet boutique. Closed Tuesday and open other days only until 4:30 or 5 p.m., so call ahead to be sure. Map H circle 7.

Village Antiques & Crafts Mall: 23331 Mavis Ave. (888-3700). This antiques promenade has everything, but it is closed Mondays, except holiday Mondays. Map H circle 8.

Bedford House: 9272 Glover Road (888-3994). This historical, ivy-covered cottage houses a dining experience worth the distance you will have to travel. The house was built in 1904 and maintained in careful detail. Brunch is served from 11 to 2 Sundays only and dinner is served seven days from 5 p.m. Reservations are recommended. Map circle 9.

Fort Langley Seafood: 9298 Glover Road (888-5820). Sometimes their fresh-from-the-water salmon is a bargain. Open seven days 9 to 7. Map H circle 10.

Albion Ferry: This free ferry leaves Fort Langley dock about every 20 minutes from 6 a.m. to 2 a.m. daily and takes cars and passengers over to Maple Ridge, in case you want to make a circle tour of your excursion. For more information, call 660-8770. Map H circle 11.

Naturally, you should make historic Fort Langley itself a part of your visit. The Fort is the original crown colony of B.C. Hours are 10 to 4:30. Call ahead for details to 888-4424. Map H circle 12.

NOTES:

Fraser 41st to 49th

International Shopping

This is a major tour for which you should budget about three to four hours, if you plan to see everything. This area is a real mix of different ethnic stores and bargain places.

Fraser is the first large street east of Main. To get there via public transportation, take the Skytrain to Science world-Main St. station and take a #3 bus southbound on Main. transfer at 41st to an eastbound bus. The next major stop is Fraser St.

For drivers, street parking is at a premium, but there is a free parking lot that runs behind the buildings on the west side of the street from 43rd to 49th.

Maria's Wool 'n Things: 5927 Fraser (327-5017). This place sells mostly wool and pattern books, but there are a few handknit baby clothes for sale, too, as well as embroidery kits and thread. Nicely-finished samples on the walls supply added inspiration. Open Monday to Saturday 10 to 5:30. Map J circle 1.

Paris Shoes & Repair: 5943 Fraser (325-3511). They repair shoes in this shop that looks completely untouched by the passage of time. Or rather -- it looks old, but unchanged by the '90s (or even this '50s for that matter!). They sell a limited range of shoes, too. Open Tuesday to Saturday 9 to 5:30. Map J circle 2.

Prairie Market & Deli: 5945 Fraser (321-6066). This steamy little shop offers some unique mid-west items, like country farm sausage. Hours are Tuesday to Saturday 9 to 5:30. Map J circle 3.

West Coast Cycles: At 5973 Fraser (324-6599) you'll find new and used bikes and accessories sold at 'discount prices'. Open Tuesday to Saturday 10:15 to 5. Map J circle 4.

St. Vincent de Paul Thrift Shop: 5985 Fraser (no phone). There's been no attempt to up-market this place, which sells clothing, knick knacks, books and furniture—all crammed into an old building. Open Monday to Saturday 9:30 to 5. Map J circle 5.

Victory General Merchandise: 6009 Fraser (324-9567) This shop sells discount men's and women's casual clothing. Jeans are advertised from 2.99 and up, there are lots of runners and thongs and Canadian souvenir t-shirts as well. Hours here are Monday to Saturday 10 to 6; and Sunday noon to 6. Map J circle 6.

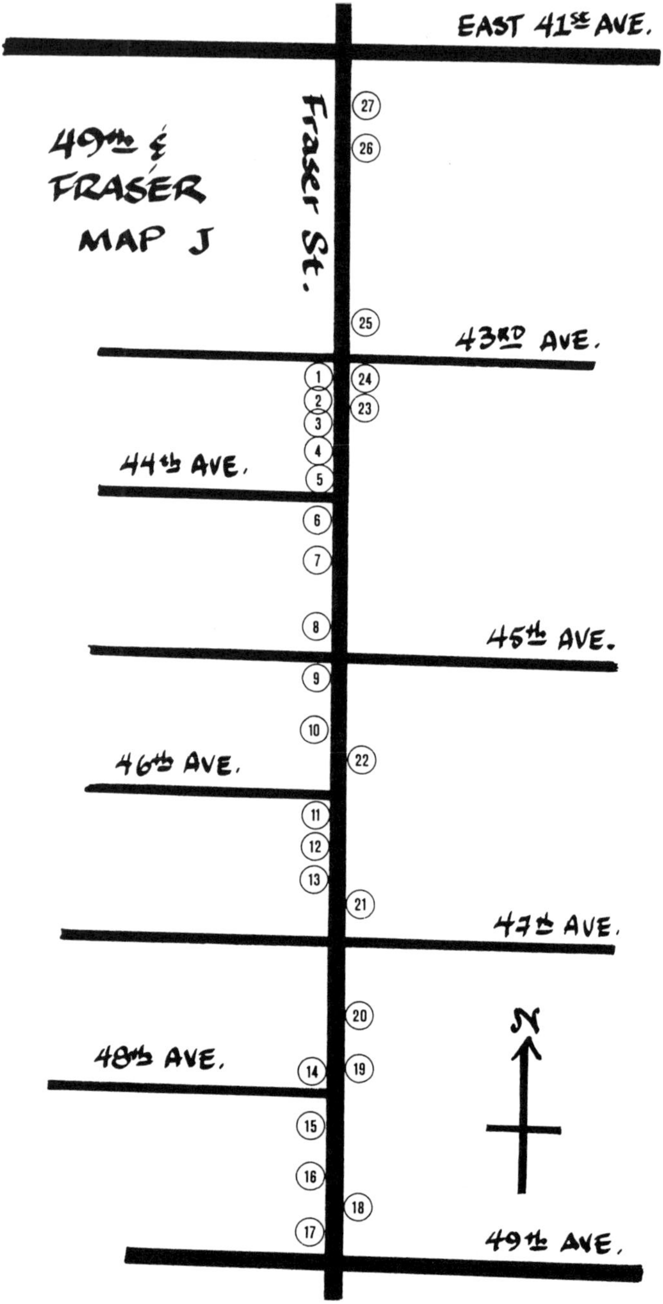
EAST 41st AVE.
49th & FRASER MAP J
Fraser St.
43RD AVE.
44th AVE.
45th AVE.
46th AVE.
47th AVE.
48th AVE.
49th AVE.
N
1
2
3
4
5
6
7
8
9
10
11
12
13
14
15
16
17
18
19
20
21
22
23
24
25
26
27

Discount Foam & Furniture: 6035 Fraser (324-2927). Here you'll find low prices on foam mattresses and wooden bed frames, camping foam pads (from $4.99) high density foam pads at $9.95 (Lorraine bought one), bags of foam chips for crafts, and queen-size pillows at two for $16.00. When Anne last visited, they had solid pine bunk beds (unfinished, but complete with mattress) for $349. Open Monday to Saturday 9:30 to 5. Map J circle 7.

Buy-Low: 6095 Fraser (597-9122, head office). This excellent supermarket offers competitive pricing and the friendliest staff around, plus there's a well-stocked garden shop around the side in warm weather. Produce is clean and fresh and there is a choice of *bottled* milk from local farms. Hours are Monday to Friday 9 to 9; and weekends 9 to 6. Map J circle 8.

U-Save Drugs: 6105 Fraser (327-1830). We think that their policy of "prescription drug price posting" means that you can check out their prices on the drugs before you order them (good for comparison-shopping. For instance, though Real Canadian Superstore has low dispensing fees, their drug prices can be high). U-Save also carries some marked down food items -- cans, juice boxes and other liquidation-type items. Open Monday to Thursday 9:30 to 7; Friday 9:30 to 8; Saturday 9:30 to 6; and Sunday 11 to 5. Map J circle 9.

Home Hardware: 6167 Fraser (327-3212). Anne really likes the service at this branch, though it's a bit of a misnomer (more 'home' than 'hardware'). They have a great many kitchen items and a very modest selection of hardware. They do stock nails and some electrical items in bulk. Open Monday to Saturday 9:30 to 5:30. Map J circle 10.

Rokko Saree & Fabrics: 6201 Fraser (327-3033). Over 6,500 square feet of fabrics -- silks, polyesters, cottons, nylons wools -- are sold here, some pre-cut to saree length but most are by the yard (not meter). Lorraine bought 24 assorted colour spools of thread in a package for only $6! Their motto: "At Rokko's all you require is good taste — not a fat purse". (For more East Indian fabrics and bargains, check out our "Little India" tour starting on page 65.) Hours here are Monday to Thursday and Saturday 10 to 6; and Friday 10 to 9. Map J circle 11.

Buckerfield's: 6219 Fraser (327-2927). Not the largest Buckerfield's we've been in, but this one is handy for in-city shopping. Their stock includes garden supplies, pet food and pet supplies, bulk grains for feeding animals, bedding plants (in season) and seeds (their brand of course) and some unusual garden tools we couldn't locate elsewhere. Hours are Monday to Saturday 9 to 5:30; and Sunday 10 to 4. Map J circle 12.

Fields: 6257 Fraser (327-2422). This looks like the family clothing stores of our childhood, with men's, women's and children's reasonably priced clothing in a store that has not undergone much modernizing. Hours are Monday to Thursday and Saturday 9:30 to 5:30; Friday 9:30 to 9; and Sunday noon to 5. Map J circle 13.

Michael's Discount Foods: 6387 Fraser (324-5778). Anne claims she loves this store because the greengrocer is so knowledgeable about his produce. "I asked for the hottest little peppers he had", she says, "and he showed me some little green Thai peppers that did not disappoint!" In addition, there are Indian specialties, bulk foods and spices, most at truly discounted prices. There's also a good selection of stainless steel cooking and serving utensils. Open seven days 9 to 9. Map J circle 14.

S.D.R. Gifts & China: 6425 Fraser (321-1121). A surprisingly-good source for giftwear, SDR also offers a permanent 50% discount on Royal Albert china. In fact, all of their housewares are competitively-priced. There's a good choice in silverware and flatware, too. Open Monday to Thursday and Saturday 9:30 to 6; and Friday 9:30 to 8. Map J circle 15.

Super Choice Foods: 6457 Fraser (321-3899). Here's an assortment of Chinese specialties, some produce, frozen seafood (squid, prawns, sea-cucumber, fish), barbecued pork and duck, fresh pork and chicken, and wonderfully strange things like pork lungs and chicken feet. They also offer take out Chinese food, deli style. Open seven days 10 to 7. Map J circle 16.

Polo Market: 6475 Fraser (321-7117). Fresh produce spills out onto the sidewalk from the front of this store, which offers an odd mix of Latin American and Indian specialty foods, bulk foods, and to top the whole thing off, rentals of videos in Spanish! Hours are Monday to Saturday 8:30 to 9. Map J circle 17.

House of Fabrics: 6468 Fraser (325-7919). Here you'll find patterns, notions, fabric, drapery material and hardware. Hours are Monday to Saturday 10 to 5:30; and Sunday noon to 5. Map J circle 18.

Krusty's Thrift Bakery: 6374 Fraser (321-2235). Until the advent of The Simpsons on TV, this seemed like a normal enough name. Now all it does is remind us of Krusty the Clown. The bargains are still there, whatever the name. There's day-old bread, fresh-baked pastries and buns, and bulk cookies at one dozen for 99 cents (3 dozen for $2.79). A few other canned and packaged marked down food items are also available. Hours are Monday to Saturday 9:30 to 5:30. Map J circle 19.

Fraser Barbeque: 6340 Fraser (324-3738). This spot features Chinese specialties, a bit of fresh produce, Chinese type vegetables, barbeque and fresh pork and duck and take out Chinese food, deli style. Open Monday to Saturday 9 to 6. Map J circle 20.

Croft's Health Products: 6262 Fraser (324-2121). Croft Woodruff has a long-standing reputation as a health expert in Canada. In fact, he's Anne's best resource in the health field -- he's that knowledgeable! Croft sells health supplements, health foods and vitamins, but with all the free advice you might need on making these substances work for your better health. Hours are Monday to Saturday 10 to 5:30. Map J circle 21.

Mason Sewing Machines: 6192 Fraser (327-3800). A long-standing favourite of ours, this unique store sells new and reconditioned (and some very antique-looking) sewing machines, plus they offer service and repairs to home and industrial machines. They sell thread and a few notions. The best part is that they have all kinds of models of sergers and you can try them all before buying. Hours are Monday to Thursday and Saturday 9 to 5; and Friday 9 to 9. Map J circle 22.

Self Help: 5920 Fraser (325-1612). The crafts of the world division of MCC efforts (see next listing) showcases crafts from developing countries in wood, fabric and woven rattan. There are wonderful (and inexpensive) Christmas decorations here from a self-help project which returns the lion's share of proceeds to the third world people who supply the items. The store is bright and has nice displays. Open same hours as next entry. Map J circle 23.

Mennonite Central Committee Thrift Store: 5914 Fraser (325-1612). Right next door is the new Vancouver location of one of the region's best thrift stores. The old one was burned pretty much to the ground in a devastating fire. We like the assortment of good used clothing, accessories and wigs, all tidy and clean in a spacious store, run by kindly volunteers. Hours are Monday to Saturday 9:30 to 5. Map J circle 24.

First Choice Discount Music: 5812 Fraser (324-6551). Here we found new and used musical instruments (lots of guitars), stereo and video repairs, plus a bulletin board inside the door with ads for music lessons, musicians looking for gigs and groups looking for a certain type of instrument player. Hours are Monday to Saturday 10 to 5. Map J circle 25.

Ample Size Park: 5766 Fraser (322-0107). This ladies consignment shop specializes in women's size 14 and larger. There are accessories and a wide range of clothing styles, including a wedding dress. There's a cute picture of Betty Boop on the wall and a nice oldtimey feel to the store. Many Province readers have written in to sing this shop's praises to the skies. Open Monday to Saturday 11 to 6. Map J circle 26.

Neptoon Records & CDs: 5750 Fraser (324-1229). Musician and lyricist Barry Greenfield tipped Anne to this place long ago. Everything is used: Records, tapes, CDs and rock videos galore, and all are in tip-top shape. Everything is neatly sorted into categories for ease of discovery. Open Monday to Thursday and Saturday 11 to 6:30; Friday 11 to 8; and Sunday 11 to 5. Map J circle 27.

NOTES:

Kerrisdale

Carriage Trade Shopping at its Best

This is one of the 'best' shopping areas in the region, with shop after shop of boutique-atmosphere, high-end merchandise and often the most accommodating sales people in town. The Kerrisdale tour takes in a great many of these shops, yet because the trade is so concentrated (and parking so convenient), we think you could manage to visit every stop on the way within 2 to 3 hours.

Street parking is free. Sometimes it's easy to find a spot, and other times it's impossible. There is a large lot, however (with free parking) behind Canada Trust off Yew St. Large signs in the area direct you to the lot. In addition, though the big lot next to Shoppers Drug Mart was redeveloped last year (eliminating parking there, of course), there are small, free lots behind many of the shops. There's one in the lane behind Buchan Stationers, for example, and few spots behind Windmill Toys, and a small lot behind Fast Feet. Thomas Hobbs has a few spaces off the lane, too. Most of these places have back doors for the convenience of customers who found parking in their back lot.

Find Kerrisdale around the intersections of West 41st Avenue and The Boulevard (variously known as East Boulevard, West Boulevard, and Arbutus Street).

For visitors travelling from the U.S., follow Hwy. 99 north until you cross the Oak Street Bridge into Vancouver. Continue north on Oak to 41st Avenue and turn left at the left turn bay there. The first major street you cross is Granville St. The next is The Boulevard, and you're there!

To get to Kerrisdale via public transit, the most direct bus routes are on #22 (either called "Knight" or "Macdonald" -- one describes the route in one direction; the other travels the opposite way). The #22 bus travels along Pender St. through part of downtown, passing just two blocks from the SeaBus terminal. If trying to catch the bus from the SeaBus, walk two blocks away from the water along either Howe St. or Granville St. and you'll see a bus stop for the #22. If you're in town for a convention at either the Pan Pacific or the Waterfront Hotel, get your concierge to point you toward Pender St. and the #22 bus. Otherwise, you can catch this bus at Clark and Broadway, Macdonald and Broadway, or Davie and Burrard in the West End. The #22 starts and ends at 41st and Carnarvon, just five blocks west of our tour's first stop. Travel time from downtown is about half an hour by bus.

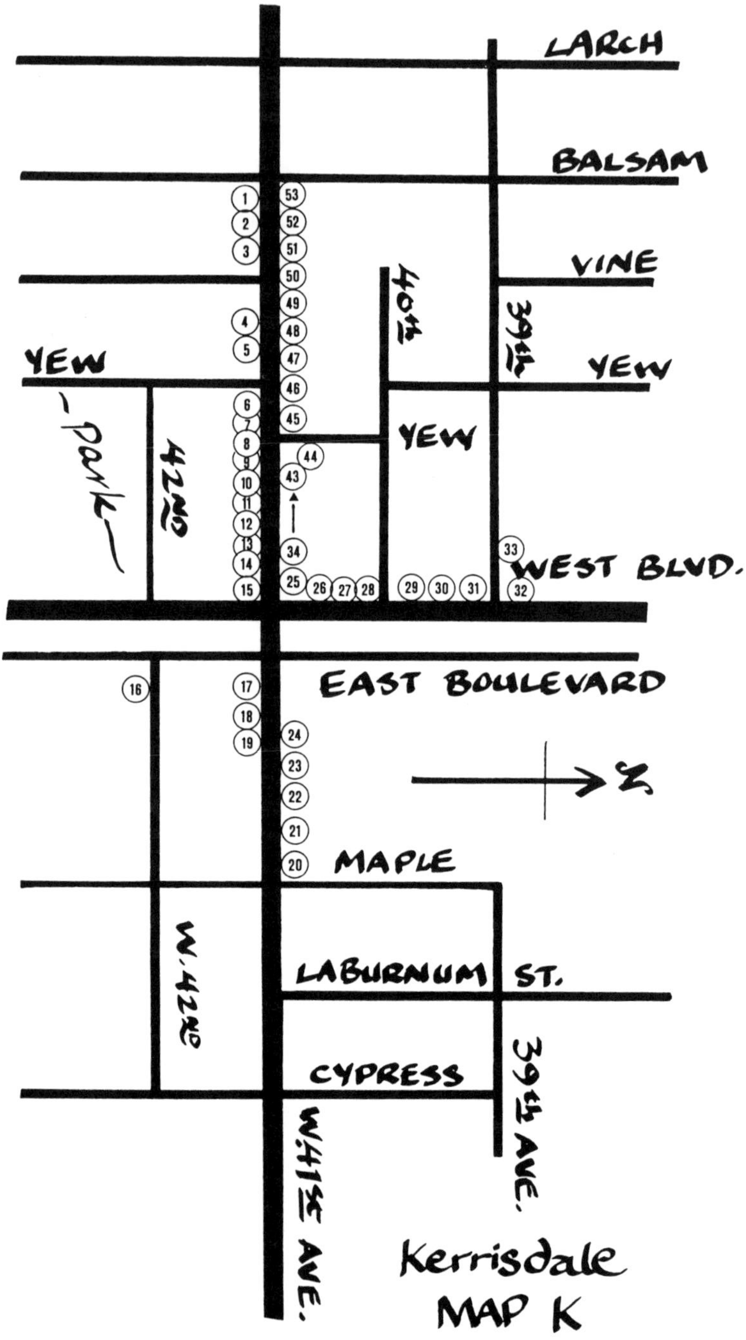
LARCH
BALSAM
VINE
YEW
YEW
YEW
40th
39th
42ND
- Park -
WEST BLVD.
EAST BOULEVARD
N
MAPLE
LABURNUM ST.
CYPRESS
W.42ND
W.41st AVE.
39th AVE.
1
2
3
4
5
6
7
8
9
10
11
12
13
14
15
16
17
18
19
20
21
22
23
24
25
26
27
28
29
30
31
32
33
34
43
44
45
46
47
48
49
50
51
52
53
Kerrisdale
MAP K

As the warm weather sets in, many shops that normally close Sundays may open from 11 or noon to 5. In addition, take note of the incredible Kerrisdale sidewalk sales (which are held periodically) and "Kerrisdale Days", a weekend-long street fair usually held in May. For details, call the Kerrisdale Business Association at 263-0351.

Oh Brothers: 2356 West 41st (263-2122). An interesting array of B.C. arts and crafts is available here, some of it appearing to be almost museum quality. There is lots of pottery, good examples of weaving, some fine prints, jewellery, stained glass work and hand-made cards. All is the work of B.C. artisans. Hours are Monday to Saturday 10 to 5:30. Map K circle 1.

Dick and Jane: 2352 West 41st (266-1090). Down a flight of ivy-trimmed stairs below Oh Brothers, this place benefits from its location, which gives it an old-world charm. Inside, you'll find stitching and needlepoint supplies, embroidery books, wool kits and the like. Open Monday to Saturday 10 to 5:30. Map K circle 2.

W.H. Puddifoot: 2350 West 41st (261-8141). This charming shop attractively showcases lovely china, crystal, giftware, dinnerware, flatware, place mats and silver frames on two floors. When we visited, there were huge ceramic geese displayed in the window. Hours are Monday to Saturday 9:30 to 5:30. Map K circle 3.

Martinique's Fashions: 2268 West 41st (266-5911). A women's fashion boutique, this one focusses on casual, comfortable-looking clothing by John Henry and Calvin Klein, among others. Just the place for gentrified country classics to wear down to Southlands for the pony shows. Open Monday to Saturday 11 to 5. Map K circle 4.

Teeter-totter Togs: 2256 West 41st (253-7540). This tiny shop sells high-quality children's clothing from infant to size 10, with emphasis on the smaller sizes. Open Monday to Saturday 9:30 to 5:30; Sunday noon to 5. Map K circle 5.

Satchel Shop: 2186 West 41st (261-8713). In its new location, here you'll find handbags, luggage, briefcases and small leather goods. Open Monday to Saturday 9:30 to 5:30; and Sunday noon to 4. Map K circle 6.

Rose Marie's of Kerrisdale: 2184 West 41st (261-7633). A Scottish-English flavour permeates this women's clothing shop, with its antiques, pictures and British bric-a-brac displayed in alcoves up on the walls. Most of the clothing is ultra-conservative designer wear. Open Monday to Saturday 9:30 to 5:30; and Sunday 10:30 to 3:30. Map K circle 7.

Kerrisdale Bootery: 2182 West 41st (261-6371). Known for its semi-annual shoe sales and traditional styles for the mature woman, this place also stocks men's and children's footwear. Hours are Monday to Friday 9:30 to 6; and Saturday 9:30 to 5. Map K circle 8.

Hager Books: 2176 West 41st (263-9412). A fine little bookstore with an excellent selection of children's titles, this one offers no bargain table, but does deliver consistently helpful and well-informed service. Open Monday to Thursday and Saturday 9 to 6; 9 to 9 Friday; and Sunday noon to 5. Map K circle 9.

Valucci: 2154 West 41st (266-3131). This shoe boutique sells its own line of exquisitely-crafted shoes -- "quality imported shoes at affordable prices". Open Monday to Saturday 9:30 to 5:30. Map K circle 10.

Basic Stock Cookware: 2150 West 41st (261-3599). It's usually a good sign when a local firm has locations elsewhere (they must be doing something right to prosper in tough times), and this place is no exception. There's a wonderful assortment of fine cookware, china, teapots, doodads and gadgets, plus a selections of coffee (available in bulk) from sources around the world. There's a wall of cookbooks (on the back wall) and always something on sale for a decent discount. Last time in, Anne was forced to buy (yes, on IMPULSE) a set of delightful salt and pepper shakers in the form of tiny cactuses. This is the perfect shop for browsing for house-warming gifts for friends or indulgences for yourself! Hours are Monday to Saturday 9:30 to 5:30. Map K circle 11.

Salar Persian & Oriental Carpets: 2134 West 41st (261-3555). Ah, yes -- high end, but worth it. They "guarantee the best selection and lowest price in B.C.", with over 4,000 antique and semi-antique Persian and Russian rugs and kelims in stock at any given time. AND, they always have at least one type of rug on sale. They also do repairs. Last time we spotted a gorgeous Persian rug there for at least 50 percent off its regular price. There's free parking in the back. Open Monday to Saturday 10 to 6; and Sunday noon to 5. Map K circle 12.

Moore's Bakery & Delicatessen: 2128 West 41st (261-2922). As much a part of Kerrisdale's history as anything else, this shop sells Scottish-type bread, cold meats, sandwiches and pastries, and provides a small eating area for dining-in. Hours are Monday to Saturday 9 to 6. Map K circle 13.

S. Lampman: 2126 West 41st (261-2750). Set back slightly from the rest of the shops, S. Lampman is both elegant and refined in its showcasing of men's label clothing from the likes of Christian Dior and

Joe Boxer. Everything from ties to socks, and casual attire to work clothes are presented in stylish splendor. Hours are Monday to Thursday and Saturday 9 to 6; Friday 9 to 9; and Sunday 10 to 5. Map K circle 14.

Forester's Fine Cheese: 2104 West 41st (261-5813). Another Kerrisdale landmark, this place sells a delightful selection of cheeses and deli selections. There are cold meats, extra-old Gouda, Cross & Blackwell comestibles, crackers and party items. Hours are Monday to Saturday 9:30 to 6. Map K circle 15.

London Drugs: 2079 West 42nd (520-9010). The big lot (enter just before you get to the liquor store) now requires that you pay for a ticket, but the cost is refunded to you in London Drugs itself. If you're lucky, you'll nab a spot out front (be sure not to park across the street or it's a $35 fine!) where the half-hour street parking is free.

Inside, you'll find every type of pharmacy item imaginable, as well as housewares, photo and (a brand new section for) computer supplies, cameras, garden equipment, hardware and a small selection of home repair supplies (job-racked screws, nails, bolts; glue guns; small tins of varnish & paint; caulking supplies; fuses and tools; etc.) and a good range of books and magazines at discount prices. In fact, most of the prices in London Drugs are really competitive, and their sale prices can't be beat -- even across the border! Anne confesses she does more than half of her shopping for EVERYTHING in this particular London Drugs location, and adds that the staff is wonderfully helpful and accommodating. Hours are Monday to Saturday 9 a.m. to 10 p.m.; and Sunday 10 to 8. Map K circle 16.

When you exit either from London Drugs' parking lot or from street parking out front, you'll be facing west on 42nd. Take a right and another right and you'll arrive in front of...

Courtyards: 2082 West 41st (261-4116). Again, Anne admits this is one of her favourite impulse-shopping meccas. She just had to have those citron-scented, two-foot-long patio candles (for driving away bugs, don't you know) and that perfect brass umbrella holder for the front hall. Anne loves Courtyards and drops in for a browse at least twice a month. Often, she buys nothing, but the staff just keep on smiling. Then, when she succumbs to some temptation or other, they still smile as she drops some major credit card charges in their favour! There is patio furniture, china, gourmet foods, gift items for outdoor living, and very clever novelties running the gamut from precious bunnies for Easter, through watermelon-motif plates and serviettes for entertaining. Open Monday to Saturday 9:30 to 5:30. Map K circle 17.

Kerrisdale Meats: 2070 West 41st (261-8755). Where would we be come Robbie Burns day without Kerrisdale Meats? They sell 26 kinds of sausage and haggis year-round. They are PST, GST and MSG free! Also available are fancy prepared entrees like chicken Kiev or chicken cordon bleu, which you merely have to take home to cook. Call ahead for custom orders. Open Monday to Saturday 9 to 6. Map K circle 18.

Qualitie Made Bakery: 2068 West 41st (261-7010). Ah, those noble Scots! Here is the winning entry in the Vancouver Sun's hot cross bun taste competition, and winner of The Province's People's Picks in the same category. They also make delicious cinnamon buns, many fine baked goods and wonderful bread. The window is filled with myriad temptations and often something is on special. Hours are Monday to Thursday and Saturday 8 to 6; Friday 8 to 6:30; and Sunday 10 to 5. Map K circle 19.

On The Go Westcoast Styles: 2007 West 41st (261-6373). Chic and colourful, this boutique features Anne Klein, plus cruise wear, costume jewellery and women's designer fashions. Hours are Monday to Saturday 10 to 5:30. Map K circle 20.

Supersave Sports Collectibles: 2009 West 41st (266-9927). This new shop sells sports cards (new and vintage), posters, magazines, books and some collectible team clothing, such as hockey jerseys. Discounts are offered for frequent buyers. Hours are Monday to Thursday 11:30 to 6; Friday 11:30 to 8; and weekends 11 to 6. Map K circle 21.

Gabriella Fashion Designs: 2033 West 41st (266-5539). Natural fibres and their own label of women's high fashion are the hallmarks of this nice boutique. Note the unique door with varathane-covered fabric. Hours are Monday to Saturday 9:30 to 5:30. Map K circle 22.

Ragfinders: 2045 West 41st (266-3611). Another great find for the uninitiated, this shop sells designer fabrics straight from the mill, which keeps prices down. They also hold great periodic sales. As well, a knowledgable staff is available to offer assistance and suggestions -- gratis! Open Monday to Saturday 9:30 to 5:30. Map K circle 23.

Danica Children's Wear: 2069 West 41st (266-1711). Yes, those yuppie puppies DO have their own store: here you'll find tiny sizes (newborn to 16) for children from labels like Mexx and Esprit, plus boys suits and hearty duffle coats and charming flower-print dresses from Mousefeathers. Open Monday to Saturday 9:30 to 6. Map K circle 24.

Torri's: 5663 West Boulevard (261-2323). Not a political position, this store instead sells ladies' clothing, loads of washable silk fashions and wools. The shop is tiny, and it has lots of stock, so the sale rack is usually on the sidewalk out front. Look for it next to the Cheshire Cheese Inn. Hours are Monday to Saturday 9:30 to 5:30. Map K circle 25.

Byron & Company: 5635 West Boulevard (266-1043). Subtitled "Objects of the World", this lovely collection includes artifacts from Indonesia, India, Thailand and the Philippines, among others. There is jewellery, home decor items, Indonesian shadow puppets, and Buddahs. Clearly one of Lorraine's favourite spots on the tour, she felt like she'd "had a mini-world tour" by the time she left. Open Monday to Saturday 10 to 5:30. Map K circle 26.

Isola Bella Designs: 5633 West Boulevard (266-8808). A top-notch kids' store, the lovely clothing runs from newborn to size 16. There are also shoes, Babar posters and other fine collectibles. Open Monday to Saturday 10 to 5:30. Map K circle 27.

The World of Gifts Shoppe: 5611 West Boulevard (261-7338). Here are lovely Japanese gift items, ceramics, plastic kiddies items (like the Hello Kitty line), Japanese magazines and greeting cards. Hours are Monday to Saturday 11 to 6:30; and Sunday noon to 5:30. Map K circle 28.

Margareta: 5591 West Boulevard (266-6211). We defy you to enter this store and not find something fabulous to buy! Gorgeous designer clothing and accessories for discerning women are showcased in a simply beautiful store -- spacious, well-lit, lovely displays, etc. We could rave on, but just drop in and see for yourself. Hours are Monday to Thursday and Saturday 10 to 6; Friday 10 to 9; and Sunday noon to 5. Map K circle 29.

Keltic Treasures: 5559 West Boulevard (264-0255). Smart folks to forego the "C" spelling, so we'll know how to say it. This shop is filled with Irish clothing and imports, hand-knit cotton sweaters (some originating in Hong Kong), men's authentic tweed hats, silver jewellery and gift items of Irish (and sometimes British) nature. Open Monday to Saturday 10 to 5:30. Map K circle 30.

Holliday's Funwear: 5507 West Boulevard (263-6821). They carry a full line of cruise wear, holiday wear and swinsuits -- even in winter. It's a bit pricey, but their sale prices are excellent and I know people in Port Moody who come all the way into Kerrisdale to shop here. Hours are Monday to Friday 10 to 6; and Saturday 10 to 5:30. Map K circle 31.

House of Brelan: 5485 West Boulevard (263-0089). This is the source for "fashionable classics", as they've dubbed them: women's designer clothing from the likes of Jones New York, and everything from coats, dresses and weekend wear to their specialty -- cotton shirts. Open Monday to Saturday 10 to 5:30. Map K circle 32.

Minka: 2101 West 39th (264-0273). This tiny shop sells Asian imports, porcelain, kimonos, china and gift items. Open Monday to Saturday 10 to 5:30. Map K circle 33.

Hills of Kerrisdale: 2125 West 41st (266-9177). This large store is one of the premier yuppie outfitters in town, carrying men's, women's and loads of teen and children's sizes (where else can you get a smart three-piece suit for your five year old?) in clothing lines like Mexx. Liz Claiborne, Ralph Lauren and Joe Boxer. There are lovely high-end shoes for the whole family, too. Hours are Monday to Thursday and Saturday 9:30 to 6; Firday 9:30 to 9; and Sunday 11 to 5. Map K circle 34.

Thomas Hobbs Florist: 2127 West 41st (263-2601). Simply the best and most creative florist in the lower mainland, Thomas Hobbs sells flowers by the stem, fresh herbs and flowers, wheat-sheaf centrepieces, dried floral arrangements and the most beautiful terra cotta planters, twig baskets and garden ornaments around. Open Monday to Saturday 9:30 to 6. Map K circle 35.

Hobbs: 2129 West 41st (261-5998). Right next door, the sister-operation sells tapestry kits, doorstops, fabulous patio furniture and outdoor accessories, and the most unique and wonderful decor items (all terribly pricey, but well worth it!) we've seen. For the unusual home and the discerning decorator, of course. Open Monday to Saturday 9:30 to 6. There are a few parking spots in the back. Map K circle 36.

Chapy's: 2135 West 41st (261-5128). The British influence is more than apparent in the U.K. souvenirs, brollies and "country weekend wardrobe for the gentlewoman" herein. Hours: Monday to Friday 9:30 to 6; and Saturday 9:30 to 5:30. Map K circle 37.

Buchan's Kerrisdale Stationers: 2141 West 41st (261-8510). This wonderful store sells some of the best greeting cards in town, such as the new releases from Saturday Night Live (featuring the likes of Wayne's World and Hans and Franz and the Church Lady). Along with all this hipness is staid and stolid flowered giftwrap, a very dignified array of art supplies, brushes and *Caran d'Ache* water-soluble crayons (the kind you need for professional face-painting results), zillions of contemporary and unusual calendars, office supplies, labels, gift novelties, helium balloons, party supplies, seasonal paper products (ie for Valentine's Day, St. Patrick's Day, Hallowe'en), fancy wrap by the sheet, gold and silver marking pens (the kind that don't clog up) and unlimited fun just browsing. There's usually a clearance table just inside the front door, and there's free parking in several spaces in the back -- and back door entry for your convenience. Hours: Monday to Saturday 9 to 5:30. Map K circle 38.

Ronson's Shoe Stores: 2145 West 41st (261-5305). Known in their branches elsewhere as "Walk with Ronson", this shop sells men's and women's comfy shoes in a huge range of sizes, and with widths from AAAA to EE. They carry Rockports, Foot Comfort and DreamAir, to mention but a few. Hours are Monday to Saturday 9 to 5. Map K circle 39.

Petite Fashions: 2153 West 41st (266-3577). Here you'll find high fashion clothing for the smaller woman, in sizes as small as 3/4. There's washable silk, Liz Claiborne and other designer lines. They have an Oakridge location, also. Hours here are Monday to Saturday 9:30 to 5:30. Map K circle 40.

Finn's Kerrisdale: 2159 West 41st (266-8358). Another conservative high-end store (though the window displays are often very avant-garde), this one sells men's and women's designer clothing, shoes, sweaters, shirts and jewellery. Open Monday to Saturday 9:30 to 6; and Sunday 10 to 5. Map K circle 41.

Peterson's: 2179 West 41st (266-5620). This has long been our favourite place to line up for their bi-annual shoe sales. Imagine our disappointment to learn they were going out of the shoe business entirely! They've replaced their old stock with country craft gift items like teddy bears and barn-shaped bird houses. They sell handbags, too. Hours: Monday to Friday 9:30 to 6; Saturday 9:30 to 5:30; and Sunday 1 to 5. Map K circle 42.

Purdy's Chocolates: 2189 West 41st (266-9311). One of the nicest of the Purdy's shops (the ladies are so patient and friendly). You know how good Purdy's chocolates are, and the ice-cream bars are a treat in the warm weather, too. Sometimes they sell seconds at half price. Hours are Monday to Saturday 9:30 to 5:30. Map K circle 43.

Vanity Hosiery: 2193 West 41st (261-0041). Yet another Kerrisdale landmark, it seems as though this one has been there forever. They have lovely lingerie of every size, colour and description -- a really extensive stock, and unusual sizes, too. They share premises with our next entry:

Price/Less: 5692 Yew (261-0041). Don't let the cheapo-discount look of the sign scare you off, the values are substantial and the stock is all designer goods from the houses of Mr. Jax, Koret and Andrea Gayle, among others. Hours for both sides of the store are Monday to Thursday and Saturday 9 to 5:30; and Friday 9 to 9. Map K circle 44.

Kerrisdale Market Place: 2233 West 41st (261-1226). This location encompasses Macfarlane's Seafood, Shaughnessy Fine Meats, Kerrisdale Scottish Bakery, and Olivieri's deli and fresh pasta items. One stop shopping for your specialty food needs. Hours are Monday to Friday 9 to 5:30; and Saturday 9 to 5. Map K circle 45.

Curran's of Kerrisdale: 2247 West 41st (261-7017). Another fine lingerie store, this one is open Monday to Saturday 9:30 to 5:30. Map K circle 46.

Borgia Fine Foods: 2255 West 41st (261-9192). A tempting assortment of ready-made take-away foods is offered in this new store -- and they do catering, too. The promise to open Sundays during the warm weather of summer, but meanwhile, their hours are Monday to Saturday 8 to 6. Map K circle 47.

Brussels Chocolates: 2257 West 41st (263-3292). Truly one of the best chocolatiers in Vancouver! You've got to try the milk chocolate hedgehogs or any one of the liquor-filled chocolates. Heaven! Hours are Monday to Saturday 10 to 9; and Sunday noon to 6. Map K circle 48.

Mode Fabrics: 2259 West 41st (266-7232). This is a lovely shop with fine quality fashion fabrics -- most natural fibres like wools and cottons. Hours are Monday to Saturday 9:30 to 5:30. Map K circle 49.

The Legh Shop: 2279 West 41st (266-9169). Pronounced "Lee", this exclusive shop has a fresh assortment of china, table lines and other gift and accessory ideas for the most discerning shopper. Here's where you'll find those bronze garden faucets (with either rose or shell handles) that you've been looking for! Hours are Monday to Saturday 9:30 to 5:30. Map K circle 50.

Norma Paterson: 2283 West 41st (266-3345). This charming shop (mainly) features its own women's fashion label, including lots of knitwear and five wide-ranging sizes from super-petite to super sizes. There's a nice selection of jewellery, too. Open Monday to Thursday 9 to 6; Friday 9 to 9; Saturday 9 to 5:30; and Sunday noon to 5. Map K circle 51.

Louise of Kerrisdale: 2295 West 41st (263-1484). Fashions here include Susan Bristol, Simon Chang and that hard-to-find petite line by Carole Little. Most stock is ladies designer wear, and all regular stock is priced to be "GST-free". Open Monday to Saturday 10 to 5:30. Map K circle 52.

Linen Collection: 2297A West 41st (261-5101). This is a great source for Battenbury lace and other cut-work white-on-white embroidered linens. There are loads of other types of table and pantry linens, as well as mini-furniture suitable for collectors or dollhouses. Hours are Monday to Saturday 11 to 5:30. Map K circle 53.

David Saba's Fast Feet: 2323 West 41st (266-3535). A good outlet for sports clothing, casual clothing and runners, this one has a few spaces in the back if you can't find easy street parking. Open Monday to Friday 9:30 to 6; and Saturday 9:30 to 5. Map K circle 54.

Yerushalem Imports: 2375 West 41st (266-0662). This is a real hidden treasure for gift-seekers: Anne found the most wonderful heavy felt alphabet hangings (26 pockets with 3-D felt shapes representing each letter in the English alphabet) -- AND -- a version with the entire Hebrew alphabet which we're sure you'll find nowhere else in town! There are books, Hebrew greeting cards, seasonal items for Jewish holidays and great gifts for people of every religious stripe, all from the Holyland. Open Monday to Saturday 10 to 6; and Sunday noon to 5. Map K circle 55.

Windmill Toys: 2347 West 41st (261-2120). Simply one of the very best toy stores in town, this one stocks the best -- and most creative -- toys available. There are books, dolls, party supplies, costumes (at Hallowe'en), stocking stuffers, and an entire area devoted to trains complete with working models and a large assortment of parts. Hours are Monday to Thursday 9:30 to 6; Friday 9:30 to 9; Saturday 9:30 to 5:30; and Sunday noon to 5. Map K circle 56.

Affordables: 2433 West 41st (266-3334). Why not end our tour on a high note? Here you'll find a fabulous collection of decorator fabrics, all at great discounts! Inside the store, you'll find it opens right into Morley Charles Interiors, so expert advice is close at hand, too. If you live in the Vancouver area, watch local papers for their (incredible) periodic sales. Open Monday to Saturday 9 to 5. Map K circle 57.

NOTES:

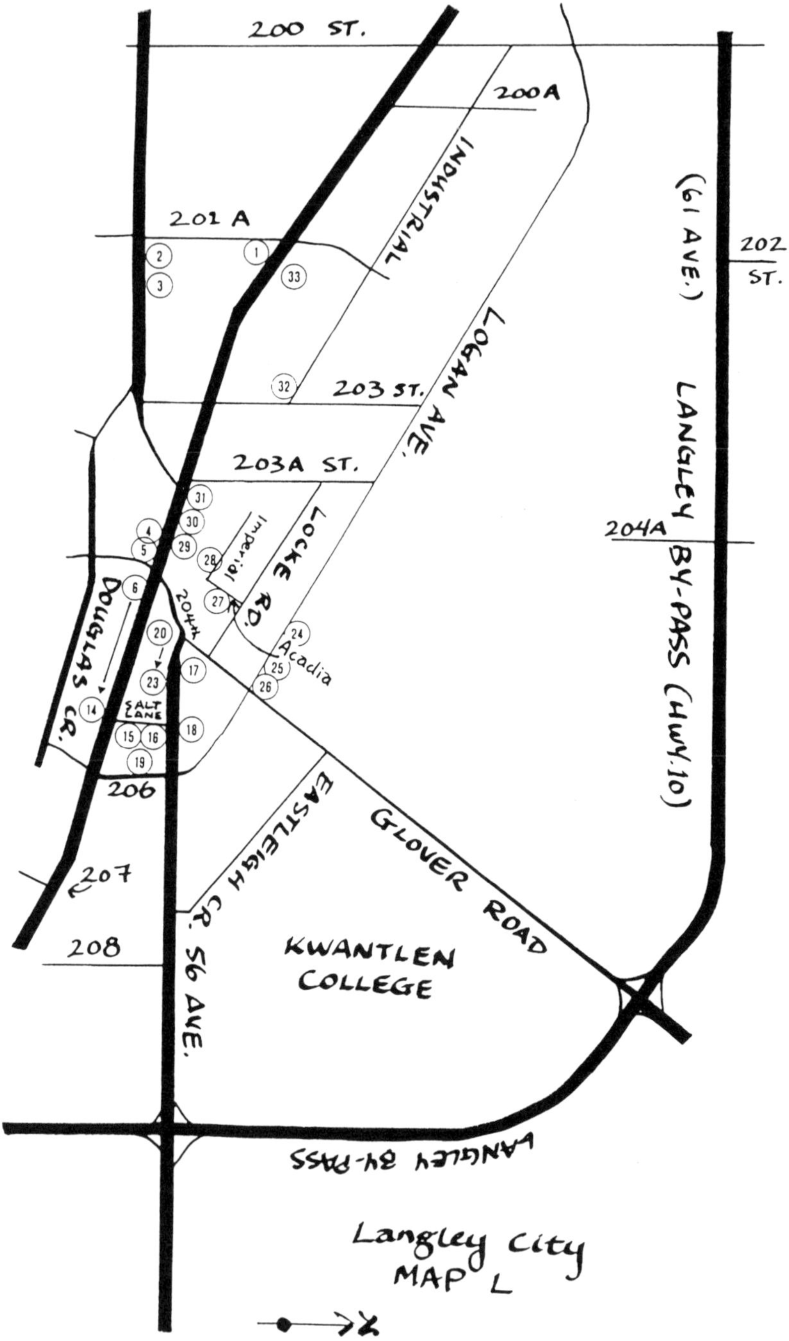
200 ST.
200A
INDUSTRIAL
201 A
(61 AVE.)
202 ST.
LOGAN AVE.
203 ST.
203A ST.
LANGLEY BY-PASS (HWY.10)
LOCKE RD.
Imperial
204A
DOUGLAS CR.
204A
Acadia
SALT LANE
206
EASTLEIGH CR.
GLOVER ROAD
207
208
56 AVE.
KWANTLEN COLLEGE
LANGLEY BY-PASS
Langley City
MAP L

Langley City

Country bargains and collectibles

This is a major tour which you should consider an all-day outing, if you want to include every stop. Many places are good for browsing, so you're likely to get stuck in a shopping time-warp if you're not careful!

Langley City can be found via any of four main routes from Vancouver: (1) Take TransCanada 1 to the Langley 200th St exit; (2) Follow Kingsway to the Patullo Bridge in New West and cross the river to Surrey. Take the King Geo. Hwy. past the Surrey Public Market to Fraser Hwy (Hwy. #10), which leads into the heart of Langley; (3) Take the Oak St. Bridge toward Richmond, but stay on Hwy. 99 and take the Hwy. #10 exit toward Langley; or (4) Drive out East Hastings, a scenic route along the Barnet Hwy., past Ioco, through Port Moody, Coquitlam and Port Coquitlam to Haney, then take the (free) Albion ferry across to Fort Langley.
The nearest U.S. border crossing is at Lynden / Aldergrove. From there, U.S. visitors should head north on 264th St. through Aldergrove and turn left at Fraser Hwy. (Hwy. #10) to continue on to Langley City.

Consider adding on a visit to Fort Langley, which is reached from Langley City by taking Glover Rd. in a northeasterly direction right into town.

People wishing to use public transit to reach Langley should take the SkyTrain to Scott Rd. Station, then change to either the #501 (Langley South) bus (which is the direct route), or the #320 (Langley), which describes a more circuitous route via Cloverdale. Either route will take about an hour from Vancouver.

Parking can sometimes be surprisingly difficult on the main streets of Langley, but there are a few mini malls with lots of space in their parking area for overflow. As always, a weekday visit yields the easiest parking.

Langley celebrates its Country Style Days during the third week of June annually, so expect crowds, a country fair and even a parade if you visit then.

<u>Sun Fresh Produce:</u> 20188 Fraser Hwy. (533-8832). What could you expect from a place that advertises "lowest prices — highest quality", and urges you to "buy by the case & save more"? We've always found a good selection of produce and excellent prices here. Open Monday to Saturday 8 to 6; and Sunday 10 to 6. Map L circle 1.

Salvation Army: 20179 56th Ave. (530-1321). This has always been a good hunting ground for bargains. Generally, furniture is on the ground floor and clothing upstairs, but on nice days, there's a rack of clothing outside as well. Open Monday to Saturday 9 to 5. Map L circle 2.

Workwear World: 20211 56th Ave. (533-1647). The usual casual and work clothing, work boots and jeans are found at this branch of the popular chain. Hours are Monday, Tuesday and Saturday 9 to 6; Wednesday to Friday 9 to 9; and Sunday 10 to 5. Map L circle 3.

Foots: 20354 Fraser Hwy. (530-5848). Here's the Langley source for coins, stamps, medals and collectables. Open Tuesday to Friday 11 to 5; Saturday 10 to 4; closed Sunday and Monday. Map L circle 4.

Madhouse: 20364 Fraser Hwy. (533-0633). This place specializes in buying, selling and trading comic, posters (comic-related themes), sportscards and comic memorabilia. Open Monday to Friday 10 to 6; Saturday 10 to 5; and Sunday noon to 5. Map L circle 5.

Pantastic Jeans Shop: 20416 Fraser Hwy. (533-2814). Here's a good assortment of jeans, sweats, T-shirts and other casual clothing, all at reduced prices. Hours are Monday to Saturday 10:30 to 5:30. Map L circle 6.

Stein Bros. Collectables: 10456 Fraser Hwy. (534-4414). This is where the serious collector goes for Bradford Exchange plates and Ashton-Drake dolls. They also sell a few needlework supplies. Open Monday to Saturday 9:30 to 5:30. Map L circle 7.

Discount Tapes & Records: 20465 Fraser Hwy. (534-5150). Here's a favourite spot for new and used tapes, records, books and CDs, all at very reasonable prices (used CDs run $9.95 and $10.95). Open Monday to Saturday 10 to 6. Map L circle 8.

Mad Dog's Ski & Sports: 20478 Fraser Hwy. (534-3913). Their ski sales are legendary. Otherwise, they have good prices on all sports equipment, bikes and some sports clothing. Hours: Monday to Thursday 9:30 to 6; Friday 9:30 to 9; Saturday 9 to 5:30; and Sunday noon to 5. Map L circle 9.

Copp Discount Centre: 20484 Fraser Hwy. (534-2314). Here's a family shoe outlet where Anne bought a spur-of-the-moment pair of short, lined, warm leather boots in the middle of a freak snow storm for peanuts! The selection is often limited but the styles are fairly up-to-date and the staff is exceptionally friendly and helpful. Open Monday to Saturday 9:30 to 5:30. Map L circle 10.

Auld-Phillips: 20500 Fraser Hwy. (534-6311). Though the clothes are a little on the conservative side, this is our kind of store: Stock is mainly women's clothing and shoes in a large (double storefront) store. The complementary coffee is always on, there's a save-on-fashion department at the back, and a nice assortment of purses and costume jewellery. Hours: Monday to Thursday and Saturday 9:30 to 5:30; Friday 9:30 to 9. Map L circle 11.

Designer Consignment: 20506 Fraser Hwy. (534-3491). A relatively-new location, this shop sells shoes, jewellery, clothing and accessories on consignment. Open Monday to Saturday 10 to 5. Map L circle 12.

Mennonite Central Committee Thrift Store: 20514 Fraser Hwy. (533-2844). Another of our favourites, added to the clean, good condition thrift items are really top-quality craft items from third world countries around the globe - all at delightfully low prices. A similar MCC operation is found in our Fraser area tour. Open Tuesday to Saturday 9:30 to 5. Map L circle 13.

United Buy & Sell: 20542 Fraser Hwy. (534-6262). Branches of these stores have been springing up around the lower mainland like mushrooms after a rain. Why? Because they sell reasonably good furniture at really low prices, without pressure. Open Monday to Wednesday and Saturday 10 to 6; Thursday and Friday 10 to 9. Map L circle 14.

Ambassador Book Buyers: 5490 Salt Lane (534-2124). Though their sign says "discount books", this is just a normal used book store, but they stand out because they also buy stamp collections, and hockey, football and baseball cards. Hours are Monday to Saturday 10:30 to 5. Map L circle 15.

Nechako Tack & Giftware: 5496 Salt Lane (530-9794). Here, the front of a vet's office has been turned into a store that sells animal-related gift items (figures, mugs, cards, etc.) and equestrian tack. Open Monday to Saturday 9 to 5. Map L circle 16.

Value Village: 5666 Glover Rd. (533-1663). This branch offers standard "VV" fare, plus a lot of toys. Anne found a great wig for a costume party here, cheaply. Open Monday to Friday 9 to 9; Saturday 9 to 6; and Sunday 10 to 6. Map L circle 17.

Saan: 20555 56th Ave. (534-1828). We've always considered this the "Fields" of the Valley — a family clothing store with lower end merchandise—a good source for reasonably-priced basics, and it's also known for really good clearance sales. Hours: Monday to Wednesday and Saturday 9:30 to 6; Thursday and Friday 9:30 to 9; and Sunday 10 to 5. Map L circle 18.

Thread & Thimble: 20568A 56th Ave. (534-9119). This small fabric shop usually has a 50 percent off table of fabrics, plus a good array of notions. Open Monday to Thursday 9:30 to 5:30; and Saturday 10 to 5. Map L circle 19.

Valley Fresh Fish: 20568B 56th Ave. (534-8717). They make fresh sushi and pack salmon for travel. They had fresh rainbow trout when we visited. The sign says "fresh fish & Japanese food". Open Monday to Saturday 10 to 6. Map L circle 19.

Langley Guns & Tackle: 20568C 56th Ave. (530-7899). This is where local hunters and fishermen "arm" themselves. Open Monday to Friday 9:30 to 5:30; and Saturday 9:30 to 5. Map L circle 19.

Orphan Annie's: 3, 20505 Fraser Hwy. (533-4322). Here's a small but intriguing collection of collectables, bears, new and used (antique) toys and dolls and greeting cards along bear themes. Open Tuesday to Saturday 10 to 4, Map L circle 20.

Tamm's Valley Stationery: 20489 Fraser Hwy. (530-4343). The sign out front says "the discount store", and we've found the prices very good indeed. There's mainly office supplies, and inexpensive photocopying, too. Hours are Monday to Friday 9:30 to 5:30; and Saturday 10 to 5. Map L circle 21.

The Hobby Hut: 20483 Fraser Hwy. (534-1125). Here you'll find model kits, painting and art supplies, every kind of craft supply, and even cake decorating supplies and books. The walkway to 56th Ave. beside the store has glass cases full of examples of things you can make and do. They run classes, too and have a big bulletin board near the entrance advertising upcoming events, suppliers and local artisans. Open Monday to Thursday and Saturday 9 to 5:30; Friday 9 to 8; and Sunday noon to 4. Map L circle 22.

Pavia Gallery: 20477 Fraser Hwy. (533-3880). We loved the items here! They specialize in hand-painted silk clothing and knitted garments and also offer charming silk earrings and gorgeous hand-painted umbrellas. Open Monday to Saturday 10 to 5. Map L circle 23.

Heritage House Gallery: 20477 Fraser Hwy. (530-0121). Mainly Canadian-made crafts are showcased here (especially lovely pottery). The store is lovely too. with beautiful stock well-displayed. Open Monday to Saturday 10 to 5. Map L circle 23.

Penny Pincher: 20470 Logan Ave. (530-3232). Here in the Rainbow Mall, is the thrift shop for the Langley Memorial Hospital —always one of our "best" sources — what Lorraine refers to as a "good old heaped-full-of-everything thrift shop". The last Saturday of each month all clothing is half price. Sometimes they have "bag day", when you purchase a standard grocery bag for $3 and you can fill it with your choice of any clothing. They also sell toys and housewares. Open Tuesday to Saturday 10 to 4. Map L circle 24.

Holland Shopping Centre: 20474 Logan Ave. (534-5111). Another shop in the Rainbow Mall, this one sells Dutch specialty foods, deli items, bulk Dutch candies, salted licorice, etc. all from self-serve jars. There's also a little coffee shop within, which serves sandwiches and coffee (ie. herring on bread —!— $2.60) and Dutch souvenirs like Delft-look china. Open Monday to Thursday and Saturday 9 to 5:30; and Friday 9 to 9. Map L circle 25.

Field's: 20500 Logan Ave. (534-7408). One-quarter of this Rainbow Mall branch is a clearance centre for clothing and a few housewares. Seniors get and additional 15% off on the last Monday of every month. Open Monday to Wednesday and Saturday 9:30 to 5; Thursday and Friday 9:30 to 9; and Sunday 11 to 5. Map L circle 26.

Coast Auctions: 5666 Acacia (530-7300). This is a great bargain find (via auction), with odds and ends, wicker, gift items, ski wear and craft supplies available on a "regular" basis — that is, when they are open. Despite their odd hours, they are always open Tuesday for all-day viewings of auction items. Auctions take place every Tuesday evening. Map L circle 27.

Langley Family Service Flea Market: 20300 Imperial (534-7921). This place hosts an inside and outside swap meet Sundays from 8 am to 3 pm. Map L circle 28.

Jack's Pawn Shop: 20337 Fraser Hwy. (533-4707). We found lots of sports equipment here. Open Monday to Friday 9:30 to 5. Map L circle 29.

Big Deal: 20331 Fraser Hwy. (533-0536). This discounter sells housewares, toys, shoes and some clothing. Basically, if they get a deal, you get a deal. Friends of Lorraine's found lots of great birthday loot-bag stuff here. Open Monday to Saturday 9:30 to 5. Map L circle 30.

Sir Plus Outdoor Store: 20305 Fraser Hwy. (530-1008). Good prices here on sleeping bags, rainsuits and camping equipment. Hours are Monday to Friday 9:30 to 6; and Saturday 9:30 to 5:30. Map L circle 31.

Jammer Zone Outlet: 102 20290 Industrial (533-1154). Advertising "active wear for active bodies, this modest-sized recent arrival features sizes 2 to adult in tye-dyed cool clothing, with well-known local labels like "Radical" and "Oh Zone". Open Monday to Thursday 9:30 to 5; Friday 9:30 to 8; and Saturday 10 to 5. Map L circle 32.

L.A.'s Warehouse Shoes: 201 20290 Industrial (533-1154). Women's, men's and children's shoes are sold in a warehouse format at discount prices here with labels like Brooks and L.A. Gear in the forefront. Sizes 2 to adult are available. Open same hours as Jammer Zone (above). Map L circle 32.

Fun Under $5: 104 20151 Fraser Hwy. (530-7866). Literally nothing here is over $5 in price - and most are well under that limit: housewares, gift items, toys, IBM shareware and a good selection of seasonal items — another good source of goodie-bag stuff. Open Monday, Tuesday and Saturday 9:30 to 6; Wednesday to Friday 9:30 to 9; and Sunday noon to 5. Map L circle 33.

Super Save Mart: 101 20151 Fraser Hwy. (533-1289). A liquidation mart, this one has constantly changing stock such as toys, housewares, lighting fixtures and more. Open Monday to Wednesday and Saturday 9:30 to 6; Thursday and Friday 9:30 to 9; and Sunday 10 to 6. Map L circle 33.

Save-on Foods & Durgs: 100 20151 Fraser Hwy. (533-1911). One of the original mass discounters, this store has a nice bulk food section (a little less jammed than some), and the usual good pharmacy, discount books, bakery, flower department - plus - a smoke house where they smoke their own bacon. Open seven days 8 to midnight. Map L circle 33.

NOTES:

Main and 49th Avenue

"Little India"

This interesting tour should take only 2 hours if you see everything.

Street parking is always difficult (even though it's free) in the area, but there is pay parking (cheap, at 50 cents for 2 hours) in the lot off the lane on the west side of Main, south of 49th.

Many stores are open seven days a week. Others are closed Tuesday, with eccentric hours -- it seems some owner-operated shops will close whenever they feel like it if business is slow, so if you want to see one in particular, please be sure to call ahead so they'll know you're planning to come by. That way, you won't find it closed and be disappointed. Here's a quick overview before we get into the main tour:

Punjabi Market at 6569 Main and 49th is an Indian mini-mall with gift shops, saree shops, jewellers and outlets selling Indian music tapes and videos (India has a gigantic film industry of course).

Food stores carry fresh produce such as the long skinny purple eggplants, okra and many varieties of chillies ranging from hot to lethal! You can buy bulk spices, legumes and nuts, canned and bottled specialties such as mango juice, rose water and chutneys, and of course milk is bargain-priced because the Indian community consumes so much of it. There are also really good values in stainless steel cookware and serving trays.

Fabric and clothing stores abound, some selling material by the entire bolt or in saree lengths (approximately 6 yards) which are often beaded or extravagantly embroidered in silver or gold. Other fabrics are sold in *shilvar kamis* (Pubjabi trouser suit) lengths of about 3 yards. Many had a good selection of raw silk and some unique woven patterned silk or jacquards.

Jewellery is mostly wrought in 22K and 24K. Places like Sungold Jewellery (6565 Main) have highly-accurate scales to weigh gold content, then a design fee is added on for custom work. Costume jewellery is everywhere, in almost every shop, so comparison-shop for the best deal. We've eliminated jewellery shops entirely from this tour because there are simply too many of them!

To reach the area from the U.S. border crossing, take Highway 99 north to the Oak Street Bridge, but take the Marine Drive East exit (marked as "City Centre" on the sign near the exit) and travel east on S.W. Marine

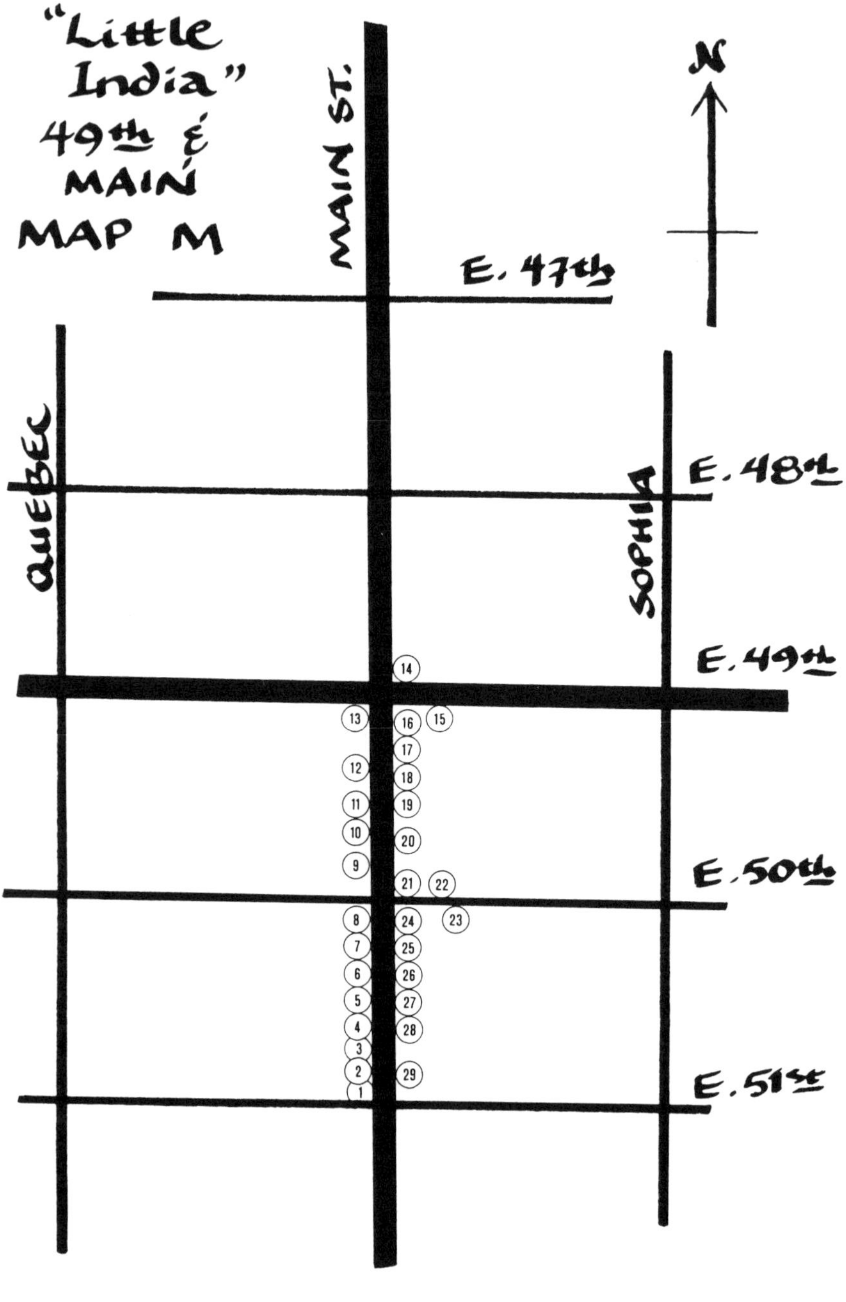
"Little India"
49th & MAIN
MAP M
MAIN ST.
N
E. 47th
QUEBEC
SOPHIA
E. 48th
E. 49th
E. 50th
E. 51st
1
2
3
4
5
6
7
8
9
10
11
12
13
14
15
16
17
18
19
20
21
22
23
24
25
26
27
28
29

Drive to Main Street. Turn left (north) onto Main and follow it right down to about 51st and Main, where our tour begins.

By public transit, you can reach the area by taking the SkyTrain to Science World-Main St. station, then transferring to the #3 bus, which runs south on Main.

Frontier Cloth House: 6695 Main (325-3515). The window displays a variety of sarees and suits. This large, busy and always-bustling store also sells bedspreads and blankets, shoes and fabrics. Hours are Monday, Wednesday and weekends 10 to 6:30; Thursday and Friday 10 to 8; and closed Tuesday. Map M circle 1.

The Video Shop: 6669 Main (321-1333). They rent Indian videos and also sell cassettes and CDs. Open Monday, and Wednesday to Saturday 10:30 to 6:30; Sunday noon to 5:30; and closed Tuesday. Map M circle 2.

Main Saree Centre: 6665 Main (322-3444). In this small shop there are sarees, slippers and vases. Open six days 11 to 6; and closed Tuesday. Map M circle 3.

Amar Cloth House: 6657 Main (324-9191). Tapes, fabric and embroidered tunics -- they have it all. They sell fabric by the yard or in suit lengths. Open seven days 10 to 7. Map M circle 4.

Flying Fashion: 6647 Main (327-9444). Opened in summer '92, this bright store sells sarees, children's suits and many sparkly trims, purses, bangles, gold belts and garlands. Usually there's something sale priced and there's a discount rack, too. Open seven days 10 to 7. Map M circle 5.

Michael's Discount Foods: 6635 Main (322-5502). One of Anne's favourites, she's entranced by the wonderful smell of spices and incense, Indian radio playing in the background and their great prices on housewares, bulk foods and produce. Last time in, milk was only $2.99 to $3.39 for a 4 litre jug! Open seven days 9 to 9. Map M circle 6.

Ashoka: 6621 Main (324-7521). Here we found a full counter of bangles at $4 a dozen, plus fabric, trims and other costume jewellery. This large store is open seven days 10 to 7. Map M circle 7.

J & B Foods: 6607 Main (321-0224). Like Galloway's with an Indian flavour, they sell cookware, pots and woks. Hours are Monday to Saturday 10 to 6; and Sunday 11 to 5. Map M circle 8.

Bombay Cloth House: 203, 6569 Main (327-4459). Another good source of silks and saree lengths. This one is open seven days 10 to 8. Map M circle 9.

Roshan's Saree Centre: 6563 Main (322-9485). A boutique operation. Hours are Monday, Wednesday, Thursday and Saturday 11 to 6:30; Friday 11 to 8; Sunday noon to 6:30; and closed Tuesday. Map M circle 10.

Mohan Cloth House: 6545 Main (321-4211). The sign says "artificial jewellery", plus they sell women's and children's clothing, trims, yard goods, and hats in a crowded little shop just like one you'd find in India itself. Open seven days 10 to 8. Map M circle 11.

Guru Bazaar: 6529 Main (327-3033). They sell ready-made Indian clothing, pre-cut saree and suit lengths, fabric and jewellery. Open seven days 10 to 7 or 7:30. Map M circle 12.

All India Foods: 6517 Main (324-2195). Find bulk foods, fresh produce, Indian spices and specialty items and unusual names for familiar products in this new location of the area's most popular supermarket. For example, "dnaniya" means cilantro, which of course is also known as coriander and Chinese parsley. Confusing, isn't it? You'll see produce outside, as well as the adjoining All India Sweets shop and cafe-sized restaurant. Open seven days 9:30 to 7:30. Map M circle 13.

Wescana House of Gifts: 6494 Main (325-2201). Here you'll find a blend of clothing, accessories, those ubiquitous bangles (well-priced, here), lamps, shoes, ceramics, purses and some very attractive bolo ties with charming slides finished with rhinestones. Open seven days 11 to 6:30. Map M circle 14.

Details: 210 East 49th (322-6066). Here's a high-end shop of men's designer silk fashions, many of them at factory clear-out prices! We saw some gorgeous silk bomber jackets last visit. Open six days 10:30 to 7; and closed Tuesday. Map M circle 15.

Ashoka Boutique: 6502 Main (322-1113). Unlike the other Ashoka earlier in this tour, this small shop is self-described as selling "highclass fashions, bridal wear and jewellery". Open seven days 10 to 7. Map M circle 16.

Shahnoor: 6510 Main (322-5411). This tiny shop is probably the most chic store in the area. It's part of a famous chain of boutiques which leads the fashion market in India, so naturally their elegant ladies' apparel is different from the traditional sarees you'll find elsewhere on

Main. A prototype Canadian version in Toronto was so successful they opened one here in early 1992. There are lovely hand-painted silk dresses and sarees, novel earrings, and many choices of golden trims and braids. Anne was captivated by the unusual "bindi" charms -- variations on the dots that Indian women often wear on their foreheads -- only these were "instant beauty press-ons", many in modern motifs that teens might use as unique faux earrings. Open seven days 11 to 7. Map M circle 17.

Rani Fashions: 6518 Main (325-3242). Jewellery and gifts are amassed here, plus brass, silver, china and other giftware. Hours are Monday to Saturday 11 to 7:30; and Sunday 11 to 6:30. Map M circle 18.

New Silk Emporium: 6542 Main (324-5650). Shelves of sarees, regional dresses, some children's apparel and fabric by the yard is sold here. Open seven days 11 to 7. Map M circle 19.

Bombay Sweet Shop: 6556 Main (874-5722). Both the divine and the dreadful of Indian sweets (a matter of personal taste, we think) are sold here. At the very least it's an interesting experience. We can agree we like the gulab jamun, kind of an Indian version of *baba au rhum*. The charming and personable owner, Nick Shukla, also operates a very successful restaurant and grocery store at this address. Open seven days 9 to 9. Map M circle 20.

Sadhna Saree House: 6580 Main (322-7666). A small shop, this one sells raw silk, unique woven pattern silks and jacquards. Hours are Monday to Wednesday and weekends 10:30 to 7; Thursday 10:30 to 8; and Friday 10:30 to 9. Map M circle 21.

Quality Shoes & Gifts: 215 East 50th (322-1494). Just around the corner, this shop sells toys and gifts, shoes, children's clothing and brassware -- something for everyone. Open six days 11 to 7; and closed Tuesday. Map M circle 22.

The Bride & Groom Shop: 216 East 50th (324-5662). We both love this shop (across the street from Quality Shoes) which is full of tacky car decorations and wedding accessories. There are small bridal gifts for Indian-style weddings, too. Open Wednesday to Monday 10 to 7:30; and closed Tuesday. Map M circle 23.

London Fashion & Fabrics: 6602 Main (325-2249). Back around the corner of 50th, fabric here is highlighted with beading and gold thread. Gorgeous embroidered sarees are in the window and there's also fabric by the yard. Hours are Monday to Wednesday and weekends 10 to 7; and Thursday and Friday 10 to 8. Map M circle 24.

Shingaar Emporium: 6610 Main (324-8127). Here you'll discover bangles galore, hairpieces, unique musical instruments, footware, decorations and other costume jewellery. This owner-operated shop is usually open seven days 10:30 to 6:30. Map M circle 25.

Mona Cloth House: 6642 Main (321-5511). We found brightly coloured sweaters on a rack outside, shoes, bedding and fabric ready-mades inside. Open seven days 10 to 7:30. Map M circle 26.

Punjab Cloth House: 6660 Main (325-8383). Here's another very popular saree shop with a good selection of yard goods. Open seven days 10 to 8. Map M circle 27.

Memsaab Boutique: 6674 Main (322-0250). This shop sells polyester, raw silk and lots of shoes so you can be fully costumed from head to toe. Open seven days 11 to 7. Map M circle 28.

Singh Foods: 6684 Main (327-4911). Huge bags of rice flour, bulk spices, produce (out front, as well as inside), cookware and pots are available here. Open seven days 9 to 8. Map M circle 29.

NOTES:

Mount Pleasant and City Hall areas

Sporting Goods and Wholesale bargains

This is a varied and interesting tour which could take four to five hours to see everything. The area was once very chic, has become badly rundown (over the past forty years!), and is now "on the way up" again. If you're looking for camping equipment or sporting goods, by the way, don't forget to check out Cheapskates (all three locations are profiled in our Almadene tour) and two brand new shops called Sports Junkies, and the Sports Exchange.

We'll give directions to start at Vancouver City Hall because it's such an easy landmark to find: City Hall was built at the crest of the hill at Cambie Street and West 12th Avenue, when the area was still partly forested and a creek ran down the hill. Nowadays, the intersection boasts a fabulous view of the city and inner waterways, and the North Shore mountains beyond.

Our first tour stop is north of City Hall, at 8th and Yukon (one block east of Cambie). To get to Broadway (equivalent to 9th Ave.) and Yukon by public transit, take the #9 Broadway bus from points on that line to Yukon and walk down the hill one block. From the SkyTrain or Sea-Bus stations, take the #17 bus (Downtown or Oak) to Cambie and 8th. With all that said, we'd recommend driving this tour because though the first few stores are close together, the rest are quite spread out.

If driving from the U.S. border, the Douglas crossing (and Hwy 99 North) will flow directly into Oak Street. Take Oak north to Broadway and turn right (east). Cambie is the next major street east, and Yukon is one block east of that. Turn left (north) at Yukon to begin the tour.

Street parking for many places on this tour is difficult. Some stores, such as Three Vets, Mountain Co-op or Canadian Tire have their own customer lots. DPC Parking at Kingsway/Main and 7th is only 50 cents an hour.

A.J. Brooks Sporting Goods: 386 West 8th (874-1117). Here you'll find trendy, quality outdoor clothing and equipment. By comparison to Taiga and Mountain Equipment, it's very modest in stock, but as we said "quality". They carry the Meindl line of imported German hiking boots and some practical and luxurious sweaters. Open Monday to Thursday and Saturday 10 to 6; and Friday 10 to 9. Map O circle 1.

Taiga Works Wilderness Equipment Ltd.: 390 West 8th (875-6655). These folks manufacture outdoor clothing, sleeping bags, back packs,

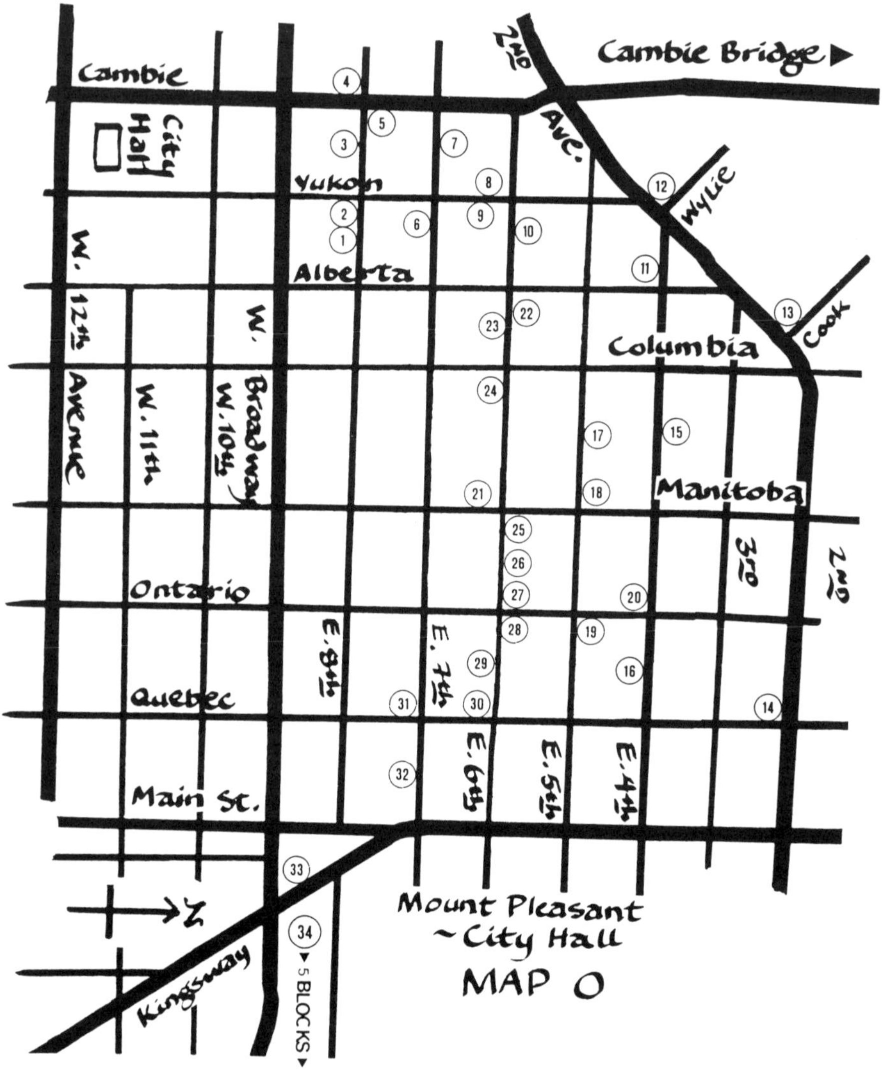
Cambie
Cambie Bridge
2nd Ave.
City Hall
Yukon
Alberta
Columbia
Manitoba
Ontario
Quebec
Main St.
Kingsway
W. 12th Avenue
W. 11th
W. Broadway
W. 10th
Wylie
Cook
3rd
2nd
E. 8th
E. 7th
E. 6th
E. 5th
E. 4th
N
5 BLOCKS
1
2
3
4
5
6
7
8
9
10
11
12
13
14
15
16
17
18
19
20
21
22
23
24
25
26
27
28
29
30
31
32
33
34
Mount Pleasant ~City Hall
MAP O

carry sacks, tents and boots. There's a 2 percent discount on cash or cheque payment (as opposed to credit card, though they do accept them) and they keep a mailing list if you're interested in their catalogue. Open Monday to Thursday 10 to 6; Friday 10 to 9; and Saturday 9:30 to 6. Map O circle 2.

Mountain Equipment Co-op: 428 West 8th (872-7858). This is open to members only, but that's easy, because anyone can join! Membership costs $5 (lifetime) and entitles you to modest discounts on outdoor equipment, climbing, hiking, cycling and camping gear and books on related subjects. There's a bulletin board of used gear-for-sale ads. Mountain Co-op has its own parking lot. Find the building by its evergreen trees painted on the side. Hours are Monday to Wednesday 10 to 6; Thursday and Friday 10 to 9; and Saturday 9:30 to 6. Map O circle 3.

Las Vegas Discount Golf & Tennis: 520 West 8th (877-1476). The name says it all: rackets, clubs and accessories. Open Monday to Wednesday and Saturday 10 to 6; Thursday and Friday 10 to 9; and Sunday 11 to 5. Map O circle 4.

Sport Mart: 2300 Cambie (873-6737). Their advertising says "We'll beat any price in Canada by 25 percent of the difference or it's yours free". That's good enough for us: This IS a discount sports store! Stock changes to reflect the season, with bikes, rollerskates and in-line rollers in summer, ski equipment in winter. Open Monday to Wednesday and Saturday 9 to 6; Thursday and Friday 9 to 9; and Sunday 11 to 5. Map O circle 5.

National Wholesale Clothing: 336 West 7th (877-1106). This true wholesaler of men's, women's and children's clothing prefers that you have an appointment, but if they're not too busy with wholesale customers, they'll help you. You tell them what you are interested in and they'll try to show you what they have, but they don't allow you to browse through their stock by yourself. There are no designer labels, but a wide selection of good quality family clothing. Please tread carefully and don't take up too much of their time, so we don't spoil it for other bargain-hunters! Hours are Monday to Friday 9:30 to 4:30. Map O circle 6.

Canadian Tire: 455 West 5th (421-9389). This Canadian success story has branches across the country. This one is smallish, but still offers a good assortment of automotive supplies and accessories, housewares and sporting goods. This City Hall branch has a Mount Pleasant cousin on Kingsway just past Fraser. Open Monday to Friday 9 to 9; Saturday 9 to 6; and Sunday 10 to 5. Map O circle 7.

Gray Beverage Inc. 2215 Yukon (875-6713). You'll find that prices at Costco and supermarkets selling loss leaders are cheaper, but this soft drink wholesaler sells case lots everyday at prices less than most stores' regular prices, making it a great source for parties. Open Monday to Friday 9 to 5. Map O circle 8.

Three Vets: 2200 Yukon (872-5475). A Vancouver icon, Three Vets sells camping equipment, totes, backpacks, hunting and fishing gear, sporting goods, good quality footwear and most everything you'd need for survival and outdoors activities, all at low everyday prices. This is where we went to equip our earthquake emergency box, and found prices lower than everywhere else. One great Three Vets surprise is the small collection (much of it for sale) of fabulous native indian art and artifacts at the far side of the store - prices on these items (many of museum quality) are also modest, considering their intrinsic and aesthetic value. Open Monday to Thursday and Saturday9 to 5:30; and Friday 9 to 9. Map O circle 9.

Neville Crosby Industries: 325 West 6th (873-4343). This interesting store sells mining, forestry and drafting supplies, plus outdoors industry supplies like backpacks, sleeping foam (at good prices), haversacks, thermoses, insect repellant, etc. When we visited they were having a buy-one, get another for a penny sale. Open Monday to Friday 8:30 to 5; and Saturday 9 to 3. Map O circle 10.

Butt & Bowes: 310 West 4th (872-8121). We've found this source of china, glassware and flatware to be hot and cold: Sometimes there are bargains, sometimes not. It functions as a restaurant supply, so you can find deals on discontinued patterns, overstock, seconds and more, plus they carry Heritage silverware and the Royal Doulton china lines used by hotels and airlines. Open Monday to Friday 8:30 to 5. Map O circle 11.

Maynard's Auctioneers: 415 West 2nd (876-1311). True, Maynard's is Vancouver's biggest auction house, but they also liquidate stock from backruptcies and surplus stock from other businesses. There is always something: clothing, sporting goods, hardware, jewellery - all worth checking out. They sold off an entire line of California sportswear a couple of years ago, and recently they cleared out stock from Neto leather at prices far below wholesale. Parking is impossible most of the time, which is why it's lucky they have their own parking in the back. Open Monday to Saturday 9:30 to 5:30; and Sunday noon to 5. Map O circle 12.

Bazaar & Novelty: 215 West 2nd (873-5241). This place is great for seasonal items (Valentine's, Christmas, St, Patrick's Day, Thanksgiving, Hallowe'en) and themes (golf, monsters, magic), plus they rent and sell costumes. This is perfect for a theme party and a good source of party favours for kids. Open Monday to Friday 8:30 to 6; and Saturday 9 to 5. Map O circle 13.

Gordon Campbell Clothiers: 78 East 2nd (879-2447). Yes, this is Mayor Gordon Campbell's relative -- his grandfather, in fact. You can buy men's and women's made-to-measure suits, skirts and pants at factory-direct prices here, plus they sell custom-tailored overcoats. There's a vast selection of fabrics and they can special-order anything else you fancy. Open Monday to Friday 8 to 4:30; and Saturday 9 to 4:30. Map O circle 14.

Radical: 163 West 4th (879-3050). This sportswear line is "wild and crazy stuff", typified by spatter-painted, tie-dyed and flourescent colours on machine-washable fabrics. There are usually factory seconds available here at their head office and periodically, they advertise in the newspapers (under Garage Sales) when they're clearing out ends-of-season or end-of-line goods. Prices are low. We spotted (no pun intended) men's shorts for $8 and kids' sweats at $9. Open Monday to Friday 9 to 5; Saturday 10 to 5. Map O circle 15.

Doug Hepburn's Gym Equipment: 38 East 4th (873-3684). This is a great place for weight-trainers and body-builders. They sell everything from weight benches to rowing machines and exercise equipment, all at discount prices. Open Monday to Friday and Sunday from noon to 5; and Saturday 1 to 5. Map O circle 16.

Moshe Paper Ltd: 151 West 5th (874-8178). Here you'll find a wealth of picnic disposables (such as plates, napkins and those holiday necessities — plastic wine glasses), which you can buy in large quantities at wholesale prices. Hours are Monday to Friday 8:30 to 5. Map O circle 17.

Doppler Computer Centre: 101 West 5th (875-0261). Though very busy with grey-suit-types at lunch time, other hours eager hackers will discuss equipment and software and provide equipment, service and repairs happily. The software includes a large selection for a wide variety of computers, and there are also classes and books for those wishing to upgrade their skills. Hours are Monday to Friday 8 to 6; and Saturday and Sunday 10 to 5. Map O circle 18.

Dunlevy Sales Ltd.: 5 East 5th (873-2231). This restaurant supply house has narrow aisles and crowded shelves, but the discounts are there on china, glassware, flatware and more. Open Monday to Friday 8 to 6; and Saturday 10 to 3. Map O circle 19.

Michael St. Clair: 44 West 4th (877-1677). A boon to locals, this hidden treasure is a dry-cleaner and laundry, open seven days, with late-night service! Map O circle 20.

La Fourchette: 2205 Manitoba (at 6th Ave.) 872-4070. This is the rest-stop for this tour. Owner Lynne Pettinger has converted the downstairs of this wonderful pink house into a restaurant with a tiny dining room and fabulous (and inexpensive) food. There's a different special for lunch every day (she's famous for her Tuesday and Thursday fresh turkey sandwiches) and the muffins are the stuff of which legends are made!

Show your copy of the Serious Shopper's Guide and when you (and any number of friends accompanying you) order your meals, you'll each receive a giant La Fourchette cookie for dessert, free. Hours are: Monday to Friday 7 a.m. to 2:30 p.m. Map O circle 21.

Action Merchandising: 227 West 6th (873-0064). If you ever wondered where to buy those souvenirs after the event, this is the place. They are licensees for the Molson Indy 500, which normally sells advertising specialities in retail stores during the event and at Christmas. Action also has caps, T-shirts, sweats, posters and pins — at the same prices as in retail stores though Indy volunteers get a 10 percent discount. Open Monday to Friday 8 to 5. Map O circle 22.

Mayer's Packaging: 210 West 6th, upstairs (875-1291). Anne found an ad in the paper and followed it to this address, and admits it's one of the few shopping experiences that literally made her mouth drop open with astonishment. She had just gotten off a place from Hong Kong (where you'd think her need-to-buy would have been satisfied), picked up her daughter, went to the store — and the two of them stood at the doorway in shock! What a wonderland of bargains! Mayer's sells gorgeous packaging, display materials, hat boxes (in fact, gift boxes of every size and shape), ribbons, tissue, novelties and the most wonderful giftwrap you'll ever find — all at wholesale prices. Naturally, if you can buy in quantity, you'll save even more, and if you have a Provincial Sales Tax license your purchases will be PST exempt. Open Monday to Friday 8:30 to 5. Map O circle 23.

Kelly Sportswear: 196 West 6th (879-8077). This manufacturer makes T-shirts and sweatshirts, and though not regularly open to the public, the do have periodic samples sales (a sign on the sidewalk signals the sales) where a friend of ours has bought "beautiful sweatshirts for as little as $2". Map O circle 24.

Wooltex West: 112A West 6th (874-5233). Here's a discount outlet for ribbons, dried flower wreaths and other accessories. Owners Hari and Warren McCuaig operate traditional hours on Mondays; other days by appointment only. Map O circle 25.

Giftcraft: 99 West 6th (873-6366). Here you'll discover all kinds of ornaments, brass items, mugs with clever sayings, stylish aprons and other good quality giftware. Open Monday to Friday 9 to 4. Map O circle 26.

Final Touch Frames: 76 West 6th Ave. (872-3023). Book specialist Allan MacDougall turned Anne on to this place, and continues to mention it at least semi-annually. She's had some great framing done here, all at bargain rates. They do custom-matting, too, they're friendly and the goods are ready for pickup when they've promised. Hours are Monday to Friday 9 to 5; and Saturday 10 to 6. Map O circle 27.

Sea Sun Sales: 25 East 6th (876-2134). This is a wholesale operation, so tread carefully. If they are not busy with a "real" customer, they will sell to the public. The stock is mainly T-shirts and sweats from kids' sizes to XXXL. In fact, it's one of the few places we've found where we can buy very large T's at very low prices. For a few dollars more thay can put a decal from their vast supply on your choice of item. This place is a personal favourite of Lorraine's — and she's awfully hard to please! They're also the authorized Casio dealer for keyboards, calculators, palm-sized TVs — all at wholesale prices. Open Monday to Friday 9 to 5. Map O circle 28.

Mount Pleasant Work Centre: 46 East 6th Ave. (876-5551). We both like this community sheltered workshop a lot. Here they make inexpensive pine bookcases, TV stands, stereo stands, night tables, magazine racks and cabinets, as well as most anything you might want on special order. They also sell aprons, pillows and canvas tote bags from the sewing workshops. We found a cloth bag filled with smooth wooden blocks for only $12.95 last time. Open Monday to Friday 8:30 to 4. Map O circle 29.

V-Com Computer Warehouse: 2227 Quebec (266-1113). This place sells its own version of the IBM computer, under the brand name "MEGA". Naturally, the price is right. Hours are Monday to Friday 8 to 4:30; and Saturday 9 to 4:30. Map O circle 30.

Cassidy's Ltd.: 2323 Quebec (879-6311). This wholesale restaurant supply house does welcome the public, but the big savings are realized by buying in quantity. Glasses are sold by the dozen, and there is china, knives, Oneida flatware, bar supplies, trays, roasting pans and bakers' supplies like tins and icing tubes (a very large selection). Seasonal specials and clear-out are common. Hours are Monday to Friday 8:30 to 5. Map O circle 31.

Marjorie Hamilton: 144 East 7th (879-9222). This clothing manufacturer periodically holds sales of their excess and sample fabrics. These sales are advertised in the newspapers. On the day of the sale a sign goes up on the front sidewalk.

Approximately four times a year there is also a sale of clothing (often from their NEXT season's stock), but these sales are advertised only by call-outs to people who have previously shopped their sales and signed a list. It's a Catch-22 because you have to go to a sale to hear about others, so if you ever pass the location and there's a queue out front, hop right in and you won't be disappointed. We used to think of Marjorie Hamilton as something of a dowdy label, but not any more! They also make the Cimone line and Ziba Petite, which are each very hip. Sale times usually start as early as 7:30 or 8 a.m. (factory time, of course). Map O circle 32.

Canadian Outfitters & Guide Supply House: 86 Kingsway (874-2839). This outdoors supply place has been here, we think, since the days of Alexander MacKenzie (a little Canadian historical note, eh?) and according to Lorraine "their windows evoke the true Canadian North spirit". Their windows also reveal such diverse items as authentic "down under" overcoats and tough-looking no-nonsense tents. Prices are very low. Parking is impossible — we've even parked at Kingsgate Mall (Kingsway and Broadway) and "hiked" back. Open Monday to Friday 9:30 to 6; and Saturday 10 to 6. Map O circle 33.

Radio Shack Discount Centre: 685 East Broadway (872-3392). Just west of Fraser on the north side of Broadway you'll find this great store — you guessed it — a super source for discontinued electronic items from Radio Shack's regular stores, plus returns, reconditioned units, and some damaged goods. Staff is extremely friendly and helpful. About 95 percent of the goods sold here are still under full warranty and a salesperson will advise you if the item you want to buy is "as is". Hours are Monday to Saturday 9:30 to 5:30. Map O circle 34.

NOTES:

New Westminster

Old World Charm & Bargains

This is a small tour which can be accomplished in 2 to 3 hours, unless you dawdle at the market or the Army & Navy. Our rest stop is at the end of this tour (on 10th St. between Agnes & Carnarvon), so if you start in the morning, this would be a good place to stop for lunch, so plan accordingly.

New West (as locals call it) was the original settlement of the British Columbia southwest coast, until the great Canadian railway pushed through instead to Vancouver. Since then, New West has remained a charming Victorian town and Vancouver has grown to its present size as Canada's third largest city. Don't think "poor New West", because the city has retained its charm and character in the face of growing industrialization, and is still a wonderful spot for historical explorations (there's a fine museum) and -- guess what? -- shopping!

There are a number of ways to reach New West by car: We both prefer the route along S.W. Marine, which flows into Marine Way, which pipes directly into Stewardson Way along the water. Be careful not to accidently cross the Annacis Island bridge as you near New West!

Another route is to follow Kingsway right down through Vancouver and Burnaby. At 10th Avenue in New West Kingsway becomes 12th Street New West. Confused?

You can also take the Lougheed Highway (eastern extension of Broadway) to North Road and take North Road south (for real!) until it becomes Columbia St, which will lead you right to our starting point at Westminster Quay. And then there's good old TransCanada 1 from which you take the Brunette exit. Brunette also takes you right downtown onto Columbia.

As you may have gathered, New West gets complicated downtown because of all those numbered streets and avenues. In fact, Woodward's is right at the corner of Sixth and Sixth, kind of a local in-joke. Generally speaking, the Avenues run (sort of) east and west, while the Streets run (sort of) north and south. As far as WE can tell, North Road is the only REAL north and south one, and it's a ROAD!

Anyway, if you're driving up from the U.S., follow 152nd St. north to King George Hwy., take King George north right through Surrey and across the Pattullo Bridge into New West.

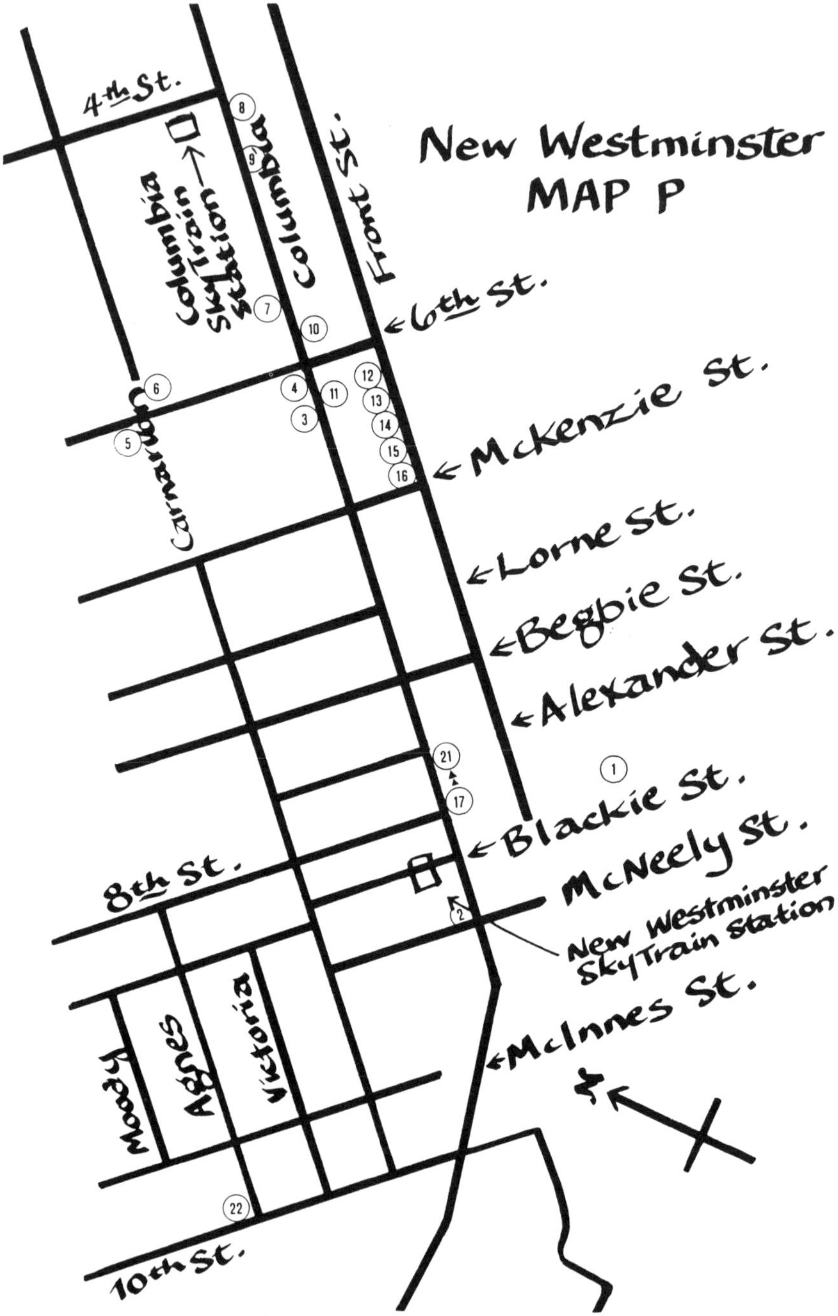
New Westminster
MAP P
4th St.
Columbia SkyTrain Station
Columbia
Front St.
6th St.
Mckenzie St.
Lorne St.
Begbie St.
Alexander St.
Blackie St.
McNeely St.
New Westminster SkyTrain Station
McInnes St.
Carnarvon
8th St.
Moody
Agnes
Victoria
10th St.
1
2
3
4
5
6
7
8
9
10
11
12
13
14
15
16
17
21
22

By public transit from Vancouver, the simplest route is via the SkyTrain and you disembark at New Westminster station. For many of us, this might well be the easiest way to get there, particularly as many of our stops are within walking distance of the Quay where our tour begins and ends.

Parking varies on the streets of New West, but there's always the two hours of free parking in the lot at the Quay (pronounced "kee"). There's also parking in a parkade off the south side of Columbia -- merchants will validate parking slips.

Westminster Quay Public Market: 810 Quayside (520-3881). This development as only a handful of years old, yet it looks like it's been there forever. At the far end of the parking lot is the New West Chamber of Commerce Visitor Info Centre in a mill house restored from 1905, which may yield some interesting information about local sights (521-7781). Don't overlook the mock tugboat left over from Expo '86 which now serves to liven up a children's play area.

A booth selling river tours is set up nearby during warm months. The three-hour cruise includes a full buffet lunch and there's a special price for Seniors on Thursday mornings. Call ahead to 732-5466 for details.

Inside the Quay is the public market, of course, with its fresh stalls of produce, meats, fish and flowers. There are also wonderful bakeries, candy shops and craft items of every description. We like the Farm Cottage Baking Company (ingredients listed on display cards in front of each baked item), KRW Turkey Specialties (which sells fresh turkey as well as turkey transmogrified into low-cal sandwich meats like salami and 'ham'), Cody's Books and Maps (which stocks those hard-to-find out-of-town papers), Adriana's (for candles and scents), I'm Impressed Inc. (artist-designed rubber stamps), Nancy Pots & Pans, Etc. (great, inexpensive wicker baskets) and of course the wonderful Fin's Waterfront Restaurant. There's also the Paddle Wheeler Neighbourhood Pub. Parking, as we've mentioned, is free for two hours while you shop. Market hours are Saturday to Thursday 9:30 to 6:30; and Friday 9:30 to 8. Map P circle 1.

Salvation Army Thrift Store: 811 Columbia St. (521-0319). This is one of our favourite Sally Anns, with an as-is department which usually yields some wonderful (cheap) find. You'll notice the once-fabulous art deco staircases that lead in opposite directions across the back of the store to the furniture floor. No refunds or exchanges are given on goods. On the last Tuesday of every month, Seniors get 10 percent off all purchases. One the last Wenesday of each month, you can "draw your own discount" for kids' clothes; Ditto the last Thursday for men's clothing, and the last Friday for women's attire. Hours are Monday to Wednesday 9:30 to 5:45; Thursday and Friday 9 to 8:15; Saturday 9 to 5:15; and closed Sunday. Map P circle 2.

Red Apple Clearance Centre: 641 Columbia (524-5257). Here's a source for discount women's, men's and childrens clothing and footwear in a large, bright store. Quality level of goods is of the K-Mart, Woolco variety. Open Monday to Wednesday and Saturday 9 to 6; Thursday and Friday 9 to 9; and Sunday noon to 5. Map P circle 3.

Chelsea Gift Shop & Royal City Dollhouse: 665 Columbia (522-4552). They sell Roger's Victoria chocolates, so we had to include them! It's a sweet little store, nicely set-up with some very pretty giftware, too. Royal City Dollhouse (which used to be in the Quay) has moved in here -- it is THE place for miniatures and dollhouses! Hours are Monday to Saturday 10 to 5. Map P circle 4.

Avalon Dance Shop: 46th 6th St. (524-2477). Here you'll find supplies for Latin and ballroom dancers, shoes, jewellery, aerobic wear and some ballet shoes for kids and adults. There's even a mini dance floor so shoes can be "test driven". Open Wednesday to Friday 11 to 7; and Saturday 10 to 5. Map P circle 5.

Creative Hobbycraft Stores: 43 6th St. (525-6644). Here are three floors of craft supplies: the top floor is entirely model kits and supplies; and on lower floors there is everything from wedding supplies to needlework, crafts and more, Hours are Monday to Thursday and Saturday 9 to 5:30; and Friday 9 to 9. Map P circle 6.

Royal City Jewellers and Loans: 515 Columbia (521-6816). This is a traditional pawn brokers, selling new and used jewellery (and they do repairs), used cameras, power tools, musical instruments, golf clubs and stereos. Open Monday to Saturday 9 to 5:30 (loan department closes at five). Map P circle 7.

The Card Exchange: 408 Columbia (522-1399). This place sells all manner of trading cards. On the day we last visited it was closed "due to Canuck's game"! Hours are usually Tuesday to Thursday 11 to 6; Friday 11 to 7:30; Saturday 10 to 6; and Sunday noon to 5. Map P circle 8.

Vibe Jewellers: 414 Columbia (526-1263). Advertising themselves as "discount jewellers", this place does manufacturing, custom work and repairs -- most finished while you shop. Open Monday to Saturday 9:30 to 6. Map P circle 9.

Army & Navy Department Store: 502 Columbia (682-6644). You'll find convenient parking in the rear on Front Street and the usual discounted clothing, housewares, sporting and camping gear, shoes and small electricals inside. Two things shine about this location: one is that their annual shoe sale is much more fun to attend than at the downtown Vancouver location (less crowded, more selection, easier parking), and the other is one of the best kept secrets around. The luncheonette in the basement level is the best deal ever! Coffee or tea is 35 cents, all desserts are priced under a dollar, there are choice sandwiches and salads -- and the most expensive item available is a huge shrimp salad, extravagantly priced at $2.50! Hours are Monday to Wednesday and Saturday 9 to 5:30; Thursday and Friday 9 to 9; and Sunday noon to 5. Map circle 10.

Downtown New Westminster Business Improvement Society: 646 Columbia (524-4996). Take advantage of their free maps and information about New West attractions and events. One of our best finds here was a set of three illustrated pamphlets called "A walking tour through history" -- self-guided tours of three different areas of New Westminster. Open Monday to Friday 8:30 to 4:30. Map P circle 11.

Community Appliance Waste Service: 611 Front St. (525-0266). This service collects discarded appliances and fixes them if possible, or recycles the freon and other parts. This is a good source of reliable, cheap, used appliances, which do carry a 90-day parts warranty. Open Monday to Saturday 10 to 6. Map P circle 12.

Shirley's Stuff: 615 Front St. (521-5448). Everything from antiques to good old junk is sold here. Lorraine describes it as a "Victorian Grandmother's heaven" with bric-a-brac galore, books, records and small furniture. Open Monday to Saturday 11 to 5; and Sunday noon to 4:30. Map P circle 13.

West Lynn Military Surplus: 623 Front (521-8033). When Lorraine checked this place, there was a group of people waiting outside for it to open! We don't know if this is common, but they do have a good selection of camping gear, uniforms, badges, medals and so on. Open Monday to Saturday 10 to 5:30. Map P circle 14.

Uptown Furniture: 633 Front St. (522-6555). Here's a nice selection of antique furniture, all well-priced. Open Monday to Saturday 10:30 to 5. Map P circle 15.

Jack's Store: 641 Front St. (521-1456). When Anne was looking for a dining room suite, she had a number of calls from people recommending this place. It's packed floor to ceiling, packed like a junk shop with everything from tatty plush animals to quite promising-looking antiques. Lorraine swore "my hands itched to go in and dig". The place has been there since before the overpass that now overshadows it. In fact it's so ancient that the faded sign still uses letters in the phone number instead of numbers. Open Monday to Saturday 10 to 5:30; and Sunday noon to 5:30. Map P circle 16.

Royal Wedding Centre: 710 Columbia (525-7457). Formerly known as Wedding Belles and Beaus in Vancouver, this one has relocated to this area. As far as we know, it's the largest wedding consignment shop, for both men's and women's items. So popular are they, in fact, that when you go to buy an expensive wedding gown in the lower mainland, chances are the sales clerk will mention that you can regain about 65 percent of the cost by consigning it here after the wedding! Hours are Monday to Wednesday 11 to 5:30; Thursday and Friday 11 to 8; and Saturday 10 to 5. Map P circle 17.

Cash for Tapes, CDs & Magazines: 740 Columbia (521-6463). This cramped little shop is full to the brim with everything in its name. Last time in, they were selling used CDs for 3 for $25. After seven years in this location, the owner still complains that many locals haven't yet discovered him -- and the bargains are there! Open seven days noon to 6. Map P circle 18.

$aveMart Store: 746 Columbia (526-9797). This place sells overstocks and "dumped" goods from grocery and housewares liquidations. Most savings over regular supermarket prices seemed to be about 50 percent when we last checked. They stock some general grocery items, picnic and barbecue supplies, kitchenware, gifts and novelties. Open Monday to Thursday 10 to 5:30; Friday 10 to 6; Saturday 10 to 5; and Sunday noon to 5. Map P circle 19.

Vijay's Boutique: 756 Columbia (522-2111) Here you'll find ladies' fashions and brass India imports all squeezed into a tiny shop. Open Monday to Friday 9:30 to 5:30; and weekends 11 to 5. Map P circle 20.

Value Village: 782 Columbia (520-6164). We like this location of "VV" as we call it at our houses. Seniors receive a 20 percent discount. Goods include furniture, clothing, housewares, electricals, books, records and bric-a-brac. On all public holidays there's a big half-price sale, just like at the other locations. Open Monday to Thursday and Saturday 9 to 6; Friday 9 to 9; and Sunday 10 to 6. Map P circle 21.

Hamburger Haven: 77 10th St. (522-8339). Formerly called "Hamburger Heaven" (and still referred to as such by many locals), this place was voted the best burger joint in the entire region by Province readers in a 1992 poll -- and with just cause! Burgers are homemade, ample, juicy and delicious (and come in seafood, vegetarian and chicken versions among many others), fries are homecut and crispy and desserts are extravagant. So isn't it wonderful luck that owner Bill Mural has agreed to a generous offer for Serious Shoppers?

Just bring along your copy of this book, and you and your shopping cohorts will receive 25 percent off any food you order (not including beverages and desserts). This offer is in effect until December 31, 1993, and applies to the owner of this book and friends accompanying that person. The offer may be used many times, but the Serious Shopper's Guide must be shown on each occasion to the server before the meal is ordered. Burger Haven hours are Tuesday to Thursday and Saturday 11:30 to 11; Friday 11:30 a.m. to midnight; and Sunday and Monday 11:30 to 10. Find it between Carnarvon and Agnes, opposite London Drugs, just two blocks from the SkyTrain station at 8th and Columbia. Map P circle 22.

NEWTS:

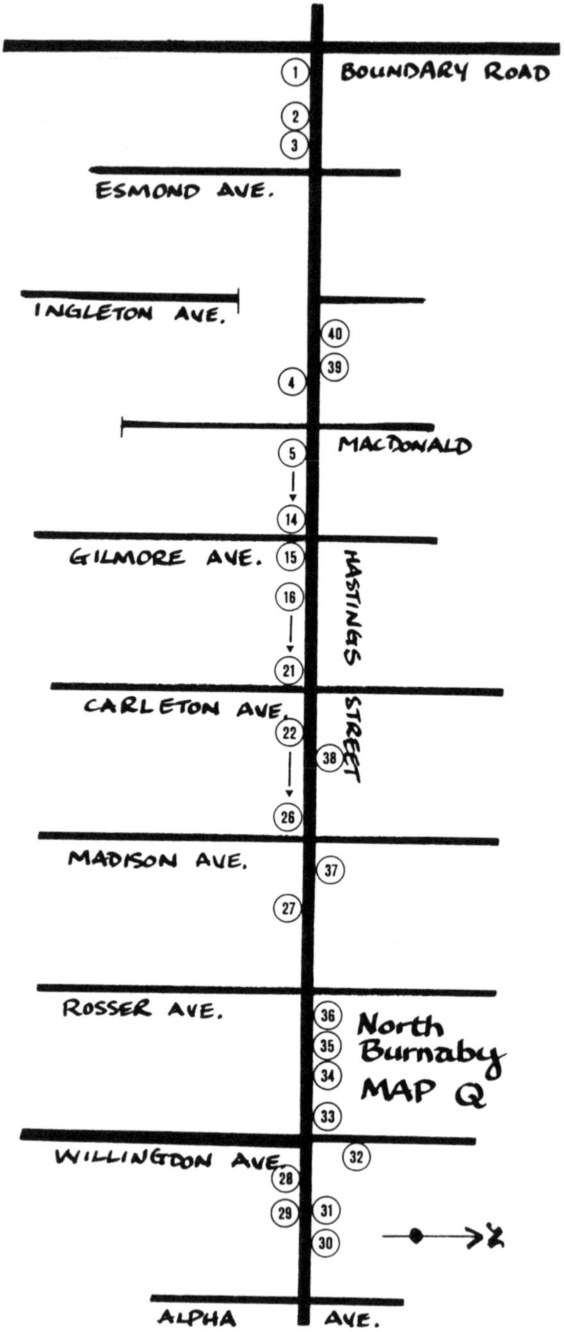
BOUNDARY ROAD
ESMOND AVE.
INGLETON AVE.
MACDONALD
GILMORE AVE.
HASTINGS STREET
CARLETON AVE.
MADISON AVE.
ROSSER AVE.
North Burnaby MAP Q
WILLINGDON AVE.
ALPHA AVE.
1
2
3
40
39
4
5
14
15
16
21
22
38
26
37
27
36
35
34
33
32
28
29
31
30

North Burnaby

More bargains in Burnaby

This is a bargain shopping tour which can be taken whole or in small outings. It should take four hours to complete.

The area itself has remained unchanged over the years ('like a time warp' says Lorraine) with (conservative) clothing stores interspersed with Italian food sources and tiny gift shops.

Street parking is easy. Where parking is tighter, shops often have parking at the rear.

To get to North Burnaby by transit, you can take a bus from anywhere on Granville Mall -- #10 Hastings Express is best, or the #14 Hastings -- either of which will take you to Kootenay Loop. From there, you can either transfer to any one of a dozen or so buses and go one stop east, or simple walk that one block over to Boundary Road, which is approximately where the tour begins. From the SeaBus, walk two blocks south on Granville to pick up the #10 or #14 bus.

Probably the most direct (though not the fastest) route up from the U.S. border crossing at Blaine would be to take Highway 99A (which becomes Kingsway) until it eventually crosses Boundary Road at Central Park in Burnaby. At Boundary, you turn right and head down (pass the Lougheed Highway and you're almost there) to Hastings St.

Vancouver drivers might find it easiest to follow Hastings eastward past the PNE grounds to Boundary. Don't take Hastings through downtown Vancouver, though, as you tend to stop at every traffic light, on every corner. We usually take 6th Avenue east until it becomes 2nd; then it's 6th again, and finally climbs that long hill past the tractor companies up to Clark. Turn left at Clark Drive and follow that route right down to Hastings, where you turn right.

Comor Ski Market: 3700 East Hastings (291-0475) This store sells ski equipment and accessories for the skier. Open 10 to 6, Monday to Thursday and Saturday; 10 to 8 Fridays; and noon to 5 Sundays. Map Q circle 1.

Hastings Comics: 3710 Hastings (299-9392). This store specializes in comic books and comic book-related collectibles. There are Star Trecker items, too, plus trading cards, books, and of course, the comics themselves. Hours are Monday to Thursday 11 to 8; Friday and Saturday 10 to 9; and Sunday noon to 8. Map Q circle 2.

Arcanum Book Shop: 3740 Hastings (294-9311). Anne had a letter from a Province reader about this place prior to Hallowe'en one year which made it sound pretty spooky, indeed, but a very sweet letter from the owner dispelled such misgivings. They sell detective mysteries, books about the supernatural, suspense, fantasy, science fiction and classic gems of literature, mostly in good, used condition, both hardcover and paperbacks. There are such must-haves as old Hardy Boys adventures, too. The closing time can be flexible (a sign says "10 to -??") but generally, they're open Monday to Saturday 10 to 6-ish. Map Q circle 3.

Wan Le Produce: 3972 Hastings (291-8236). This place sells fresh fruit and vegetables at reasonable prices, plus there are always specials outside in bins. There are also some basic groceries and really fresh and attractively-displayed fruit in crisp baskets inside. Hours: Seven days 9:30 to 6:30. Map Q circle 4.

Old Dutch Country Bakery: 4016 Hastings (291-0229). This is one of Anne's son's favourite bakeries -- he even has his special cheese buns on the agenda before we go in. There are buns and bread (bargain-priced at just 79 cents a loaf), cakes, pies and doughnuts and an ice cream counter for further temptation. Open Monday to Thursday and Sunday 9 to 6; and Fridays 9 to 8. Map Q circle 5.

Regent Fish Market: 4020 Hastings (298-9825). This place always features a special price on something, whether it's the tins of salmon for 99 cents or a special on frozen shrimp, or on fresh squid and oysters. We found smoked salmon priced at 99 cents per 100 gm and a wide selection of fresh fish and seafood. Open Monday to Thursday and Saturday 9 to 6; Friday 9 to 7: closed Sunday. Map Q circle 6.

Auld Scottish Larder: 4022 Hastings (294-6616). Here's the source for your Robbie Burn's Day haggis, as well as blood puddings, steak and kidney pies, Melton Mobray, bridies, oatcakes and scones. They also stock Barr brand imported Scottish soft drinks, such as ginger beer and operate a full service butcher store, too. Hours are Monday to Saturday 9 to 6. Map Q circle 7.

Woolworth's: 4050 Hastings (298-4944). Here's where the time-warp factor really shines -- you won't see a lot of upgrading here. In fact, it feels like you've just slipped into 1958. Low prices, too. Open Monday to Thursday and Saturday 9:30 to 5:30; and Friday 9:30 to 9. Map Q circle 8.

Robertson Hardware: 4052 Hastings (298-1255). This fine example of a Home Hardware store offers fittings, bolts, screws, nuts, washers and other small items from a large cabinet with drawers, so that customers can buy a single unit instead of the usual assortments or bubble-packs of too-many of a good thing. They also sell bulk nails, for the serious builder. The place manages to retain that old-timey feeling. Open Monday to Thursday and Saturday 9 to 5:30; and Friday 9 to 9. Map Q circle 9.

The Valley Bakery: 4058 Hastings (291-0674). You'll find bread, pastries and all the goodies here. Our friends swear it's the best place for cakes. The selection is extensive. Hours: Monday to Thursday and Saturday 9 to 6: and Friday 9 to 9. Map Q circle 10.

Glenburn Meats: 4066 Hastings (298-1919). This upmarket meat store sells fancier cuts, such as chicken neptune (ie with crab or shrimp), chicken or veal cordon bleu, chicken royale, Kiev, Wellington, cuts and puff pastry, Scotch meat pies, English pork pies, English rasher-style bacon and freezer beef. Select cuts of beef are also sold, in addition to those specialty chicken items just mentioned, which are sold solo or in dozens for $39.95. Open Tuesday to Saturday 9:30 to 5:30. Map Q circle 11.

Angkor Jewellery: 4068 Hastings (299-5277). This small shop features a vast selection of watches, gold chains and bracelets, plus watch and jewellery repair while-you-wait. Open Monday to Saturday 10 to 5:30. Map Q circle 12.

Lucy's Fashions: 4088 Hastings (298-8050). Here's a spot for woman's clothing in both standard sizes and those for the larger figure. Lines include Koret-Cami, plus classic styles and sexy lingerie. Hours: Monday to Friday 9 to 5; Saturday 9:30 to 5. Map Q circle 13.

Picco's Men's Wear: 4098 Hastings (298-5417). We like this store for its mens' clothing, suits (made-to-measure and formal rentals), plus women's and men's alterations. There is a wealth of sweaters, shirts, underwear and both casual and dressy garments. Open Monday to Thursday and Saturday 10 to 6; and Friday 10 to 9. Map Q circle 14.

Abbey Arts & Crafts: 4118 Hastings (299-0115). We're not just drawn by the drawers and drawers full of beads and findings, but the craft supplies for a wide variety of projects, craft videos (2 days $5) and everything else for the home hobbyist. Drop in craft classes Wednesday evenings from 7 to 10 p.m. cost $5. Open Monday to Saturday 10 to 5:30; and Sunday noon to 5. Map Q circle 15.

Helen's Children's Wear: 4142 Hastings (298-5141). This store -- the one with the neon sign of the girl on a swing -- has been there as long as either one of us can remember. Their stock is available in sizes from newborn to 14, and includes everything from little boys' suits to Oshkosh overalls -- much of it is on the conservative 'dress-up' side. Open Monday to Thursday and Saturday 9 to 5:30; and Friday 9 to 9. Map Q circle 16.

Bob's Sporting Goods: 4150 Hastings (298-8551). Here you'll find hunting and fishing supplies, rods n'reels n'rifles, lures, hooks, weights and bait (dew worms, salmon roe and herring). Hours: Monday to Thursday 9:30 to 6; Friday 9:30 to 8; and Saturday 9 to 5:30. Map Q circle 17.

Cioffi's Meat Market & Deli: 4152 Hastings (291-9373). This is a good source for Italian sausage, frying rabbit, lamb, veal, Italian buns, salt cod, deli meats and cheeses and Italian specialty foods. Open Monday to Saturday 8 to 6. Map Q circle 18.

The Original Compact Disc Exchange: 4162 Hastings (299-6466). They rent, sell and trade new and used CDs and Nintendo games. There are over 8,000 CDs in stock at any given time, priced from $4.99 to $9.99. Hours: Monday to Saturday 11 to 6. Map Q circle 19.

Red Apple Market: 4170 Hastings (299-6544). This mini-grocery store offers lots of resh fruit and vegetables. Open Monday to Wednesday and Saturday 9 to 6; Thursday and Friday 9 to 9; and Sunday 10 to 6. Map Q circle 20.

Italian Florist & Gifts: 4190 Hastings (291-7191). Here you'll find cookware, crystal, silver, china, porcelain knick-knacks, cappuccino cups, and some flowers, plants and other gift items. Open Monday to Thursday and Saturday 9 to 6; and Friday 9 to 9. Map Q circle 21.

CC's Clothing Co.: 4226 Hastings (294-2600). Featured here is new and consignment clothing for women, including some for the larger figure. They also offer alterations and dressmaking services. Open Monday to Saturday 10 to 5:30. Map Q circle 22.

Castelo Bakery: 4240 Hastings (298-9611). This is the source of 'the original' Portuguese buns. They also sell bread, cookies, Italian specialty foods -- AND -- there's a huge wedding cake in the window with a "rent me" sign on it! Hours are Monday to Saturday 8 to 6; and Sunday 8 to 4. Map Q circle 23.

Azzara's Italian & Canadian Deli: 4242A Hastings (299-1911). In addition to the expected Italian specialty foods, they sell fresh pasta, Milano fruit loaves and seeds for growing your own (hard-to-find)

Italian vegetables. Open Monday to Saturday 9:30 to 5:30; and Sunday 10 to 2. Map Q circle 24.

Kea's Meats Ltd.: 2424B Hastings (298-6828). Mediterranean specialties are the highlight here, along with meats, cheeses, Greek olives and feta cheese. Hours: Monday to Thursday and Saturday 9 to 6; and Friday 9 to 8. Map Q circle 25.

Fruit Basket: 4282 Hastings (298-9330). An ideal spot for good, fresh produce. Open Monday to Friday 9:30 to 7; Saturday 9 to 7; and Sunday 10 to 6. Map Q circle 26.

Rocky's Meats: 4342 Hastings (298-8943). Nothing too close to Sylvester Stalone, this, but you will find fine smoked meats hanging in the window and fresh eggs sold in bulk. This is a classic: an old-fashioned butcher shop. Open Tuesday to Thursday and Saturday 9 to 6; Friday 9 to 9; closed Sunday and Monday. Map Q circle 27.

The Tazmanian Comic Connection: 4520 Hastings (298-6208). This is a great find -- perfect for the comic book hobbyist or simply a couple of hours' worth of browsing on a rainy Saturday. There are comics, of course, as well as comic-subject books, illustration and sports cards. Hours are Monday to Wednesday 11 to 6; Thursday and Friday 11 to 9; and Saturday 11 to 5; and Sunday 1 to 5. Map Q circle 28.

Life Force Ecology Store: 4530 Hastings (299-2822). Right in step with the '90s, this new arrival offers free slide and video shows to the as yet unconverted and items meant "for people, animals and the environment". Open Monday to Friday noon to 6; and weekends noon to 5; but please call before you go there as they are "frequently out on emergencies". Map Q circle 29.

Dolphin Cinemas: 4555 Hastings (293-0321). This double theatre is worth a separate visit, but we put it into our tour so you could place its location for next time. After the big movie houses get pictures on their first-run, but long before the films are released in video format, they play here -- and for the bargain price of only $1.50. Call ahead for what's-on info and show times. Map Q circle 30.

Scoff's Hockey Shop: 4543 Hastings (298-5630). Here you'll find hockey and lacrosse equipment and repairs. They have literally everythng for the hockey and lacrosse player. It's a large store and we've included it because lacrosse is not an easy sport for which to find supplies and equipment. Open Tuesday to Thursday 9 to 5:30; Friday 9 to 8; Saturday 9 to 5; and Sunday 10 to 5; closed Monday. Map Q circle 31.

The Scout Shop: Rm. 33, 250 Willingdon (293-1964). Located in an old school, you'll find the Burnaby edition of the Boy Scouts of Canada (the Vancouver version is on West Broadway near London Drugs). They sell campling supplies, uniforms and everything you could possibly want that has to do with scouting in Canada. Open Monday to Friday 9:15 to 5; closed weekends. Map Q circle 32.

King's Nutrition Shoppe: 4455 Hastings (298-3626). This is a good source for discount vitamins, health and lifestyle books, and bulk herbs and spices. Open Monday to Thursday and Saturday 10 to 6; Friday 10 to 9; closed Sunday. Map Q circle 33.

Nana's Selectables: 4449 Hastings (291-2711). This ladies' consignment shop (bring your consignment goods in by appointment, please) sells fashionable clothing and accessories, plus a few children's coats and some new items. There are also a few books and assorted bric-a-brac which brings down the tone of what is otherwise a very nice shop. Open Tuesday to Saturday 10 to 5. Map Q circle 34.

Burnaby Books: 4435 Hastings (298-0038). This is a wonderful store full of used books in good condition. There's an extensive (not EXPENSIVE) selection and a very friendly cat which greeted Lorraine at the door and kept her company as she browsed the shelves. Hours are Monday to Thursday and Saturday 9:30 to 5:30; Friday 9:30 to 9; and Sunday noon to 5. Map Q circle 35.

Tailwagger Boutique: 4427 Hastings (298-4411). So the name fooled you too? We can only assume this is clothing for animal lovers, because -- except for the carved animals at the top of each rack-pole -- this seems a standard women's clothing store. Another difference is that most items are for the petite figure. Hours are Tuesday to Friday 10:30 to 6; Saturday 10 to 5:30; closed Sunday and Monday. Map Q circle 36.

Vancouver Pet Centre: 4371 Hastings (294-8933). Yes, this IS a pet supply store, and one which sells all the major brands in bulk and at discount prices. There are also pet accessories and supplies. Open Monday to Wednesay and Saturday 10 to 6; Thursday and Friday 10 to 9; and Sunday 11 to 6. Map Q circle 37.

The House of Granite: 4249 Hastings (294-4044). Anne thought this might be a source of pillars and mantels, but instead it's filled with curling supplies -- rocks, brooms, clothing and shoes. Open Tuesday to Saturday 10 to 5:30. Map Q circle 38.

Bella Idea Gift & Furniture: 3959 Hastings (299-8885). This is a source of Italian-style giftware and furniture with a good selection of crystal, linens, area rugs, tea trollies and ornate furniture. Hours are Monday to Wednesday and Saturday 10 to 5; and Thursday and Friday 10 to 9. Map Q circle 39.

Jon's Plant Factory: 3951 Hastings (294-3000). Garden supplies for both indoor and outdoor gardeners are featured here, plus a nice selection of bonsai trees and an interesting idea for the economy-minded smoker: a tobacco plant starter kit which costs $15.95 for 200 seeds, soil, planter and complete instructions. One plant in three months will yield seven ounces of cured tobacco, so it's worthwhile if you're patient and if you don't mind rolling your own! Hours are Monday to Saturday 10 to 5:30. Map Q circle 40.

Phil Mattia, 3722 Hastings (294-3014). NOTE: THIS PLACE HAS RELOCATED IN MAY 1992 TO CHARLES & BOUNDARY. No longer on Hastings, but so interesting, we had to tag it on at the end, this place sells a fascinating collection of plaster moldings and fireplaces, marble-topped pedestals finished with ornate flowers and gilt. There are also luxe marble columns, fabulous rococo flowered ceiling mouldings and remarkable finishing touches for walls, corners and ceilings, which prompted us to say "So that's where you buy this stuff!" This is not impulse shopping, but a place to add to your memory banks for when you really need one of these pieces. Open 4 to 6 Monday to Friday; and 9 to 4 Saturdays.

NOTES:

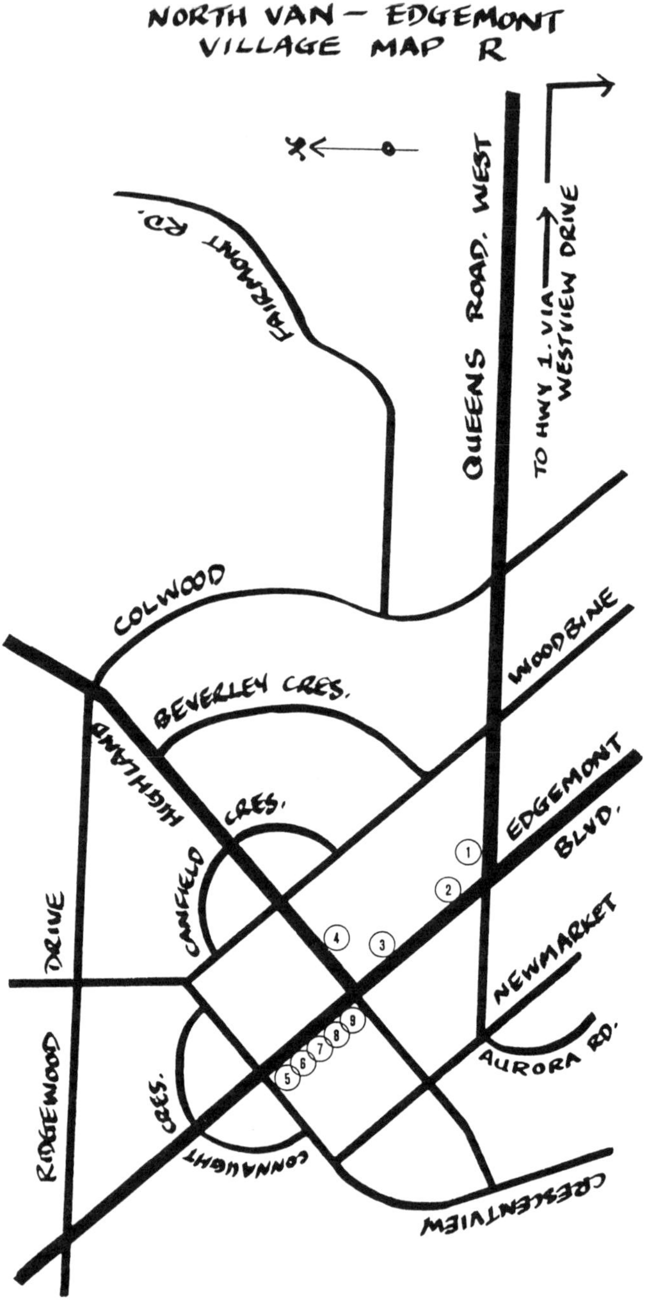
NORTH VAN – EDGEMONT
VILLAGE MAP R
N
QUEENS ROAD. WEST
TO HWY 1. VIA WESTVIEW DRIVE
FAIRMONT RD.
COLWOOD
WOODBINE
BEVERLEY CRES.
HIGHLAND
CRES.
EDGEMONT
BLVD.
CANFIELD
DRIVE
NEWMARKET
AURORA RD.
RIDGEWOOD
CRES.
CONNAUGHT
CRESCENTVIEW
1
2
3
4
5
6
7
8
9

North Van - Edgemont Village

Consignment, specialty, decor

This is a small tour which could take as little as one hour to complete, unless you dawdle.

Edgemont Village must be one of the best kept secrets in the region. We only discovered it ourselves about two years ago. It's simply full to the brim with charming shops with unique, well-priced (often bargain-priced) merchandise.

To reach Edgemont Village by car from Vancouver, take one of the bridges to the North Shore, and head toward a half-way point between those bridges in North Van. If you cross the Lions Gate, exit toward North Van and take the Capilano cut up to Ridgewood, then turn right onto Ridgewood and you're virtually there. From the Second Narrows, stay on Highway 1 (west) and exit at Westview (right after Lonsdale). Head north (up the mountain) on Westview to Queens, take a left there, and continue just past Highland where Queens flows into Ridgewood and Edgemont.

By public transit, take the SeaBus to Lonsdale Quay and transfer to bus #246, which takes you right there.

From the U.S., make your way to Highway 1 via the King George Highway (if you cross at Douglas- Peace Arch), or up 264th St. (if you cross at Aldergrove). Highway 1 wil take you across the Second Narrows bridge (eventually). Follow directions above.

Street parking in Edgemont Village is usually easy and free, but at peak shopping times (such as Saturday afternoon), you may have to resort to side streets.

Luxury Rags: 1010 West Queens (984-7247). This place has a large stock of lovely party frocks, fancy sweaters and other upmarket fare -- also consignment. Hours are Monday to Thursday 10 to 6; Friday 10 to 8; and Saturday 9:30 to 5:30. Map S circle 1.

The Comeback: 3050 Edgemont (984-2551). Just around the corner is another contender: We wish we had a dollar for every reminder from a fervent fan of this place, surely one of the classiest consignment shops in the region. Fashions are crisp and tidy, very designer-y and current -- and did we say inexpensive? Hours are Monday to Saturday 10 to 5. Map S circle 2.

Sylvan Crafts & Pottery: 3080 Edgemont (986-4863). This mother and daughter-run shop next to Highland Produce and kitty-corner from Edgemont Bakery is like a fantasy world of hangings, candles, pottery, incense and crafts, mostly hand-wrought in the area. Entering the shop is not unlike moving into another dimension! Open Tuesday to Saturday 10 to 6; and closed Monday in July & August. Map S circle 3.

Highland Produce: 3114 Highland (987-5163). Here's the source for farm fresh eggs, great bargains in produce and free fortune cookies for children! Open Monday to Saturday 10 to 6; and Sunday 11 to 5. Map S circle 4.

Peter Rabbit Market: 3171 Edgemont (985-3556). You wouldn't think a toney area like this one would have such bargains in produce, but they do. It's an unpretentious, family-run grocery store, with a swell selection of penny candy. Open seven days 10 to 10. Map S circle 5.

Garnier Hardware: 3139 Edgemont (988-8010). This place seems to have changed hands recently, but we still find some elements of their famous welcoming atmosphere. Open Monday to Saturday 9 to 6; and Sunday 11 to 4. Map S circle 6.

Trims: 3151 Edgemont (986-8746). Likely the gem in the platinum setting of this tour, Trims is a wonderful new-ish store to this area. It's filled with the brilliant dried floral arrangements of the talented importer-turned-designer Marlene Tate, with unabashed bargains in giant silk irises for a price so low we can't quote it here! The other flowers, which look like traditional dried ones are instead a kind of heat-fried polyester flower known in the trade as "perma-dried". Of course they outlast "real" flowers and it's almost impossible to tell them from the real thing. Hours here are Tuesday to Saturday 10 to 6; and Monday 10 to 5. Map S circle 7.

Edgemont Bakery: 3153 Edgemont (986-0961). Famous for miles around for their Edgemont pizza by the slice, this place also makes a host of other wonderful baked goods. Open seven days 9 to 7. Map S circle 8.

Starbucks: 3127 Edgemont (985-8750). A new location of this ever-spreading coffee phenomenon has become the local meeting place for the *cognoscenti*. In addition to at-the-counter specialty coffees, muffins, dessert squares and the like, there's a plethora of stay-hot mugs, dashboard coffee-holders, carafes, filters, and of course great imported coffee beans. Open weekdays 6:30 a.m. to 10p.m.; and weekends 7 a.m. to 10 p.m. Map S circle 9.

North Van - Lower Lonsdale

Antiques, crafts and bargains

Lower Lonsdale is a medium-sized tour. If you plan to visit each and every place we've listed, then consider this a half-day tour. If you add in Lonsdale Quay, the time-frame would stretch to approximately five to six hours. Please also see Upper Lonsdale (next) for more shopping in the area.

From downtown Vancouver, it's easy (and fun) to take the SeaBus right to the foot of Lonsdale and the beginning of our tour. In fact the SkyTrain can take you right to Waterfront Station, where the SeaBus is located. The SkyTrain travels from Surrey, through New West and Burnaby into downtown Vancouver. For transit info in Vancouver, call 261-5100.

For cars, the only bridges to North Vancouver are located in the West End (Lion's Gate or First Narrows Bridge) and in East Van not far from the border of Burnaby (Second Narrows Bridge). It is wise to avoid either during rush hours, and you will generally find the Second Narrows a little faster most of the time anyway. Tune in to radio traffic reports (the FM stations all have good traffic coverage from about 3 or 3:30 pm onward) to be sure you're not going to run into slowdowns from an accident on one of the bridges.

Once you're on the North Shore, you have two principal choices to get to Lonsdale: either via TransCanada 1 (quit the highway at Lonsdale and travel southbound to start the tour); or via Marine Drive. If coming from the Lion's Gate, keep to the right as you leave the bridge and the road will lead you naturally right onto Marine Drive. Stay on it (and bear right) until the road splits -take the right fork in the road, which leads you to 3rd St. and follow that right through until it intersects with Lonsdale.

If travelling across the Second Narrows, you have many choices to leave the highway. The simplest is to take the second right after you leave the bridge (DO NOT go to Deep Cove!) and follow the loop all the way around until you're on Main St. This will lead right into Esplanade or 3rd St. (your choice) which each eventually intersect with Lonsdale.

If arriving from the U.S. via Sumas (entering Canada at Aldergrove), stay on the same highway (13) until just past the 56th Ave. exit to Langley, and you'll see big signs heralding the exit to Hwy 1 EAST. Stay on Hwy 1 right through Surrey, across the Port Mann Bridge, past Coquitlam and through Burnaby. Don't take the Vancouver exits, but proceed right into North Van. To keep things simple, We'd advise you

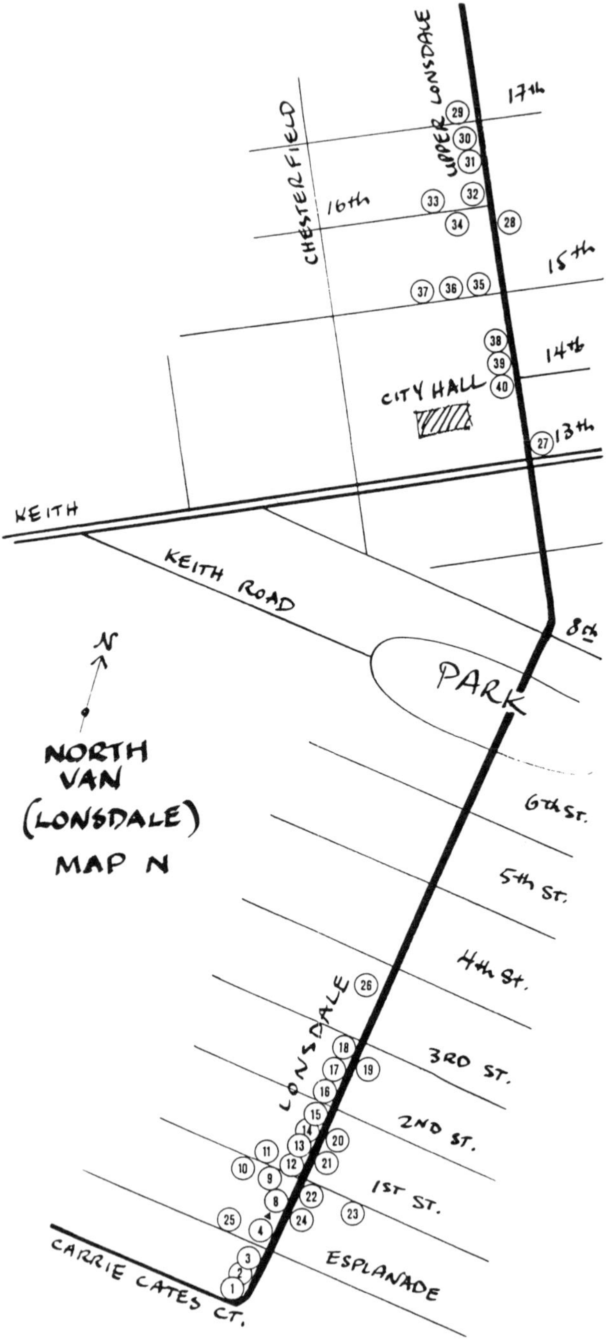
UPPER LONSDALE
CHESTERFIELD
17th
16th
15th
14th
13th
CITY HALL
KEITH
KEITH ROAD
8th
PARK
N
NORTH VAN (LONSDALE) MAP N
6th ST.
5th ST.
4th St.
LONSDALE
3RD ST.
2ND ST.
1ST ST.
ESPLANADE
CARRIE CATES CT.
1
2
3
4
8
9
10
11
12
13
14
15
16
17
18
19
20
21
22
23
24
25
26
27
28
29
30
31
32
33
34
35
36
37
38
39
40

to just stay on the highway until you get to Lonsdale. You'll see a couple of signs for Lonsdale before you get there.

If crossing through U.S. border points at either Douglas or Pacific Highway, it's more complicated. Basically, you'll have to travel through most of the municipalities between your arrival point and the North Shore. The easiest routing might be to stay on Hwy 99A (North), which is also known as King George Hwy. You'll take this road right across the Pattulo Bridge into New Westminster and then either McBride (which flows in a circuitous route into Canada Way) or Columbia St. (which becomes North Road) will take you to Hwy 1 (East), which in turn leads to North Van (see previous paragraph for directions once in North Van on Hwy 1). If, instead, you find yourself on Hwy 7 (Lougheed Hwy), don't panic. The Lougheed itself crosses Hwy 1 (take Hwy 1 Eastbound) again before the approach to the Second Narrows Bridge, so you can get back on the correct highway without difficulty.

As you've probably gathered from the preceding (long-winded) directions, the primarly focus of this tour is on Lonsdale Ave., from below Esplanade to 16th St. We've included the intersecting side-streets, too. For shops in Lonsdale Quay, please see our section on Public Markets. Please also see Upper Lonsdale (which follows this section), and the section on Edgemont Village.

Paper-Go-Round: 9 Lonsdale (988-9932). Here's a source for recycled papers, jewellery made from used paper, writing and office paper and business supplies. Computer paper is sometimes on special. Hours are Monday to Saturday 10:30 to 6; and Sunday noon to 5. Map N circle 1.

Lonsdale Antiques and Clocks: 11 Lonsdale (987-3371). This place welcomes consignments of antiques and clocks and offers "expert clock and watch repairs". Items you wish to sell may sometimes be bought outright. There's a nice collection of old and reproduction glass bottles, brass fittings and lots more if you follow the stairs to the second floor balcony. Hours are Monday to Saturday 10:30 to 5:30; and Sunday noon to 5. Map N circle 2.

Antix: 13 Lonsdale (987-9272). There's a sister store at 1072 Davie (682-4161) which, like this one, sells consignment fashions, jewellery and accessories, ladies' and men's discount and designer clothing, jeans and some trendy designer duds, too. Open Monday to Saturday 10:30 to 6; and Sunday noon to 5. Map N circle 3.

Hangers: 51 Lonsdale (980-2965). Lots of trendy sportwear here, plus a wide assortment of jeans. Open Monday to Saturday 10 to 6; and Sunday noon to 5. Map N circle 4.

Carol's Costume Corner: 55 Lonsdale (upstairs) (986-4880). Carol Ahern has collected a great variety of high-quality costumes, suitable not just for Hallowe'en, but for fancy dress and other outings. Carol has designed costumes for TUTS, opera and theatre companies for years. Most assembled costumes will rent for $40 to $50 per day. Examples are saloon girl, Southern belle, Viking. Hours are Monday to Saturday 10 to 6. Map N circle 5.

Opulence Silks and Dyes: 55 Lonsdale (upstairs) (980-2120). This delightful adventure into another world includes fabric paints, dyes, brushes for painting on silk, findings, markers, "Ro Ketsu Fude" waxing brushes, fabric, T's, aprons, pongee silk scarves and cosmetics - often sale-priced. Classes in various silk painting and batik techniques run just about year-round, and there's lots of printed material on hand to help you mull over the many choices. Open Monday to Saturday 10 to 5. Map N circle 5.

Pine Design: 61 Lonsdale (984-3012). We loved the pine cerubs, rocking horses, bird cages and duck decoys (Anne bought a hand-painted, cow-motif, wall-mounted key hook -- "had to", said she), but there's a winning assortment of fine old and new pine furniture in supply, too. Hours are Monday to Saturday 10:30 to 6; and Sunday noon to 6. Map N circle 6.

Comics Scene: 73 Lonsdale (987-8213). Here's a great comic store selling collectors' comics (Rocketeer, super heroes), plus the usual (and unusual) posters, books and paraphrenalia. Hours are Monday, Tuesday and Thursday 12:30 to 5:30; closed Wednesday; Friday 11:30 to 6:30; Saturday 11:30 to 5:30; and Sunday 1 to 4:30. Whew! Map N circle 7.

Woodland's Natural Foods: 93 Lonsdale (985-9328). Owned by the same people (natch) who operate the Kits store and restaurant, this is the North Shore's primary source of natural foods, health foods and remedies. It's big and well organized, like a supermarket in a gorgeous white heritage building with burgundy awnings. Open Monday to Saturday 10 to 8; and Sunday 10 to 6 (restaurant part is closed Sunday). Map N circle 8.

Above Average Lingerie: 109 West 1st St. (988-0445). Here's a unique source for high-fashion lingerie "for the full-figured woman". Hours are Monday to Friday 10 to 5:30; and Saturday 10 to 5. Map N circle 9.

Martin Marine: 121 West 1st St. (985-0911). An ancient grey building houses this assortment of boat hardware, life jackets and other sea-going supplies. Navigation, seamanship, varnish and paint how-to videos are rented for $3.50 a day. Hours are Monday to Friday 9 to 5:30; Saturday 9 to 5; and Sunday 10 to 2. Map N circle 10.

The Glass House: rear, 121 West 1st St. (980-5611). This space (which is actually right behind the Keg) doubles as the studio of Campbell, MacFarlane & Co. You'll see the Bavarian/Tudor facade and neat window boxes in the lane. Inside, there are supplies of gold leaf, glass blocks, new windows, repairs, supplies for stained glass work and classes available. Hours are Tuesday to Saturday 8:30 to 5:30; and closed Monday. Map N circle 10.

The Food Warehouse: 108 West 1st St. (985-3506). This distributor of clear-outs, canned goods, day-old bread, and even some "President's Choice" items usually found only at the Superstore, can offer great prices - or not. Check prices carefully. Open Monday to Saturday 9 to 5:30; and Sunday 11 to 4. Map N circle 11.

Highwater Tackle Ltd.: 113 Lonsdale (986-3239). Another fisherman's paradise, this one sells fishing gear, licenses, rods, T-shirts, and that "stainless steel fillet glove" you've been looking for. Open Monday 9:30 to 5:30; Tuesday 9:30 to 6; Wednesday to Saturday 9 to 6; and closed Sunday. Map N circle 12.

Imperial Books: 115 Lonsdale (988-4950). This store sells new and used (buy, sell, trade) books and includes an adult section (over age 18, please). Open Monday to Thursday 10 to 6; Friday 10 to 8; and Saturday 10 to 5. Map N circle 13.

Tesla Pawn Brokers & Electronics: 123 Lonsdale (984-9222). Moved last year to this new location from its previous place across the street, this place sells good condition used tools, electronics gear, stereo equipment, answering machines and the like. Hours are Monday to Thursday 9:30 to 5:30; Friday 9:30 to 6; and Saturday 9:30 to 5. Map N circle 14.

Cash's New & Used Home Furnishings: 139 Lonsdale (980-1912). This standard 2nd hand store has some interesting extras: new kitchen items (like the portable range-top stove we saw) and novelty items and gifts, like an old-style pay phone. Hours are Monday to Saturday 10 to 5:30; and Sunday noon to 3. Map N circle 15.

Great Outdoors: 201 Lonsdale (980-3313). This large store always has something on special. They carry gore-tex, sleeping bags, footwear and hiking boots, tents and other camping equipment. Hours are Monday to Thursday 10 to 6; Friday 10 to 9; Saturday 10 to 5:30; and Sunday 11 to 4. Map N circle 16.

Granny's Tea, Coffee & Spices: 205 Lonsdale (985-4813). The little tea room inside will offer an unofficial rest-break if you're tired from all your shopping so far. The store part sells tea, coffee, china, strainers, spice jars and espresso makers. Open Monday to Friday 7 to 6; Saturday 8 to 6; and closed Sunday. Map N circle 17.

The Salvation Army Thrift Store: 241 Lonsdale (980-4413). One of the best "Sally Ann" stores in the lower mainland, this one always has a fresh stock of clothing, toys, TVs and stereos, drapes and linens, books and records -- and it's still Anne's best source of cheap costume wigs. The only annoyance is that they usually display a few wonderful goodies in the window that you can't buy until the date announced by a window sign. We guess this assures repeat business, but it's irksome when you have to travel there from some distance away! Hours are Monday 9 to 4:45; and Tuesday to Sunday 8:30 to 4:45. Map N circle 18.

The Serenity Shop: 228 Lonsdale (987-8726). This very unusual bookstore carries titles dedicated to helping you "clean up your act". There are lifestyle guides, books on quitting addictions of various kinds and ecological tomes. We feel less serene having to mantion all these hours, but they are: Monday, Wednesday and Thursday 10 to 5:30; Tuesday 10 to 7; Friday 10 to 8; Saturday 10 to 5; and Sunday noon to 5. Map N circle 19.

Vitamin Discount Store: 152 Lonsdale (988-3454). A good assortment of vitamin supplements, shampoos, energy boosters and diet plans is offered here. Open Monday to Saturday 9:30 to 5:30. Map N circle 20.

The Plum Clothing Co.: 128 Lonsdale (988-1754). A sister-operation to the well-known Pt. Grey shop, this one also sells off-price women's attire at 30 to 70 percent off retail. Stock encompasses casual to elegant apparel in a pleasant environment with helpful staff. Open Monday to Thursday and Saturday 10 to 6; Friday 10 to 8; and Sunday noon to 5. Map N circle 21.

Cal Streets: 92 Lonsdale (984-8559). The neon decor may seem incongruous in this beautiful, old, former bank building, but apparently times change: here you'll find surfing fashions, snowboards, skates and surfboards. Open Monday to Thursday and Saturday 10 to 5:30; Friday 10 to 7; and Sunday noon to 5:30. Map N circle 22.

Sylvia's Place: 115 East 1st St. (987-1991). A good consignment store, run by nice folks. This place also features Liz Sport and London Fog lines. Hours are Monday to Saturday 10 to 6; and Sunday noon to 4. Map N circle 23.

Paine Hardware: 90 Lonsdale (987-2241). Repeatedly voted best hardware store in town in Province polls, this is one of the few places around where you can buy "one at a time" nails, bolts, washers, etc. And their stock is staggeringly vast! And the salespeople are knowledgeable and helpful. Hours are Monday to Saturday 8:30 to 5:30; and Sunday 10 to 4. Map N circle 24.

Midland Liquidators: 110 West Esplanade (986-7277). This great potpourri of goods includes tools, gardening stuff, stacking baskets, lawn furniture, toys, housewares, and an ever-changing variety of surplus items. Open Monday to Saturday 9:30 to 5:30 (sometimes 6). Map N circle 25.

Two Stops between Lower & Upper Lonsdale:

If you're going to continue on to do the Upper Lonsdale tour, these are en route:

Fabricland: 341 Lonsdale (980-4433). They offer their fabric club for greater savings of 10 percent off regular-priced fabrics and notions, and special "insider" tips and sales unavailable to non-club members. They have special two-fer sales like buy a meter of fabric, get two free; buy one pattern, get two free, and so on. Membership costs $10 for two years, but even non-members can save - there's usually a bargain area at the back. Open Monday to Wednesday and Saturday 9:30 to 5:30; Thursday and Friday 9:30 to 9; and Sunday noon to 5. Map N circle 26.

Presentation House: 333 Chesterfield (986-1351). This wonderful gallery also schedules public performances and gives patrons a break with their special "pinch penny nights". Call for details, to see if there's one planned for on the date of your planned tour of Lonsdale.

NOTES:

North Van - Upper Lonsdale

More bargain goodies...

This companion tour to the preceding Lower Lonsdale one should take only about one hour, if you visit each stop.

For directions from the border and public transit, please see the previous tour's introduction.

Street parking is usually easy -- and it's free. Some stores have additional parking in the rear, and side streets offer other parking options, also free.

Please also see Lower Lonsdale (previous) for more shopping in the area, and Edgemont Village, another North Shore area.

This tour starts at 13th St., which is one block north of Keith Road, a major artery leading back to Marine Drive.

New Choice Specialty Foods: 1320 Lonsdale (985-3214). This was a Galloway's store, and now under a new name they still carry much the same stock as before: bulk and pre-packaged spices, grains, nuts, sauces, hard-to-find condiments, etc. Open Monday to Saturday 9:30 to 6; and Sunday noon to 5. Map circle 27.

The Bon Style Shop: 1564 Lonsdale (986-2988). Prices seem reasonable at this Hong Kong import shop. Among the offerings are childen's and women's clothing, angora sweaters and washable silks. Open Monday to Friday 10 to 5; and Saturday 10:30 to 5. Map circle 28.

Boomers & Echoes: 108 West 17th St. (984-6163). Quality consignment goods for children, babies and families are sold here. They also carry that rare commodity: Consigned maternity wear. A bulletin board near the door offers space for local ads for furniture for sale and available babysitters. Open Monday to Saturday 9:30 to 5. Map circle 29.

Lewis Hands-On Arts & Crafts: 1641 Lonsdale (988-5266). Supplies for a vast range of craft projects are available here, plus they offer their own classes. There is knitting wool, and kits they have packaged themselves with supplies for projects which can be completed in just a few hours, or less. Open Monday to Friday 9:30 to 5; and Saturday 9:30 to 6. Map circle 30.

North Shore Ski & Sailboard: 1625 Lonsdale (987-7245). Enthusiasts for these sports will find a motherlode of clothing and equipment here, varying naturally, on whether it's summer or winter. Hours are Monday to Thursday and Saturday 10 to 6; Friday 10 to 9; and Sunday 11 to 5. Map circle 31.

Fangle: 1603 Lonsdale (987-6543). They promote their wares as "creative living accessories" -- which turn out to be gift items with an Oriental flair: handbags, brass accent pieces and quite a good selection of bonsai plants. It's an odd mix of things, but it works. Open Monday to Saturday 10 to 5. Map circle 32.

Apollo Hobbies: 142 West 16th St. (273-3642). Here you'll find model kits, and bits and pieces to help finish or customize you own projects. Open Tuesday to Friday 11 to 6; and Saturdau 10 to 6. Map circle 33.

Skyline Sports: 119 West 16th St. (985-9161). Every sport is represented here. Upstairs, the space is entirely devoted to ski stuff; downstairs, there's everything from world-class frisbees to badminton birds and shoes for running, tennis and more. Open Monday to Thursday and Saturday 9:30 to 5:30; Friday 9:30 to 9; and Sunday noon to 5. Map circle 34.

Deja-Vu Fashions Consignment: 116 West 15th (985-5358). This is a small, narrow shop, but we liked the sale rack selection and the shoes. Hours are Monday to Saturday 10 to 4. Map circle 35.

MacGillycuddy's: 124 West 15th St. (984-8081). Anne's friend Sharon Clark owns this place, which has been in business for ages -- in fact, they've been at this very location for almost a decade! Among other top labels, they seem to have a lot of Simon Chang. MacGillycuddy's is the secret closest-clearing area for a great many West Vancouverites too proud to resell their finery closer to home! Prices are extremely low, too. Open Monday to Saturday 9:30 to 6. Map circle 36.

Lion's Gate Hospital Auxiliary Shop: 128 west 15th St. (984-5734). This place has low-end clothing and housewares, in typical thrift shop fashion, but it is bright and clean and on occasion we've even found a little treasure (cheap!) here. Hours are Tuesday to Thursday 10 to 4; and Friday 10 to 1. Map circle 37.

Nicole Adrienne: 1451 Lonsdale (980-2288). This used to be a location of Marc Downs, and has been transformed into yet another discount designer clothing outlet, with some lovely, current fashions for women. Open Monday to Thursday and Saturday 10 to 6; Friday 10 to 7; and Sunday noon to 4. Map circle 38.

Swedish Antiques: 1449 Lonsdale (980-6113). This beautiful store houses wooden furniture, wardrobes, tables and accessories, with the accent on solid pine pieces. Hours are Tuesday to Saturday 11 to 5:30; closed Sunday and Monday. Map circle 39.

Echo's Discount China: 121, 1433 Lonsdale (980-8011 or 985-4825). Another North Shore institution, owner Joan Howell has been babying this business along for years -- people come from all over North America (a mail order service is available, too) to match lost or broken pieces from their china or silver patterns. The store is beautifully maintained and chockablock full of antiques and fine tableware. Open Tuesday to Saturday 9 to 5; closed Sunday. Map circle 40.

NOTES:

Point Grey and UBC Gates

High quality without snobbery

This pleasant half-day tour is best taken when it's sunny, as you'll find you will park and walk for stretches, then return to your car and repark further on.

Street parking is usually easy, or you can try the sidestreets with success. Otherwise, there's a large Safeway lot down at the 4500 block of West 10th, for patrons of the supermarket and smaller shops nearby. Parking is hardest to find on Saturday.

To get to West 10th Avenue, either follow West 12th until it curves into 10th at MacDonald (and keep on going, past Dunbar and up the hill), or follow Cornwall and Point Grey Road along the water to Alma (where the road curves southward), and drive right up Alma to West 10th, where it's a right hand turn (westward).

If driving in from the U.S., follow Hwy. 99 north until you cross the Oak Street Bridge into Vancouver. Take the exit for westside-bound traffic (NOT the one marked "City Centre") which will take you under another bridge. Right after that, you'll see a left turn bay, so get into the line. You'll turn left, then left again at S.W. Marine Drive (follow the traffic flow). Then you follow Marine Drive through all its winding curves. The third traffic light is Dunbar St. Turn right there and follow Dunbar right down to 10th and turn left at 10th and proceed up the hill.

By public transit, the #10 bus leaves Granville Mall in downtown Vancouver and eventually travels toward UBC (and along West 10th) to take you into the heart of West Point Grey.

We start at West 10th and Discovery:

Valucci: 4331 West 10th (222-3122). A very chic store, this place specializes in boots, handbags, accessories and its own label shoes. Open Monday to Saturday 10 to 6. Map S circle 1.

Form & Function: 4357 West 10th (222-1317). This firm manufactures most of the furniture they sell. Some is Quaker-inspired; some more contemporary. Among the choices are tables, chairs, stools, cupboards and bedroom suites and each may be custom-made to your preference of size or finish. Three doors down is their bedroom showroom. Hours: Monday to Saturday 9:30 to 5:30. Map S circle 2.

Lee's Candies: 4361 West 10th (224-5450). A local legend, this place

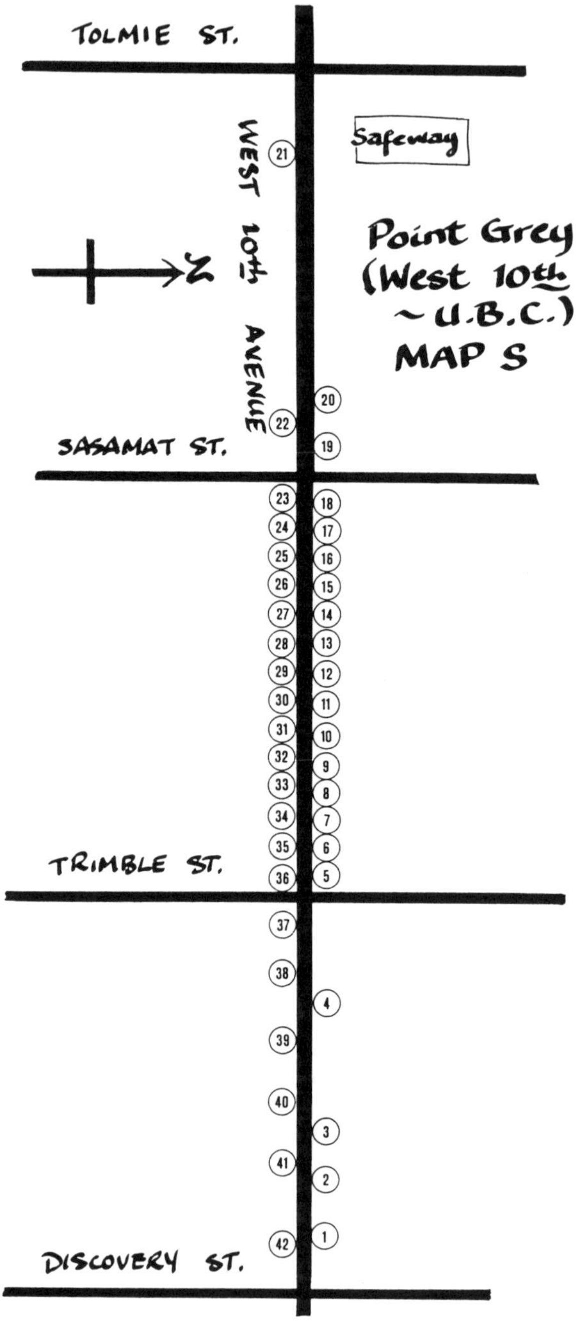
TOLMIE ST.
Safeway
WEST 10th AVENUE
N
Point Grey
(West 10th
~U.B.C.)
MAP S
SASAMAT ST.
TRIMBLE ST.
DISCOVERY ST.
1 2 3 4 5 6 7 8 9 10 11 12 13 14 15 16 17 18 19 20 21
22 23 24 25 26 27 28 29 30 31 32 33 34 35 36 37 38 39 40 41 42

specializes in home-made, hand-dipped and rolled chocolates. It's a small store, with great stuff and warm and friendly staff. We know someone who drives in regularly from Burnaby to this shop! And they got top marks in a Province poll for fine candy. Highly recommended! Open Monday to Saturday 10 to 5. Map S circle 3.

Cap's Bicycle Stores: 4387 West 10th (222-8200). Another Province poll-topper, this store sells bikes, biking accessories, helmets, carriers, locks and more. Hours are Tuesday to Thursday and Saturday 9:30 to 6; Friday 9:30 to 9; closed Sunday and Monday. Map S circle 4.

The Cloth Shop: 4415 West 10th (224-1325). Behind the windows full of different patterned quilts, there's a store full of enterprise and inspiration: quilting supplies, gift items (cards, candles), fabrics, sewing notions and stencilling supplies. Classes are given in subjects such as bearmaking, advanced bearmaking, applique, cross-stitch, how-to make boxer shorts, pillows, and of course, quilting. Seasonal classes spotlight Christmas, Valentine's Day and Easter. Open Monday to Saturday 10 to 5; and Sunday noon to 5. Map S circle 5.

Peasantries: 4429 West 10th (224-7196). Country accessories shine here. We found an antique butter churn and old milk bottles, fine antiques and new country-look reproductions. There were lots of gift ideas and decorations, too. They are self-described as "country with an old world touch". Open Monday to Saturday 10 to 5:30. Map S circle 6.

The Upper Crust Gourmet Kitchenware: 4431 West 10th (222-1566). This is a good spot for hard-to-find kitchenware, gadgets and cooking equipment, plus kitchen gift goodiess and practical items like pots, pans and china. They sell reprodcutions of Anne Adams lovely view of Point Grey for just $25. Hours are Monday to Saturday 10 to 6. Map S circle 7.

The Last Romantics: 4437 West 10th (222-2717). Old Eaton's catalogue pages fill the windows and there are strains of old romantic music in the air. It's not a time warp, it's a special shop selling new clothing, hats, Victorian styles, valentines and gifts, all replicated to look like goods from past eras. Hours are Monday to Thursday and Saturday 9:30 to 5:30; and Friday 9:30 to 7:30. Map S circle 8.

Better Buy Books: 4443 West 10th (224-4144). Quite a good used book store, this, with both new and gently used volumes - new ones sometimes discounted. Children's books are conveniently divided and displayed according to age levels. Open Monday to Saturday 10:30 to 5. Map S circle 9.

Ford's Flowers & Nursery: 4445 West 10th (224-1341). This florist, established in 1929, sells gardening supplies, gift items, bedding plants and even stuffed animals. For example, we found stuffed carousel ponies on poles for $79. Anne fell in love with the verdigris (weathered green copper-look) $185 birdbath, complete with coppery birds perched ready to bathe. Hours are Monday to Saturday 9 to 5:30. Map S circle 10.

Kaboodles: 4449 West 10th (224-5311). Once co-owned by the Hon. Darlene Marzari, this neighbourhood toy store features kits, cards, books, Far Side T-shirts and neat stuff for the young and the young at heart. There's a whole wall of stickers for enthusiasts, collectors and kids. Hours are Monday to Thursday and Saturday 10 to 6; Friday 10 to 9; and Sunday noon to 5. Map S circle 11.

Plum' Full: 4451 West 10th (222-4991). This beautiful shop is filled with Victorian laces, tableware, bedding, linens and accessories. There's also Grandma's linen cupboard inside and a bargain barrel (in a real barrel) at the door. Don't overlook Plum' Full's Lace Club which offers periodic newsletters and increasing discounts as your purchases mount up. Open Monday to Thursday and Saturday 10 to 6; Friday 10 to 9; and Sunday noon to 5. Map S circle 12.

Hewer's Home Hardware: 4459 West 10th (224-4934). This fine version of a Home Hardware store sells the usual housewares, hardware items and home repair supplies, but the thing that sets it apart is its fine selection of baskets in wicker, cane, twig and grasses at really low prices. One palm-cloth basket we found in an antique store on Main Street for $25 cost under $10 here! Anne buys all her Christmas basket fixings at Hewer's. Hours: Monday to Saturday 9 to 6. Map S circle 13.

Connoisseur Cards: 4469 West 10th (228-9911). A nice little card shop, this one sells the usual cards, wrapping paper, cards on recycled paper, Medici cards and writing paper by the sheet. Open Monday to Saturday 10 to 5:30. Map S circle 14.

Splish Splash Bath Boutique: 4471 West 10th (224-3888). One of our region's few stores devoted exclusively to the bathroom, this one has everything imaginable for private moments in the tub, as well as designer bed linens (at discount prices), towels, shower curtains and hard-to-find bathroom fittings, holders and scales. Hours are Monday to Thursday and Saturday 9:30 to 5:30; and Friday 9 to 6. Map S circle 15.

Panache: 4475 West 10th (224-2514). Here they create their own handcrafted silverware. Besides, they sell lovely giftware, harmony balls on chains or just to hold "created by Druids as meditation devices", crystal, china and fine jewellery. Open Monday to Saturday 10 to 5:30. Map S circle 16.

Mollie's Stationery: 4479 West 10th (224-4643). This is a handy source of office, school and stationery supplies, plus partyware, cards and a nice selection of candles. Open Monday to Saturday 9:30 to 5:30. Map S circle 17.

University Bakery: 4487 West 10th (224-3848). A local favourite, this place has little in the way of cakes, but they do a booming business in bread (20 varieties, fresh daily!), buns and doughnuts. Open Monday to Friday 9 to 6; and Saturday 9 to 5:30. Map S circle 18.

Clozzone: 4511 West 10th (222-0107). Clozzone is known for being able to fit small sizes - and all at discount prices. The Carol Little label for petites is featured and with their policy of "labels for less", they suit sizes 4 to 14 with great style. They also showcase local designers prominently. Hours are Monday to Friday 10 to 6; and Saturday 10 to 5:30. Map S circle 19.

Jan's Lingerie & Hosiery: 105, 4545 West 10th (224-2114). Here's the best place in Pt. Grey for undergarments, offering every size, shape, style and colour (including wonderful florals for sock-addicts like Anne) of stocking and socks. It's around the corner from Muffin Break, facing the Safeway parking lot. Open Monday to Friday 10 to 6; and Saturday 9:30 to 5:30. Map S circle 20.

Pascal's Bakery Shop: 4530 West 10th (228-9914). Another fine bakery, this one sells bread, pies, bagels, scones and lots of other baked goods. There were also yummy-looking mini-pizzas when we last visited at $2 each, and a special of five loaves of bread for $3.99 (10 for $7.89). Hours: Monday to Thursday and Saturday 8:30 to 7; and Friday 8:30 to 7:30. Map S circle 21.

Exeter Deli: 4512 West 10th (224-0113). This place doubles as a coffee shop (serving breakfast 8:30 to 11:30) and deli. Stock includes deli meats and cheeses, home-baked pies and pastries and fresh bread and buns. Hours are Monday to Saturday 8:30 to 6. Map S circle 22.

Turn Me Loose: 4476 West 10th (224-5050). This men's shop began selling just consignment items. Now the stock has expanded to include new "designer discount" fashions, too. Hours are Monday to Saturday 10 to 6. Map S circle 23.

TVS Sports: 4466 West 10th (222-2607). The only actual sports equipment sold here is tennis racquets and tennis balls, but they have a good assortment of sports clothing, shorts, warm-ups and runners designed for joggers and court sports. Open Monday to Saturday 10:30 to 6. Map S circle 24.

Bali Bali: 4462 West 10th (224-2347). Anne's pal Gayle's friend Mooh owns this eccentric and wonderful store, which (when they have 'em) has some of the best sales in town! They carry a lot of women's clothing and a few items sized for children. Much of the stock originates in Bali, or -- like the local Moratti line -- LOOKS as though it did. Colours are vivid and many different looks are possible by mixing and matching. There are also carved wood puppets, masks, Indonesian handicrafts and a vast and delightful selection of unusual earrings. One of our favourite shops! Open Monday to Thursday and Saturday 10 to 6; Friday 10 to 9; and Sunday noon to 5. Map S circle 25.

Natural Life Styles: 4460 West 10th (222-2202). For all the earth conscious among us, here's a source for organic cosmetics, handmade papers, Australian wool slippers, Birkenstock shoes and Aussie outerwear. It now incorporates Good Life, which used to be down the block, adding its stock of vitamins, organic produce, etc. Open Monday to Saturday 10 to 5:30. Map S circle 26.

Lisa B.: 4456 West 19th (224-6544). Wonderful designer clothing and shoes (two stores in one) shine here, with Impo shoes and Mary Rose clothing among the selection. Other designer clothing and accessories are available, enabling you to coordinate shoes and outfit in one stop. Hours are Monday to Saturday 10 to 6. Map S circle 27.

Covers: 4454 West 10th (224-5116). This store, as might be expected, specializes in bedding, towels, tablecloths and shower curtains in a positive riot of colours and textures. Custom-duvet service is available for duvet covers perfect for your bedroom decor. Open Monday to Thursday 10 to 6; Friday 10 to 8; and Saturday 10 to 5:30. Map S circle 28.

Delectables Fine Foods: 4448 West 10th (222-2253). Anne designed the logo for this business when her old friend Linda Meinhardt first started it. She's on to bigger things at the Bread Garden and Gallery Cafe, but Anne's work lingers on. At least those years of art school training didn't go to waste! Anyway, they sell wonderful preserves and homemade take-out goodies and do catering, too. Open Monday to Saturday 9:30 to 6. Map S circle 29.

<u>Duthie Books:</u> 4444 West 10th (224-7012). This is our favourite of Duthie's branches, largely because the staff is so knowledgeable and it's easy to park (free, too). There's always a bargain table of mark-downs, and if you don't see what you want, they'll order it in, naturally. Open Monday to Friday 9:30 to 9; Saturday 9:30 to 5:30; and Sunday noon to 5. Map S circle 30.

<u>Lesley's:</u> 4440 West 10th (222-4900). There's "always something new" a Lesley's, where ladies' designer clothing in sizes 4 to 16 is highlighted. There's a nice selection of belts, too. Hours are Monday to Wednesday and Saturday 10 to 6; Thursday and Friday 10 to 8; and Sunday noon to 5. Map S circle 31.

<u>High Five:</u> 4438 West 10th (222-3001). A newish addition to the area, this place sells sports cards (new in packages; old in cases), plus framed sports posters and pictures. Open Monday to Saturday 11 to 5:30. Map S circle 32.

<u>Michael Mcbride:</u> 4426 West 10th (222-4433). This is a pricey spot for men's casual clothes, sweaters, shirts, suspenders and socks, but maybe he's worth it! We particularly liked the bow ties printed with European money -- for men who want to put their money (nearly) where their mouth is. Open Monday to Saturday 10 to 6. Map S circle 33.

<u>Zig Zag Boutique:</u> 4424 West 10th (224-2421). Why is it everything we want is so expensive? Here we found tempting shoes, handbags, socks, tights, belts and accessories, a few lovely pieces of clothing and novelty shirts embroidered with cows. Hours: Monday to Thursday and Saturday 10 to 6; Friday 10 to 9; and Sunday 1 to 5. Map S circle 34.

<u>Tayari:</u> 4412 West 10th (224-5589). They carry some of their own label goods (Tayari International, that is) with a distinctive look: bowler hats, flowered tops, plain skirts -- very '90s. Open Monday to Thursday 10 to 6; Friday 10 to 7; Saturday 10 to 5:30; and Sunday 1 to 5. Map S circle 35.

<u>The X Factor:</u> 4408 West 10th (222-3321). This is where the yuppie puppies are clothed in sizes 8 to 18, boys and youth styles and labels such as Mexx and Red Eraser, team logo hats and jackets and casual attire running the gamut from jeans and T-shirts to jackets and sweats. There's a walk-through to Lil'Putian's, next door. Open Monday to Saturday 10 to 6; and Sunday 1 to 5. Map S circle 36.

<u>Lil'Putian's:</u> 4406 West 10th (222-3321). A sister-operation to the previous entry, this one carries infants wear and sizes up to boys' 6x and girls' wear to size 16. Featured labels are Mexx, Guess, Oshkosh and all the other top designer labels for tots. Same hours and map circle as X Factor.

Le Papillon Boutique: 4390 West 10th (222-8282). A small shop with ladies' designer clothing, this one showcases lots of European imports in elegant decor -- note the gorgeous Persian rug on the floor. Open Monday to Saturday 10 to 5. Map S circle 37.

Francoise: 4376 West 10th (222-2190). This little wool shop sells knitting supplies, patterns and hand-knit items ready-made. We liked the knit slippers with leather soles available in child to adult sizes. Open Monday, Tuesday, Thursday and Saturday 10 to 5:30; Wednesday and Friday 10 to 6. Map S circle 38.

Dead Write: 4374 West 10th (228-8223). Don't be scared away by the 3D paper skeleton reading children's mysteries in a rocking chair -- this is a wonderful source for crime and mystery books -- all new paperbacks and hardcovers and many hard-to-find titles. Hours are Monday to Thursday noon to 6 (apparently their patrons rise late); Friday noon to 8; Saturday 11 to 6; and Sunday 1 to 5. Map S circle 39.

White Dwarf: 4368 West 10th (228-8223). Another sister operation (this time to Dead Write) in the neighbourhood, this one features all new fantasy and science fiction books, children's fantasy selections and role-playing games. Open Monday to Friday 10 to 8; Saturday 10 to 6; and Sunday 1 to 5. Map S circle 40.

Enda-B Fashion: 4346 West 10th (228-1214). Always slightly ahead of the pack, this place is carving out a reputation based on its collection of natural fibre, designer, womens' fashions and accessories. They have a good selection of fine shoes, too. This large store is divided into sections -- ie. shoes, lingerie, etc. Among the labels are Jones New York (Anne's favourite), Peter Nygard, Liz Claiborne, Adrienne Vittadini, Alfred Sung and pieces from the wonderful Steilmann line. Open Monday to Wednesday and Saturday 10 to 6; Thursday and Friday 10 to 9; and Sunday noon to 5. Map S circle 41.

Time After Time: 4330 West 10th (228-8636). Here's where Ruth (who bought out Jeanette's on Dunbar) moved her consignment women's clothing operation. There are also hats and jewellery and brand new lingerie. Open Monday, Tuesday, Thursday and Friday 10 to 6; and Saturday 10:30 to 6. Map S circle 42.

NOTES:

Port Coquitlam

Collectibles, kiddies and the unusual

Just 2 Km from the bustle of the strip-malls and mega-mall Coquitlam Centre, sits Port Coquitlam itself, almost like a small, sleepy village. When we ventured out to do this research, it was a hot day "and there were several people relaxing in the shade on benches in the park in front of City Hall."

This is a medium-sized tour which times out to about three to four hours, all inclusive.

Find Port Coquitlam by driving the Lougheed Highway (extension of East Broadway out of Vancouver) through Burnaby, past New Westminster, through Coquitlam and on; or take Hastings Street east until it runs into Barnet Hwy., which in turn runs through St. Johns in Port Moody and eventually again intersects with the Lougheed. TransCanada 1 goes out to Port Coquitlam (watch the signs carefully, as it's easy to end up in Surrey by mistake if you cross the Port Mann Bridge). Note: All Highways out to Port Coquitlam after 3:30 p.m. on any weekday are jam-packed!

From the U.S. Peace Arch border, take 152nd St. through White Rock straight north. After you pass 104 Avenue in Surrey, watch for signs to TransCanada 1, which will take you across the Port Mann bridge toward Port Coquitlam.

By public transit, it's a long trip, but a relatively simple one: Take the SkyTrain to Columbia Station in New Westminster, then transfer to the #100 bus which eventually wends its way to Port Coquitlam centre at Wilson and Shaughnessy.

If you drive, street parking anywhere in Poco is relatively easy.

Salvation Army Thrift Shop: 2275 Elgin (942-0505). Not quite as classy as the new one in Richmond, but not far off the mark, either. Store display racks hold a selection of handbags and the bric-a-brac can yield some interesting finds. Open Monday to Saturday 9 to 5:15. Map T circle 1.

Batty's Casual Connection: 2646 Shaughnessy (464-6454). Advertising "Fashions for women on the go", this place naturally spotlights active wear, casual clothing (jeans, shorts) and some dresses that are downright stylish -- some quite suitable for work. There were even a few sequined tops. We found a nice selection of clothing and good sale

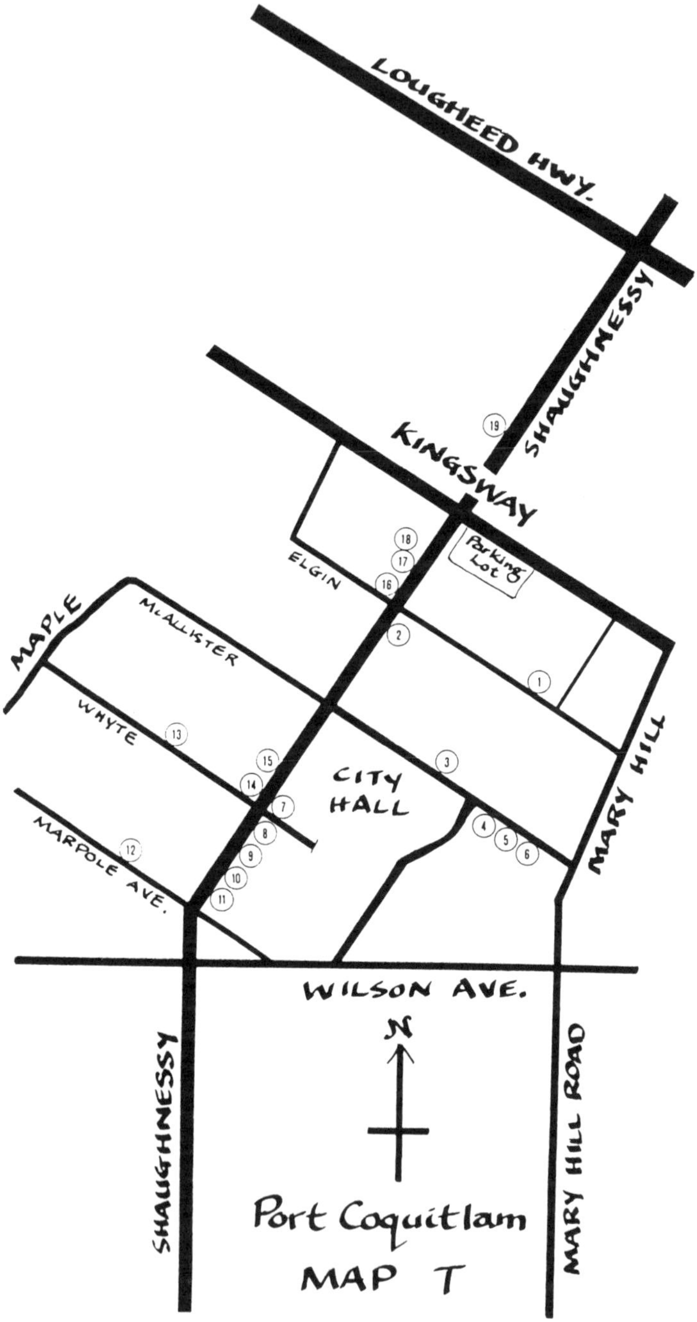
LOUGHEED HWY.
SHAUGHNESSY
KINGSWAY
Parking Lot
ELGIN
MAPLE
McALLISTER
WHYTE
CITY HALL
MARPOLE AVE.
MARY HILL
WILSON AVE.
N
SHAUGHNESSY
MARY HILL ROAD
Port Coquitlam
MAP T
1
2
3
4
5
6
7
8
9
10
11
12
13
14
15
16
17
18
19

racks -- the place was recommended to us by one of our best spies. Open Monday to Thursday and Saturday 9:30 to 6; and Friday 9 to 9. Map T circle 2.

The Perfect Gift: 2283 McAllister (941-1626). We were both impressed with this place: Owner Pat Dale carries Le Chocolate Belge Daniel, fine wrapping paper by the sheet, cards, a machine to enclose gifts in a balloon and charming burl boxes. The place in general is well-decorated, with colour-coordinated displays and interesting items. Open Monday to Saturday 10 to 5:30. Map T circle 3.

Tiger Sports Collectibles: 2232B McAllister (942-2276). Dave and Sharon Murray run this place which sells sports cards and magazines, 1958 CFL cards, back copies of Sports Illustrated, new sports card packs, and so on. Hours are Monday to Thursday 11 to 6; Fridau 11 to 7; Saturday 10 to 5; and Sunday 11 to 5. Map T circle 4.

Jaymer's Fly & Tackle: 2232A McAllister (944-2479). The small store next door to Tiger Sport is a source for rods and reels, flies for salt or fresh water fishing, tackleboxes and crab traps. Open Monday to Saturday 9 to 5:30. Map T circle 5.

Violet Fashion Artists: 101, 2228 McAllister (942-8399). This place specializes in 100 percent silk and sandwashed silk casual clothing. They sell ready-made items and will also custom-tailor their designs to your choice of colour and size. The offer professional tailoring/sewing courses and will custom-create a pattern and/or sew to your design -- BUT they will NOT make up Simplicity or other commercial patterns. Oopen Monday to Saturday 11 to 5:30. Map T circle 6.

Europe Bakery & Delicatessen:2552 Shaughnessy (942-5955). There are lots of bargains here in foodstuffs: A ham sandwich was $2.50 when we stopped by, a turkey sandwich $2.95. There are bulk self-serve buns, European rye bread, sourdough, cold cuts, cheese, salads, some terrific-looking baked goods (cheap -- muffins 39 cents each!) and mocha cakes (Amaretto, Gran Marnier) by the slice or whole. It was very busy (with good reason) and we had to take a number for service. Hours are Monday to Saturday 8:30 to 6. Map T circle 7.

Sophie's Gold & Gift Shop: 2550C Shaughnessy (941-9119). Moved to larger quarters here from their old location next to Tiger Sports, this place has been doing business in Poco for a dozen years. They sell a wide variety of 10 and 14 carat jewellery, some costume jewellery, clocks, candle holders, pewter boxes and more. You must ring a buzzer and wait to be admitted. Open Monday to Saturday 10 to 6. Map T circle 8.

Midland Liquidators: 2550A Shaughnessy (941-9139). We found housewares, hardware, toys, tools and such bargains as a "professional" curling iron for $4.99 and comic books at 50 percent off. On a separate voyage of discovery, Lorraine found auto repair manuals. They make keys cheaply, too. Hours are Monday to Saturday 9 to 5:30. Map T circle 9.

Kids Stuff: 114, 2540 Shaughnessy (941-8385). A mother and daughter team (Ivy Perodie and Michele Nishio) run this nice children's shop. Some items are consigned, but there's lots of new stuff too, like Baby Bunch clothing, hand-made bows and barrettes for little girls and custom-made three-storey painted and wallpapered dollhouses ($250) or cloth balloons for a child's wall at only $2.50. Used goods include good condition Fisher-Price items, doll cribs, board-puzzles, doll clothes and other very clean toys and shoes. Larger equipment like carseats, cribs and highchairs (all checked to meet current safety standards) are available, too. This is a large, bright, clean store, and there's a children's play area to keep the tots busy while you browse. Open Monday to Friday 10 to 5:30; and Saturday 10 to 5. Map T circle 10.

John Bull's English Meat Pies: 112, 2540 Shaughnessy (464-2099). Here's a wholesale/retail operation with a small store front and the main production at the rear. In a small eating area, they sell pies and soft drinks (meat pies for $2.50 include steak and mushroom; barbecued beef; curried chicken; steak and vegetable; and beef and onion). There are also cornish pasties and sausage rolls, and of course, what you can buy in quantity is further discounted. Open Tuesday to Saturday 9 to 5:30. Map T circle 11.

Playthings: 107, 1331 Marpole (941-7315). An "adult" store (though many of us are still not grown-up enough for THIS!), this place sells sex toys, lingerie, "marital aids" and dirty cards. Open Monday noon to 5; Tuesday to Thursday and Saturday 10 to 6; and Friday 10 to 9. Map T circle 12.

Poco's Natural Food: 2329 Whyte (942-5612). Here you'll discover herbs galore: eye-bright, red clover blossom, feverfew, skullcap and nettles, to name just a few. There are self-serve natural nuts and grains, organic produce, vitamins, foot-health shoes and those herbs, arranged in industrial size mayo jars sideways on shelves. We hear that folks come from far and wide for hard to find items, which are stocked regularly here. Open Monday to Saturday 10 to 5. Map T circle 13.

Wm. Simpson Jewellery: 1551 Shaughnessy (942-0121). This is the only place Lorraine could find City of Port Coquitlam souvenirs, including "official" coffee mugs. There is also an assortment of cups, saucers, plates, crystal, jewellery, grandfather clocks and gift items. Open Tuesday to Saturday 9:30 to 6. Map T circle 14.

Home Hardware: 2557 Shaughnessy (942-7720). One of those great old-fashioned hardware stores that sells wood screws, brass screws, washers, nuts and bolts by the piece, this place also stocks housewares, hardware and even electrical and lighting findings by the piece. It's a relatively large store for the area, and well patronized by locals. Hours are Monday to Saturday 9 to 6. Map T circle 15.

Batty's Shoes: 2657 Shaughnessy (942-8416). This is a good source for hard to fit feet, with a wide selection of men's women's and children's regular and orthopedic shoes. It is THE local source for properly fitted kids' shoes, says our source, and we also learned that customers travel for miles for their orthopedics. Hours are Monday to Thursday and Saturday 9 to 6; and Friday 9 to 9. Map T circle 16.

Haida Office Supplies: 2663 Shaughnessy (942-7014). This big office supply store has great discounts when their seasonal flyers come out periodically (especially summers), plus they do the usual office printing, stationery and photocopying. They sell office furniture, too. There's free parking at the back of the store. Open Monday to Friday 8:30 to 5:30; and Saturday 10 to 5. Map T circle 17.

M & R Sports Den: 2669 Shaughnessy (941-4814). This place looks like its business is built entirely on supplying local teams, but there's certain to be more to it. The carry baseball and hockey shirts and jackets with local lacrosse and baseball team logos, equipment for those sports and more. Open Monday to Thursday and Saturday 9 to 5:30; and Friday 9 to 8. Map T circle 18.

T.J.'s Kiddies Korner: 2807 Shaughnessy (464-9190). If you're a local shopper, you probably know these folks from their stores on Fraser Street in Vancouver and on the King George in Surrey. They have a long-standing reputation for family service. They sell children's furniture, car seats, strollers, highchairs, playpens, cribs, and they rent similar items, too. Hours are Monday to Thursday and Saturday 9 to 5:30; Friday 9 to 9; and Sundays noon to 5. Map T circle 19.

NOTES:

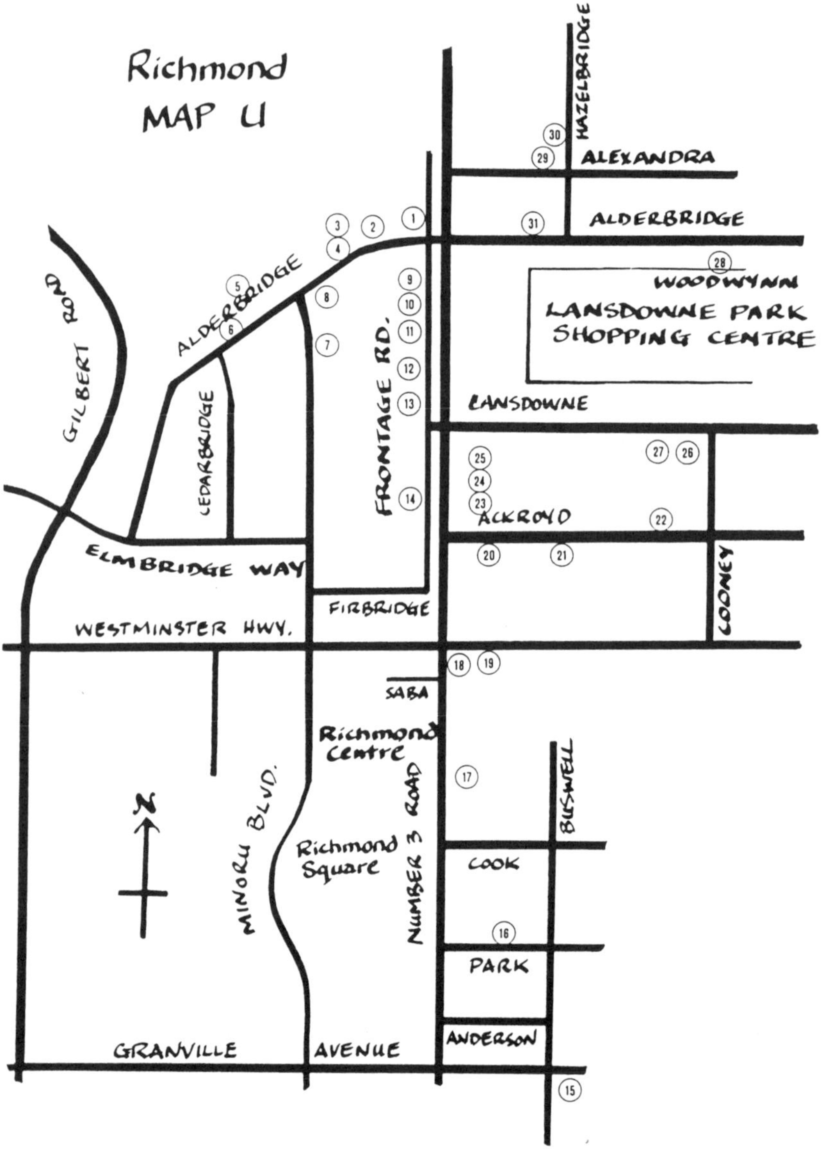
Richmond
MAP U
HAZELBRIDGE
30
29
ALEXANDRA
1
2
3
4
31
ALDERBRIDGE
28
WOODWYNN
LANSDOWNE PARK
SHOPPING CENTRE
ALDERBRIDGE
5
6
8
7
9
10
11
12
13
14
FRONTAGE RD.
GILBERT ROAD
CEDARBRIDGE
LANSDOWNE
25
24
23
27
26
ACKROYD
22
20
21
ELMBRIDGE WAY
FIRBRIDGE
COONEY
WESTMINSTER HWY.
18
19
SABA
Richmond
Centre
17
BUSWELL
N
MINORU BLVD.
Richmond
Square
NUMBER 3 ROAD
COOK
16
PARK
ANDERSON
GRANVILLE
AVENUE
15

Richmond

Bargains and the unusual

This is probably the best bargain area (thus the best bargain tour) in the book. Allow four to five hours if you must see everything.

This is not a walking tour because -- besides the great distance between stops -- there are very few sidewalks! Richmond is Strip Mall Heaven, so there is almost always adequate parking (except Aberdeen Centre's lot which is impossible!) Addresses are sometimes misleading because though the store faces onto a major road, the MALL's actual address is from another corner. It is confusing, so just try to follow the numbers on our map.

Richmond is the next municipality south of Vancouver. Driving from Vancouver, you can enter via either the Arthur Laing Bridge (extension southward of Granville Street), the Oak Street Bridge (Oak, obviously), or the Knight Street Bridge (Clark Drive flows into Knight at about 15th Avenue and Knight goes to the southernmost part of Vancouver, and across the bridge).

If you enter Richmond from the Knight Street Bridge, don't take the first (Bridgeport Road) exit, but stay on the freeway until the next exit, which says "Richmond Centre". This puts you onto Westminster Highway (westbound) into the heart of Richmond, and our tour. You will pass No. 4 Road, Shell Road and Garden City Way on this highway and the next major street is No. 3 Road, where our tour starts.

If driving up from the U.S. border, the simplest route is to follow Hwy. 99 North through White Rock, Delta and Ladner and cross into Richmond via the Deas Tunnel (also known as the George Massey Tunnel). Take the Westminster Highway exit and proceed westbound to No. 3 Road, as described above.

Our tour begins at Alderbridge Way and No. 3 Road, opposite the northwest corner of Lansdowne Park Shopping Centre.

<u>Blockbuster Video:</u> 120, 4991 No. 3 Road (278-3849), We've always liked this store, simply for the sheer magnitude of its offerings: previously-owned videos from $8.88, laser discs and some movie-ish accessories. They buy multiple copies of new movies, then when the rental demand declines, they sell off the extra copies. You can often buy copies of new releases still on the "New Release" shelves, such as "Fival Goes West", which Lorraine bought there last time for $8.88. Open seven days 10 to midnight. Map U circle 1.

Fabricland: 7971 Alderbridge (270-7767). Good for regular fabric and sewing needs, this place becomes even better if you're a member ($10 for two years) because some special discounts are just for members. Anne more or less paid for her membership when she was buying dress patterns because the deal offered to members was two free patterns with one bought. Since she needed three different patterns, each About $9 in price, she laid out $19 (membership plus the price of one pattern) and received $27 worth of goods at once. Since then, she's received monthly newsletters and enjoyed savings of 50 percent and more off selected items she probably would have paid full price for otherwise. At the back of this store there's a $2 as-is centre with some good values even for non-members. Open Monday to Friday 9:30 to 9:30; Saturday 9:30 to 5:30; and Sunday noon to 5. Map U circle 2.

The Shoepermarket Discount Footwear: 120A, 7931 Alderbridge (129-1991). This is a discount outlet for Rockport and other brand names, boots, men's, women's and children's shoes and sandals. Open Tuesday to Saturday 10 to 5; closed Sunday and Monday. Map U circle 3.

La Joanne Merchandises Discounts: 7911 Alderbridge Way (278-9238). This place is up on the second floor of the building, but a large banner proclaims its whereabouts. You'll discover handbags, leather men's and women's clothing (leather skirts from $19.99 last time we checked) and up to 70 percent off leather and linen women's fashions everyday. Hours are Monday to Saturday 10 to 6. Map U circle 4.

Shoe Warehouse: 160, 7771 Alderbridge Way (278-7781). Sales of 50 percent off are common here on women's, men's and children's shoes (including kids' dress shoes), sports footwear and boots. There's often a very good selection of men's and women's sample size shoes and VERY loud music as a backdrop to it all. Open Monday to Thursday and Saturday 10 to 6; Friday 10 to 9; and Sunday noon to 5. Map U circle 5.

Mr. Jax Fashion Fabrics: 7771 Alderbridge (276-8222). Vancouver's foremost national fashion house rarely sells samples to the public -- except -- here! There's a tidy selection of fabrics, remnants, shoulder pads, buttons and findings and seasonally-changing racks of clothing seconds from the Mr. Jax and Evan Picone lines. Entire racks are dedicated to $10, $15, $20 and $25 reductions and most seconds are clearly marked to divulge flaws. Stock is less picked-over than at their downtown location. Open Monday to Wednesday and Saturday 9:30 to 5:30; Thursday and Friday 9:30 to 7; and Sunday noon to 5. Map U circle 6.

The Westway Discount Store: 5400 Minoru (270-1516). This is a great source of men's, women's and children's clothing, plus discounted housewares, brass, glassware, china and kitchen gadgets. There are always "dollar" bins ($1 to $3) with hardware, stationery, housewares, fridge magnets and so on. The clearance centre is against the rear wall. We find this a good place to shop for stocking stuffers, party favours and gifts for children's parties (loads of inexpensive but sturdy toys). There are both brand names and generics in just about every category. Open Monday to Thursday and Saturday 10 to 5:30; and Friday 10 to 9. Map U circle 7.

Ed's Linen Warehouse: 7800 Alderbridge (270-3318). We've always liked this place for discount linens, towels and bathroom accessories. There are even some brass beds and always good discount areas and sales. Open Monday to Wednesday and Saturday 9:30 to 5:30; Thursday and Friday 9:30 to 9; and Sunday noon to 5. Map U circle 8.

Dots Discount Ladies' Wear: 5355 No. 3 Road (276-9646). Discounted labels here include Adrienne Vittadini, Marc D'Alcy, Anne Pinkerton, Radical, Michael Sport and others, with possible savings of up to 70 percent off regular retail. Not all styles are current season, however, so we find it best to shop for basics or classics only. They carry some larger sizes, too. There's everything from casual tie-dyed shorts or blue jeans to elegant evening wear. Parking is free in the lot out front. Hours are Monday, Tuesday and Saturday 9:30 to 5:30; Wednesday to Friday 9:30 to 9; and Sunday noon to 5. Map U circle 9.

Sport Mart: 5381 No. 3 Road (244-0317). They claim never to be undersold, and we've found their prices very competitive, indeed. Their changing stock reflects the current season (skiwear in winter, beachwear in summer). Included are athletic shoes, in-line skates (excellent prices on these), bikes, sportswear, camping supplies and accessories like sunglasses. Open Monday to Wednesday and Saturday 9 to 6; Thursday and Friday 9 to 9; and Sunday 11 to 5. Map U circle 10.

Save-on-Diapers: 5421 No. 3 Road (599-0642). They sell bulk cloth and disposable diapers in newborn to adult sizes. They also carry baby food, large equipment (like playpens, highchairs, cribs) and many national brand names -- all at competitive or discount prices. Naturally, bulk purchasers receive wholesale prices. They do mail orders too, which is handy if you're from far away and wish to reorder. Open Tuesday to Saturday 9:30 to 5:30; and Sunday noon to 5. Map U circle 11.

Salvation Army Thrift Store: 5491 No. 3 Road (278-5997). We've always liked this edition of the Sally Ann because it's so clean, carpeted and upmarket. GST is included in the already-low prices. Monday and Tuesday are half price days for all colour-tagged clothing, plus there are other daily specials. Generally speaking, they seem to get the deluxe Sally Ann goods. Open Monday to Wednesday and Saturday 9 to 5; and Thursday and Friday 9 to 9. Map U circle 12.

Pro Golf: 5611 No. 3 Road (273-5530). Their motto is "We discount everything but the service", which seems to hold true. Among the offerings are bags, clubs, grips and how-to-videos. Open Monday to Wednesday and Saturday 9 to 6; Thursday and Friday 9 to 9; and Sunday 11 to 5. Map U circle 13.

Buy & Sell Weekly: 5791 No. 3 Road (280-1000). Forget getting through on the phone lines. The trick is to pick up some ad forms on one trip, drop them in on the next. This paper is distributed throughout the lower mainland. People looking for stuff to buy purchase the Buy & Sell (for $1.98 including GST), but most of the ads in it are free. If you want a fancy display ad or a picture ad to sell your car, there's a fee, but it's a low one.

The paper comes out every Monday and Thursday, so savvy bargain-hunters drive out to pick it up in Richmond then, then dash right to the phones. Included are sections for autos, trucks and vans; household; and auto parts and RVs. The office is open Monday to Friday 8:30 to 4:30; and weekends 10 to 4; insertion deadlines: Sunday 4 p.m. and Wednesday 4:30. Map U circle 14.

Great Canadian Office Supplies Warehouse: 8240 Granville Ave. (270-3151). Ah, yes: the place with the impossible-to-remember name. The place itself is hard to forget because the discounts on office supplies and furniture are pretty good. It's a large warehouse-type operation with friendly staff and excellent after sales service. This is where Anne bought her wonderful Mitsubishi fax machine (receives over 100 faxes a week -- no problems in two years and it cost under $400!). Hours are Monday to Friday 8 to 9; Saturday 8 to 7; and Sunday 10 to 6. Map U circle 15.

China Can Enterprises: 8131 Park Road (270-3425) -- a second location is at 8095 Park Road (270-4499). This whole shopping strip has Chinese restaurants -- like a mini-Hong Kong, if fact people downtown have taken to calling this area and Aberdeen Centre nearby "The New Chinatown". Whatever your name for it, if you're into Asian import foodstuffs, this is the place. Lorraine visited on a Sunday and it was really busy. Sales coupon books are sometimes available in the store. Open seven days 9 to 7. Map U circle 16.

London Drugs: 6390 No. 3 Road (520-9011). Here you'll find all manner of competitively-priced drugstore items, plus housewares and London Drugs regular deal of 10 percent off all books and magazines. The computer centre here has helpful staff with the time to talk to you. Open Monday to Saturday 9 to 10; and Sunday 9 to 8. Map U circle 17.

The Spare Room: #9, 6040 No. 3 Road (no phone). This has long been one of our favourite finds because it's hidden upstairs in what must be the most decrepit building around. BUT -- we figure 97 percent of the stock is priced at under $5 and there's everything from antiques and collectables to toys to good old "junque". Open Monday and Tuesday noon to 5; Thursday to Saturday 1 to 5; and CLOSED Wednesday. Map U circle 18.

Nevada Bob's Discount Golf & Tennis: 8080 Westminster Hwy. (279-0015). They are the complete outfitters for the two sports at a discount, with stock including clothing, footwear, clubs and racquets. Lorraine's Aussie guests adored the place. Open Monday to Wednesday and Saturday 9:30 to 6; Thursday and Friday 9:30 to 9; and Sunday 10 to 5. Map U circle 19.

Saffy's Shoes: 160, 8100 Ackroyd (276-2700). This place is a must for the hard-to-fit. Though prices are not discounted on regular stock, there is always a bargain section. They can fit sizes 4 to 13 and widths 5A to WW. They have Keds in narrow widths, too. Included in the stock are Easy Spirit and New Balance, among other brands. Open Monday, Tuesday and Saturday 10 to 6; Thursday and Friday 10 to 9; and Sunday 1 to 5. Map U circle 20.

Save-on Foods & Drugs: 8200 Ackroyd (278-3229). The "original" mega-supermarket, this one has a great book department (Lorraine's favourite, actually) with 10 percent off all books and magazines, and even bigger discounts on red-tag books. There's also a well-planned bulk foods section, which we both prefer to the other stores'. Open seven days 8 a.m. to midnight. Map U circle 21.

Buns Master: 150, 8291 Ackroyd (278-0729). Here's one we've always liked: they offer a dish of sample cookies at the counter, plus a community bulletin board. Prices are great on buns, bagels, bread, cheese twists, pizza bread, pita-shells, mini-cookies, croissants, cheese and onion buns and pies. Hours are Monday to Thursday 7:30 to 5:45; Friday 7:30 to 9; Saturday 9:30 to 6; and Sunday 10 to 5. Map U circle 22.

Consumers Distributing: 180, 8171 Ackroyd (276-2407). Though their catalogue is billed as the guide to the lowest prices, we often find they don't have what we want available and we have to return time after time to get the item in question. The do seem to offer good prices on housewares, toys, guftware and jewellery, but we have to add a cautious caveat emptor for the record. Open Monday to Friday 9:30 to 9; Saturday 9 to 6; and Sunday 1 to 5. Map U circle 23.

Bi-Way Stores: 180A, 8171 Ackroyd (276-2249). This is a Field's, K-Mart type store with toys, clothing, housewares, snack-food items (cookies, crackers, coffee, etc.) with some brand names if they can get a deal on quantities, and generic fill-ins. Open Monday to Friday 9:30 to 9; Saturday 9:30 to 5:30; and Sunday noon to 5. Map U circle 24.

Kitmond Arts & Crafts: 155, 8171 Ackroyd (278-8708). Here's a source for inexpensive Asian imports: jewellery, embroidered kimonos, toys and kids runners among other cheap things. Open Monday to Saturday 10:30 to 5:30. Map U circle 25.

Village Stitchery: 150, 8380 Lansdowne (278-3666). This is not really a bargain spot, "But," says Lorraine, "Oh so lovely." This is a craftperson's dream: cross-stitch and needlework supplies and kits, artsy rubber stamps, gift items -- all beautifully displayed. It's a great place to get ideas since there are some great examples made up for display. There's always an old wheelbarrow and group of baskets full of marked down items outside. Lorraine hasn't been able to just drive by it yet -- last time out she bought an ornament kit marked down from $19,95 to 99 cents! Hours are Monday to Wednesday and Saturday 10 to 5:30; Thursday and Friday 10 to 9; and Sunday noon to 5. Map U circle 26.

Egghead Discount Softwear: 120, 8380 Lansdowne (273-9770). We know this is an international chain, but the people are so nice. They sell computer software -- not always at a discount, but they will match prices. A free "CUE" (Custom Update News) card gives return customers an additional 5 percent off both regular and sale prices, plus a regular quarterly newsletter, invites to seminars and sales, etc. Open Monday to Saturday 9 to 6; and Sunday noon to 5. Map U circle 27.

Woodwynn: 326, 5300 No. 3 Road (270-9683). Though we've avoiding touring the malls store by store, we couldn't resist adding this one on the Alderbridge side of Lansdowne Park Shopping Centre because the staff is SO helpful and friendly, and the store so clean and well laid-out. We've found it a wonderful source for inexpensive comforters, sheets and towels. They also carry low-price family footwear, some housewares and fashions discontinued from Woodward's stores, their parent operation. Open Monday, Tuesday and Saturday 9:30 to 5:30; Wednesday to Friday 9:30 to 9; and Sunday noon to 5. Map U circle 28.

<u>MacGillycuddy's:</u> 165, 4811 Hazelbridge Way (270-9230). This is the sister operation to Sharon Clark's North Van location, selling high quality women's consigned items, plus shoes, jewellery and accessories. Hours are Monday to Thursday and Saturday 10 to 6; Friday 10 to 9; and Sunday noon to 5. Map U circle 29.

<u>Fabricana:</u> 4811 Hazelbridge Way (273-5316). Here you'll find nice quality fabric (home decor fabrics upstairs) plus a handy children's play area. Patterns are always half-price when the required fabric is purchased at the same time. Open Monday, Tuesday and Saturday 9:30 to 5:30; Wednesday to Friday 9:30 to 9; and Sunday noon to 5. Map U circle 30.

<u>Shoestrings:</u> 124, 4940 No. 3 Road (273-3420). Save up to 50 percent on discounted runners, walking shoes, golf shoes, kids', women's and men's shoes, aerobic clothing, T-shirts, socks, shorts and more. Not all styles are available in all sizes (some broken lines). Hours are Monday to Wednesday 10 to 5:30; Thursday and Friday 10 to 9; Saturday 9:30 to 5:30; and Sunday noon to 5. Map U circle 31.

NOTES:

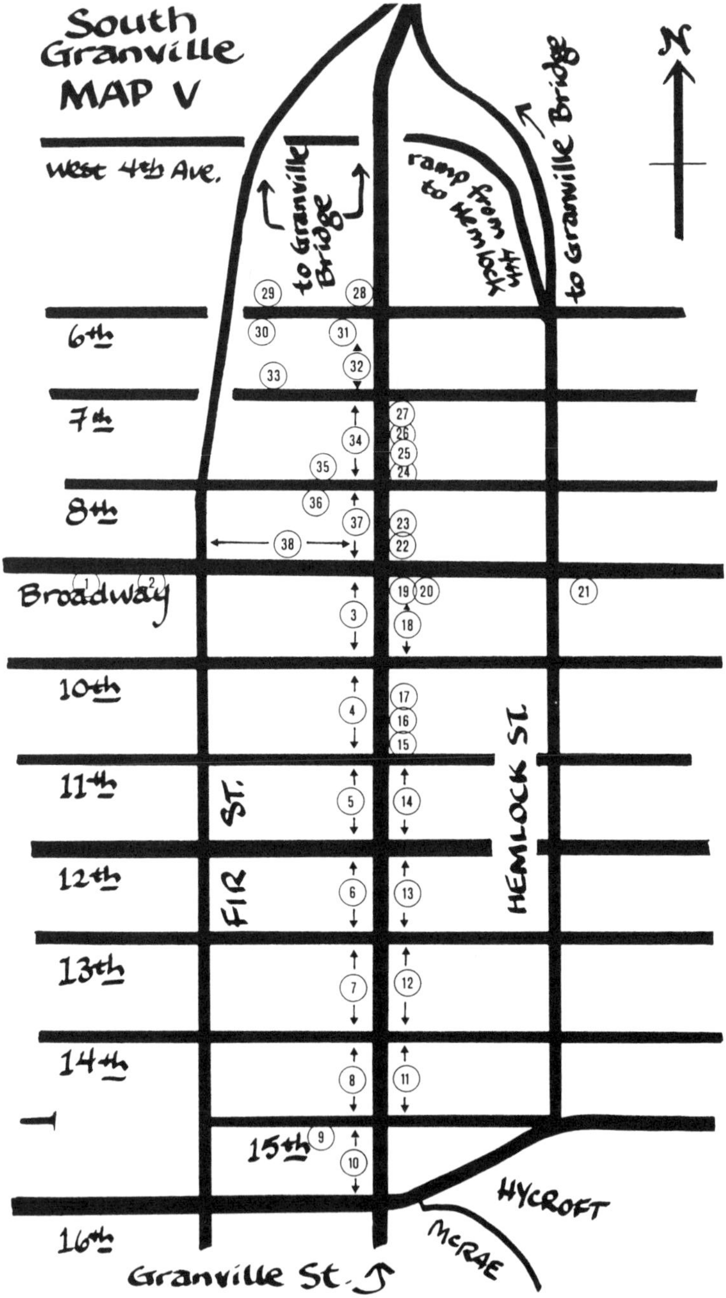
South Granville MAP V
West 4th Ave.
to Granville Bridge
ramp from 4th to Hemlock
to Granville Bridge
N
6th
7th
8th
Broadway
10th
11th
12th
13th
14th
15th
16th
FIR ST.
HEMLOCK ST.
HYCROFT
MCRAE
Granville St.
1
2
3
4
5
6
7
8
9
10
11
12
13
14
15
16
17
18
19
20
21
22
23
24
25
26
27
28
29
30
31
32
33
34
35
36
37
38

South Granville

Fine clothing, furnishings, carpets -- and bargains!

This half-day tour could be completed in two to three hours, depending on whether or not you get swallowed up in a time-vortex in one of the incredibly elegant antique stores in the area. You'll note we give little information about the carpet, antique and designer clothing boutiques, because so much of what you'll discover is one-of-a-kind -- and a matter of personal preference.

South Granville has a reputation for "top dollar" prices, which is certainly true when it comes to the fine imported antiquities, fine art, objets d'art, handmade silk carpets, decor accents and the sylish fashions and shoes available there. On the other hand, there are some surprising bargain delights, too, like Turnabout, Bruna Coiffures, Dress 4 Less and Mister Liquidators. At the corner of Broadway and Granville stands the somewhat decayed and less-than-elegant Aristocratic Restaurant, which in its heyday was quite the "in" place. Nowadays, it's still a landmark, but more of a smoky cafe (with a good breakfast special, mind you) than anything else.

We do not give driving directions to the area because Broadway and Granville are such major crossroads. If you can't find this area, you can't really be a Serious Shopper!

By Transit, the Broadway #9 bus (connecting to Broadway Station on the SkyTrain line) stops there, but if you were travelling from downtown, that's certainly the long way around. From downtown Vancouver, almost any bus on Granville Mall southbound will get you there. For transit info, call 261-5100.

Our tour starts and ends near Broadway and Fir, to simplify parking, as it's very difficult to park on either Broadway or Granville - and even when you can find parking on the main streets, it's at expensive short-term meters.

<u>Compumax:</u> 102, 1668 W. Broadway (731-2828). For the computer-minded, here's a small selection of software and accessories. Open Monday to Saturday 10 to 6. Map V circle 1.

<u>Goldilocks Bake Shop:</u> 1606 W. Broadway (736-7744, 736-2464). An incredible experience even if you just browse, this bakery has Chinese good-luck cakes, opulent wedding cakes and a variety of baked goods you'll never see elsewhere, such as their famous purple potato cake! Part of the bakery is a Filipino restaurant called Galing Galing (we

always think "Galing Galing, Gone") where you can point to buffet items and dine like royalty for pocket change. Open Tuesday to Sunday 10 to 7. Map V circle 2.

Aristocratic: 2501 Granville (733-1515). Right at the corner of Broadway, this flashback is notable as a local point of interest. Their cheap breakfast special is in effect till 11 a.m. Open Monday to Friday 7:30 to 7; and weekends 8 to 6. Map V circle 3.

Turn the corner (head south) onto Granville here.

For Legs Only: 2517 Granville (732-5535). This place sells a huge assortment of wild and traditional hosiery, lingerie and accessories. It's sister operation Exposee is located at Lougheed Mall. Open Monday to Thursday and Saturday 10:30 to 6; and Friday 10:30 to 6:30. Map V circle 1.

La Bon Soup: 2523 Granville (737-1437). This great take-out (or dine-in) spot serves breakfast, desserts and refreshing coffees like latte, cappuccino and iced mochaccino (if you haven't tried the last, you haven't lived!). Open Monday to Thursday 7 to 6:30; and Friday 7 a.m to 8 p.m. Map V circle 2.

The Quality Custom Shirtmakers: 2531 Granville (731-9190). Here's a great source for bargain-priced, custom-made men's shirts: How about 2 x 2 100 percent Egyptian cotton broadcloth from England custom-made into shirts for only $65 to $85? Or pure cotton or poly-cotton casual shirts for $38 to $55? Open Monday to Friday 10 to 6; and Saturday 10 to 5. Map V block 3.

Mister Liquidators: 2543 Granville (731-9544). This shop makes keys and carries a hodge-podge of discounted goods including carpets, hoursewares, electricals, and a weird dart-board clock for which you might know the perfect recipient. Open Monday to Saturday 9:30 to 6. Map V block 3.

Duke's Gourmet Cookies and Cappuccino: 2561 Granville (736-9191). Duke's is well-known in the area for great cookies and muffins. They also sell cappuccino, lattes, mochas and their two-dollar deal varies according to the day of the week: Monday it's hot chocolate and a muffin; Tuesday it's a latte and muffin; Wednesday it's cafe mocha and a cookie; and so on. Open Monday to Friday 7 to 6; and Saturday 8 to 6. Map V block 3.

Van den Bosch Patisserie Belge: 2567 Granville (731-0023). Another South Granville favourite, this one sells wonderful pastries. They have branches also at Granville Island and Arbutus Centre. Open Monday to Friday 8 to 6; and Saturday 9 to 5:30. Map V block 3.

Bogart Discs: 2579 Granville (739-1124). Longtime Vancouverites will remember this place from its old location on Commercial Drive. It's a tiny store, but crammed with records, CDs, tapes (both new and used), posters and paraphenalia. Open Monday to Friday 11 to 7; Saturday 10 to 6; and Sunday noon to 6. Map V block 3.

Network Apparel: 2585 Granville (736-0801). This discount fashion shop carries women's and children's clothing with some items priced at $5 or less. Last time in we noticed some lovely Hong Kong hand-knit cotton sweaters for $50 and $60. Open Monday to Friday 9:30 to 6:30; Saturday 10 to 6; and Sunday noon to 5. Map V block 3.

Mexico Arte: 2617 Granville (739-9275). This place offers a charming collection of glass, pottery, small furniture and hangings. Open Monday to Saturday 10 to 6; and Sunday noon to 5. Map V block 4.

Leathers for Less: 2625 Granville (731-8188). They claim 30 to 70 percent off everyday prices, plus special reductions for stock clearances. We'd caution you to be selective. Open Monday to Saturday 10 to 5:30; and Sunday noon to 5:30. Map V block 4.

Sicklemore's Flowers: 2633 Granville (733-9188). We find Sicklemore's somewhat pricey but their work is certainly worth it. They are the florist of choice for most of the business people in the area, with a long-standing reputation for quality and workmanship. Open Monday to Saturday 8:30 to 5:30. Map V block 4.

Gala Fabrics: 2637 Granville (731-7815). A good assortment of moderately-priced fabrics are found in this small store. Open Monday to Saturday 10 to 6; and Sunday noon to 5. Map V block 4.

Nicole Adrienne: 2705 Granville (738-8187). Formerly Marc Downs, this location now promises slightly more upmarket women's fashions. Open Monday, Tuesday and Saturday 10 to 6; Wednesday to Friday 10 to 9; and Sunday noon to 5. Map V block 5.

Ming Wo: 2707 Granville (737-7885). This recently-opened branch of Vancouver's most famous housewares store is surely *numero uno*. They've eschewed the usual bric-a-brac and kitchen gadgets for fabulous wrought-iron pedestal candle holders, chunky glassware, stylishly-huge baskets and "statement" decor accents. Open Monday to Saturday 10 to 6; and Sunday noon to 5. Map V block 5.

Mondo Uomo: 2709 Granville (731-2387). This stylish shop sells everything from women's casual wear to formal attire and furs. Trendy outfits bearing the "Anita Belle" label originate in China, and other imports come from France, Italy and Britain. Anne found the salespeople "totally stuck-up and pretentious", but the stock is worth a look-see. Open Monday to Thursday and Saturday 10 to 6; and Friday 10 to 8. Map V block 5.

Mackinnon's Bakery: 2715 Granville (738-2442). Scottish baking is obviously the focus here, but they also sell wonderful Milano coffee, wedding cakes and their special, distinctive pastries. Open Monday to Saturday 10 to 6. Map V block 5.

Jackson Meats: 2717 Granville (738-6328). Jackson Meats has a reputation for excellence a mile long in Vancouver. They sell meats, fresh fish, chicken or steak pies and their famous cornish pasties. Open Monday to Thursday and Saturday 9 to 6; Friday 9 to 7; and Sunday 11 to 5. Map V block 5.

Canada Produce: 2712 Granville (738-5168). This is a great place to buy fresh, unblemished fruit, and their flowers are reasonable, too. Open seven days 8:30 a.m. to 10:30 p.m. Map V block 5.

Sun On Market: 2723 Granville (738-2105). Their pricing is naturally very competitve (since they're right next door to Canada Produce) and their floral bouquets are lovely. Open seven days 8 a.m. to midnight. Map V block 5.

Sheppard Shoes: 2799 Granville (736-4935). We've getting tired of saying "the best", but this truly is a great shoe store. Open Monday to Friday 10 to 6; and Saturday 9:30 to 5. Map V block 5.

Ronson's For Shoes: 2825 Granville (736-8183). Again, they have a great reputation and also offer a wide range of sizes for men and women. Open Monday to Saturday 9 to 5:30. Map V block 6.

The Write Place: 2843 Granville (732-7777). Recently moved just two doors from its former location, this place specializes in custom stationery, gift cards, novelties, gift wrap and so on. Open Monday to Friday 10 to 6; Saturday 10 to 5:30; and Sunday noon to 5. Map V block 6.

The Plum Clothing Company: 2845 Granville (737-0246). This is a designer discount source for women's (and some unisex) casual clothing -- mainly cottons. They are open Monday to Thursday and Saturday 10 to 6; Friday 10 to 9; and Sunday noon to 5. Map V block 6.

Abaca Fashions: 2861 Granville (738-2883). Here they sell washable silks, sweaters and casual wear for women. Open Monday to Thursday and Saturday 10 to 6; Friday 10 to 8; and Sunday noon to 5. Map V block 6.

Freedman Shoes: 2867 Granville (731-0448). Yet another classic South Granville shop with wonderful shoes. Open Monday to Thursday and Saturday 9:30 to 6; and Friday 9:30 to 8. Map V block 6.

Szasz Restaurant & Delicatessen: 2881 Granville (738-7922, 738-7925). A well-known local dine-in deli, this place also sells take-out food and has a tempting assortment of petits-fours. Open Monday to Saturday 8 to 7; and Sunday 10 to 4. Map V block 6.

Kim-John China & Gifts: 2903 Granville (732-7311). One of the best sources for hard-to-find and discount fine china, flatware and crystal, this place is open Monday to Wednesday and Saturday 9:30 to 6; Thursday and Friday 9:30 to 9; and Sunday noon to 5. Map V block 7.

Gisele Shoe Boutique: 2911 Granville (736-0821). Yet another good shoe store for women. Open Monday to Thursday and Saturday 10 to 5:30; and Friday 10 to 6. Map V block 7.

Barney's Caffe & Bakery: 2975 Granville (731-6446). Known in the area simply as "Barney's", this chic spot is the nexus for the South Granville crowd, with weekend line-ups out into the street far from uncommon. Open Monday to Saturday 8 a.m. to 10 p.m.; and Sunday 9 to 5. Map V block 7.

Cottonental: 2977 Granville (733-6553). Here's the source for casual cotton separates and exercise clothing for women. Hours are Monday to Thursday and Saturday 10 to 6; Friday 10 to 8; and Sunday noon to 4. Map V block 7.

On-Going Kids: 2985 Granville (736-3703). As the name suggests, this is a clothing, toy and gift store for growing children. Open Monday to Saturday 10 to 6; and Sunday noon to 5. Map V block 7.

Minaret Oriental Carpets: 3003 Granville (733-6414). One of Vancouver's high-quality imported carpet stores. Hours are Monday to Saturday 10 to 6; and Sunday noon to 5. Map V block 8.

Hampshire Antiques: 3007 Granville (733-1326). Another of South Granville's fine antique stores, this one is open Tuesday to Friday 11 to 5; Saturday 10 to 6; or by appointment. Map V block 8.

Vancouver Antiques International: 3025 Granville (737-0013, 737-9913). Perfect for antique browsing, this one is open Monday to Saturday 10:30 to 6; and Sunday noon to 5. Map V block 8.

Esmode Boutique: 3035 Granville (732-4209). Upmarket women's fashions here. Hours are Monday to Saturday 10 to 6. Map V circle 35.

Bau-Xi: 3045 Granville (733-3211). One of Vancouver's top art galleries, this one also represents a number of avant-garde artists. They feature sculpture, prints, paintings and offer expert crating and shipping services, too. Open Monday to Saturday 9:30 to 5:30. Map V block 8.

Atkinson's: 3057 Granville (736-3378). Here they sell fine imports, china, glassware and crystal like Lalique, Lladro, Limoges and Rosenthal. Open Tuesday to Saturday 10 to 5:30. Map V block 8.

Country Furniture: 3097 Granville (738-6411). We found weathervanes, butter churns, quilts, wrought iron arboretum furniture, room-screens and decor accents here, all with a focus on country style. Open Monday to Saturday 9:30 to 5:30. Map V block 8.

Pacific Oriental Rugs: 1520 West 15th (731-6699). This is an importer of fine rugs. They have free customer parking at the side. Open Monday to Saturday 10 to 6; and Sunday 1 to 5. Map V circle 9.

The House of Fine Carpets: 3109 Granville (731-3724). They do indeed sell fine carpets here. Hours are Monday to Saturday 10:30 to 5:30; and Sunday 1:30 to 5. Map V block 10.

Presents of Mind: 3135 Granville (736-6463, 738-2287). They have customer parking at the rear. They sell fine china, glass, decor accents and amusing china and teapots with whimsical motifs. Open Monday to Saturday 9:30 to 5:30. Map V block 10.

Dorian Rae Collection: 3151 Granville (732-6100). They too, offer parking in the rear. Among the treasures: Asian antiques, jewellery, oriental art, North American antiques, pottery and unique imports. Open Monday to Saturday 10 to 6. Map V block 10.

Suki's: 3157 Granville (738-7713). Probably the best-known and trendiest of Vancouver's hair stylists, Suki's might be worth a stop for a new look (call ahead to book and appointment). Hours are Monday to Wednesday and weekends 9 to 5; and Thursday and Friday 9 to 9. Map V block 10.

This is the "bottom" of our tour, so now you cross Granville and head back in the direction you've just travelled, only on the other side of the street. There are no shops across from Suki's, so resume the tour on the next block up.

Portobello Antiques: 3050 Granville (734-2275). Owner Jytte Allen has a wonderful reputation for good taste and fair dealings in the buying and selling of top calibre antiques and jewellery. She'll take on estate sale merchandise, too. Open Monday to Saturday 10 to 5. Map V block 11.

Arkay Antiques: 3040 Granville (734-8422). Offering a very fine collection, this place is open Monday to Saturday 10 to 5. Map V block 11.

Panache Antiques & Objets d'Art: 3030 Granville (732-1206). As the name implies, they sell antiques and objets d'art. Hours may vary but they're usually open Monday to Saturday 10 to 5; and Sunday noon to 4 -- call ahead! Map V block 11.

Martin Antiques: 3022 Granville (736-3884). The focus here is on imported antiques and decor accents. Open Tuesday to Saturday 10:30 to 6. Map V block 11.

Lount's Tapestries & Fine Art: 3012 Granville (734-3314). Besides fabric treasures, they collect and sell old lace. Hours are Tuesday to Friday 10:30 to 6; and Saturday 11 to 6. Map V block 11.

Christie's Antiques: 3010 Granville (736-4454). Not to be confused with the auction house back east with a similar name, this one does trade fine antiques. Open Tuesday to Saturday 10:30 to 5:30. Map V block 11.

Hearts Merchants & Traders: 3002 Granville (732-4405). Jim Mathias and his cohorts have created an island of serenity and healthy living in the middle of bustling South Granville here, with bulk foods and organic produce taking the spotlight. Open Monday to Friday 7:30 to 9; Saturday 7:30 to 6; and Sunday 9 to 6. Map V block 11.

Booktique: 2960 Granville (736-3727). For some reason, we've passed this by without seeing it on occasion, but once you know where it is, you'll be glad you found this little bookstore, with its surprisingly good selection of new books. Open Monday to Saturday 10 to 6; and Sunday noon to 5. Map V block 12.

La Cache: 2956 Granville (731-8343). Stock here includes pillows, loungewear and loads of decor accents. Open Monday to Thursday and Saturday 10 to 6; Friday 10 to 8; and Sunday noon to 5. Map V block 12.

Diane's Lingerie & Loungewear: 2950 Granville (738-5121, 738-3936). Just what the name implies, this place sells lingerie. It's open Monday to Saturday 9:30 to 5:30. Map V block 12.

Harrison Galleries Fine Art: 2932 Granville (732-5217). Here's a place for fine framing and conservation -- they specialize in preserving and restoring wood and canvas paintings and both painted objects and paper items. Open Monday to Friday 9:30 to 5:30; and Saturday 10 to 5:30. Map V block 12.

The Art Emporium: 2928 Granville (738-3510, 738-4510). A nice collection. This one opens Monday to Saturday 9:30 to 5:30. Map V block 12.

Thomson & Page Fine Furnishings: 2914 Granville (738-5144). This is an outstanding source for fine upholstery, accessories, fabrics, wallpapers, carpets, classic furnishings and art. Open Monday to Thursday and Saturday 9:30 to 5:30; and Friday 9:30 to 9. Map V block 12.

M.J. Jewellers: 2832 Granville (736-6016). Very up-market, this one, with some lovely original designs. Open Monday to Saturday 10 to 5:30. Map V block 13.

Bratz: 2828 Granville (734-4344). Aptly named, this is the place for those expensive yuppie-puppy clothes. Too rich for our blood, but worth a visit. Open Monday to Saturday 9:30 to 5:30. Map V block 13.

Modern Bazaar: 2822 Granville (731-6199). Here's a place for toys, gifts, costume jewellery and novelties. Open Monday to Saturday 10 to 6. Map V block 13.

Valnor Studio: 2818 Granville (733-0331). These folks will copy or restore your treasured old family photos. Open Monday to Saturday 10 to 6. Map V block 13.

Timothy Piehl Jewellers: 2812 Granville (732-1500). They do some really unusual pieces here -- quite original. Hours are Tuesday to Friday 10 to 5:30; and Saturday 10 to 5. Map V block 13.

Byblos: 2790 Granville (737-0368). Stylish women's clothing and expensive shoes are the main attraction here. Hours are Monday to Thursday and Saturday 9:30 to 5:30; and Friday 9:30 to 8. Map V block 14.

Bacci's: 2788 Granville (732-7317, 733-4933). We find the salesclerks pretty snooty here, but the women's designer apparel and shoes are top-notch. Open Monday to Thursday and Saturday 9:30 to 5:30; and Friday 9:30 to 8. Map V block 14.

Boboli: 2776 Granville (736-3458). The fabulous Italian stone doorway and facade foretell the lovely designer fashions and footwear for men and women here. Open Monday to Thursday 9:30 to 6; Friday 9:30 to 9; and Saturday 9:30 to 5:30. Map V block 14.

Look for the Stanley Theatre (if it's still there), Vancouver's "best" movie house until it was closed and put up for sale recently.

Chevalier Creations: 2756 Granville (731-8746). This very exclusive men's wear shop (they do a lot of fine custom work) is open Monday to Saturday 9:30 to 7. Map V block 14.

Torri's Fashions for Less: 2714 Granville (733-0642). Mixed right in with the *creme de la creme* is this shop which offers clearance prices on some very upmarket clothing for women. Hours are Monday to Thursday and Saturday 9:30 to 5:30; Friday 9 to 9; and Sunday 11:30 to 4:30. Map V block 14.

Speiser Furs: 2706 Granville (731-2181). Yes, some people are still wearing fur, and if you're so inclined, this is one of Vancouver's most prestigious sources. Open Monday to Saturday 9 to 5:30. Map V block 14.

Jeda Bottega Discount Shoe Outlet: 2694 Granville (734-2858). This elegant women's shoe store sells exquisite designs at great discounts. It is not uncommon to find sample size sixes selling for $39 to $49 (regularly up to $125). In addition, the sales people are particularly friendly and accommodating. Hours are Monday to Saturday 10 to 6. Map V circle 15.

House of Fabrics: 2676 Granville (736-5004). First-quality fabrics are available here, as well as a wide range of traditional weights and fibres in yard goods. There are imported woollens and linens and a good selection of "grad fabrics". Thursdays, Seniors receive a 10 percent discount. Open Monday to Thursday and Saturday 10 to 6; Friday 10 to 8; and Sunday noon to 5. Map V circle 16.

Peggy Speer: 2658 Granville (737-0330). This upmarket women's fashion boutique and bridal shop also sells costume jewellery, hats and hair ornaments. Open Monday to Saturday 10 to 5:30. Map V circle 17.

Edward Chapman Ladies Shop: 2596 Granville (732-3394). One of Vancouver's best women's clothing shops, this one sells top lines and classic styles. Hours are Monday to Saturday 9 to 5:30. Map V block 18.

Harrison: 2574 Granville (737-4303). This fine optics store has been operating in Canada since 1857! Here they sell telescopes, binoculars, microscopes, weather instruments, etc. Find it up the street-side staircase. Open Tuesday to Friday 9:30 to 5:30; Saturday 10 to 5; and closed Sunday and Monday. Map V block 18.

Balfour's Lingerie: 2566 Granville (733-6444). Fine lingerie here, but you must go down a short flight of stairs to find it. Open Monday to Friday 10 to 6; and Saturday 10 to 5:30. Map V block 18.

Bubble Gum Clothing Co.: 2546 Granville (737-7897). You'll find trendy ladies' and men's upmarket clothing here, with the focus on casual and sports attire. Open Monday to Wednesday and Saturday 10:30 to 7; Thursday and Friday 10:30 to 9; and Sunday 12:30 to 6. Map V block 18.

Welch's Candy & Card Shop: 2506 Granville (733-7434). Another Vancouver institution, this shop has been doing business on this corner for as long as anyone can remember. They sell candies by the pounnd or in pre-packed selections and can send gifts anywhere. Open Monday to Friday 7:30 a.m. to 7 p.m.; Saturday 10 to 6; and Sunday noon to 5. Map V circle 19.

Turn the corner onto Broadway here.

Jordan's Interiors: 1470 W. Broadway (733-1174). This is the place for fine furnishings, carpets, drapery, reupholstery and decor accents for home and office. Hours are Monday to Thursday and Saturday 9 to 5:30; Friday 9 to 6; and Sunday noon to 5. Map V circle 20.

Egghead Software: 1368 W. Broadway (731-6255). You'll have to cross Hemlock to reach this place, which is the easternmost stop on our tour. Yes, we know it's a chain operation, but their prices are deeply discounted and they provide mail order service as well, so you can add in components you remember after you've returned home. Open Monday to Saturday 9 to 6; and Sunday noon to 5. Map V circle 21.

Cross Broadway now, and double back onto Granville, headed north. Do not cross Granville yet.

Ars Longa: 2410 Granville (731-9779). Here's a nice collection of women's fashions. Open Monday to Saturday 10 to 6. Map V circle 22.

Lee's Jewellers: 2446 Granville (734-2549). Formerly known as Axum Jewellers, this shop has been in this location for years. They do speedy repairs (the last watch Anne took in was a two-minute job, no charge!) and also custom-design jewellery. Open Monday to Saturday 10 to 5:30. Map V circle 23.

McKeller's Traditional Furniture: 2354 Granville (734-1671). They advertise themselves as selling "fine traditional furnishings for the elegant home and office", and that's exactly what they carry. Open Monday to Saturday 10 to 6. Map V circle 24.

Arts 'N'Lite Studio (Tiffany Lights): 2342 Granville (737-8821). Here's an interesting and recent addition to the South Granville experience: a source for fine Art Nouveau and Arts & Crafts period reproductions of light fixtures and statuary reflecting the Tiffany style. Prices are steep, but the work is gorgeous: we spotted a Tiffany-inspired bronze lily-pad motif floorlamp with authentic-looking glass shades for $2,200 and a "Sleeping Beauty" lamp (also faux Art Nouveau) for $750. Hours are Monday to Friday 10 to 5; and Saturday noon to 5. Map V circle 25.

Julius Antiques: 2310 Granville (738-9614). More fine antiques to browse through. Hours vary (call ahead). Map V circle 26.

Industrial Revolution: 2306 Granville (734-4395). A good source for shelving and high-tech items. Open Monday to Saturday 10 to 6; and Sunday noon to 5. Map V circle 27.

Cross Granville Street (kitty-corner) at 6th Avenue:

Brave Interiors: 2199 Granville (731-4426). Ah, here's a find: They sell some bizarre (yes, you must be brave) and highly eccentric forms of home furnishings - items that look as though they might have come out of the '30s or '40s, but first they had to pass through the Twilight Zone. Don't get us wrong: We love this store! Open Monday to Saturday 11 to 5. Map V circle 28.

Turn the corner and stroll west on 6th:

M.P. Morris Wholesale: 1575 West 6th (731-4674). A great surprise and delight when we found it, this place sells gift-wrap, packaging, excelsior, display items and more -- and there's an entire room devoted just to ribbon! It's a true wholesale, so to get the most from their stock you must be prepared to buy in bulk (share with a friend?). Open Monday to Friday 8:30 to 5. Map V circle 29.

Woltjen Udell Gallery: 1558 West 6th (736-8900). Across the street, you'll find this excellent art gallery. Open Tuesday to Saturday 10 to 5. Map V circle 30.

Acme Plating & Silver Shop: 1530 West 6th (733-3317). Need your silver service replated? Here's where. Open Monday to Friday 8 to 5; also open Saturdays in winter months only, 9:30 to 3. Map V circle 31.

At the corner you turn south again onto Granville.

Ararat Oriental Rug Co.: 2221 Granville (733-5616). Long considered Vancouver's best rug dealer, this is certainly the place most often recommended for the cleaning of fine rugs. They also do excellent repair and restoration work. Open Monday to Saturday 9 to 5. Map V block 32.

Aban Persian Carpets: 2229 Granville (736-8550). Another reputable dealer, this one has some sensational seasonal sales. Open Monday to Saturday 9 to 5. Map V block 32.

Granville Native Art: 2241 Granville (731-7719). Upstairs, you'll discover this collection of high-quality native Indian art and crafts. Open Tuesday to Saturday 11 to 4:30. Map V block 32.

Kupczynski Studio Gallery: A-2243 Granville (734-5673). Upstairs at this address is the working studio and gallery of one of Vancouver's prominent artists. Kupczynski's work is dramatic and distinctive and well worth a look. Hours are usually Monday to Saturday 11 to 6, but they suggest you call ahead to be certain. Map V block 32.

Heffel Gallery: 2247 Granville (732-6505). Another prominent gallery, this one specializes in "important Canadian art", which they both buy and sell. Open Tuesday to Saturday 10 to 6. Map V block 32.

Turn the corner and proceed west on 8th for the next stop:

Diane Farris Gallery: 1565 W. 7th (737-2629). Farris is considered one of British Columbia's most gifted gallery owners, with a sharp eye not only for what is collectable now, but for the work of emerging artists before it is priced out of young collectors' budgets. Hours are Tuesday to Saturday 10 to 5:30. Map V circle 33.

Return to Granville and continue southbound:

Malacca: 2301 Granville (732-8838). If you thought rattan and wicker furniture was just for casual patios, think again. This place carries some very elegant pieces in this most humble of materials, plus gorgeous pillows, vases, stands and other decor accents you're sure to find irresistible -- one of the best furniture collections in town. Open Monday to Saturday 9:30 to 6; Sunday noon to 5. Map V block 34.

Equinox Gallery: 2321 Granville (736-2405). Another really "important" gallery, we know top collectors who would never dream of missing an opening at the Equinox. Hours are Tuesday to Saturday 10 to 5. Map V block 34.

Derek Simpkins Gallery of Tribal Art: 2329 Granville (732-4555). Featured here is fine art of the Northwest coast, Papua New Guinea and Australia, among other excellent aboriginal pieces. Hours are Tuesday to Saturday 10 to 6. Map V block 34..

Simon Patrich International Art & Multiples: 2331 Granville (733-2662). Fine art and imported work, here, as the name suggests. Hours are Monday to Saturday 10 to 5:30. Map V block 34.

Ann Sacks Tile & Stone: 2349 Granville (737-7966). Mere words cannot adequately describe how wonderful this store is! It's filled with decorative tiles, coves and stone facing material of the most exquisite kind, from authentic Victorian-era and Art Nouveau motifs to contemporary Italian patina stone. If you're looking for some fine tiles to add to a renovation, we've never seen so varied and elegant a source. Hours are Monday to Friday 9 to 5; and Saturday 10:30 to 1. Map V block 34.

Turn the corner and venture westward down 8th a little.

Threshhold Gallery: 1521 West 8th (736-1427). A brand new gallery, this one opens Tuesday to Friday 10:30 to 5:30; and Saturday 11 to 5. Map V circle 35.

La Viola Ladies Design: 1544A West 8th (731-9199). We keep wanting to say "La voila!", but this little boutique has its own eccentric spelling and a nice collection of women's fashions. Open Monday to Friday 9:30 to 5 BY APPOINTMENT ONLY. Map V circle 36.

Leg-A-See Fashions: 1542 West 8th (731-8715). Odd spellings must have something to do with this street. Anyway, this place specializes in hats, hosiery, lingerie, accessories and giftware. Open Monday noon to 4; and Tuesday to Saturday 11 to 4. Map V circle 36.

Turnabout Collections: 1544 West 8th (734-5313). Owner Joy Lapka was the first in Vancouver to really make a business of consignment clothing. They have a super computer system and very high-fashion merchandise. This is the head office. A sister-operation is closer to the end of this tour. Open Tuesday to Saturday 10 to 6; closed 1 to 2 daily for lunch; and sometimes closed in July/August (call ahead). Map V circle 36.

Return to Granville and continue southward:

Bravo Factory Outlet: 2415 Granville (253-4612). This is a space the Bravo factory rents for periodic sales (they also use an address on West Broadway when it's available). The clear-out store sells kids' clothing and some women's casuals. They keep a mailing list, so if you find them open when you tour the area, drop in to sign up. Map V block 37.

A'Knit Above Wools: 2427 Granville (734-0975). Naturally, it's a wool shop. Open Monday to Friday 10 to 5:30; and Saturday 10 to 5. Map V block 37.
8
Craftsman Designs: 2435 Granville (733-1011). Specialties here are interesting lamps and lighting fixtures. Open Tuesday to Friday 9:30 to 5; and Saturday 10 to 4. Map V block 37.

CLOSED

Kibun: 2443 Granville (738-3008). [illegible] for women in the Japanese mode is [illegible] [illegible]urs are Monday to Saturday 11:30 to 5:[illegible] [illegible] 37.

Turn the corner and head west on Broadway to complete the tour:

Bruna Coiffures: 110, 1501 W. Broadway (731-0132). Bruna's one of our favourite shops, and Bruna herself one of our favourite people. She sells a wide range of professional hair products for wholesale and often in large sizes you can't find elsewhere. Frankly, we wouldn't dream of buying hair products anywhere else! Among the brands are Nexxus, Rajoc, Paul Mitchell, Redken, TRI and Sebastian, to name but a few. Open Monday 11 to 2; and Tuesday to Saturday 10 to 6. Map V block 38.

Le Bijoux Place: 1509 W. Broadway (731-8871). A wonderful source for faux gems and real accessories. Open Monday to Saturday 10:30 to 6. Map V block 38.

Dress 4 Less: 1513 W. Broadway (737-2844). This is a factory outlet store with most items at or under $10! Open Monday to Friday 10 to 5:30; and Saturday 10 to 5. Map V block 38.

Mocha Cafe: 1521 W. Broadway (734-5274). While not one of our designated rest stops, this place sells bargain muffins if you're peckish. New owners are Don and Shanti McDougall. Open Monday to Friday 8 to 3 and 5 to 9:30. Map V block 38.

Oscar's Art Books & Books: 1533 W. Broadway (731-0553). This is a book remainderer, which means everything in the store is discounted from retail. Open Monday to Friday 10 to 8; Saturday 10 to 6; and Sunday noon to 6. Map V block 38.

Mayfair News: 1535 W. Broadway (738-8951). Hard-to-find magazines? No problem. Out-of-town newspapers? Ditto. If you've given up on finding a source, try this one. Open Monday to Friday 8 to 10:30; and weekends 9 to 10:30. Map V block 38.

Tilley Endurables: 1537 W. Broadway (732-4287). Their men's and women's clothing is guaranteed never to wear out! They're famous for their hats, of course (an alternate number is 604-SEA-HATS). Open Monday to Saturday 10 to 5:30. Map V block 38.

U San Gifts: 1539 W. Broadway (731-8399). A great assortment of housewares is available here: carpets, baskets, brass, giant fans, windchimes, rice-paper blinds, wicker and umbrellas, among much, much more. Open Monday to Saturday 10 to 6; and Sunday noon to 5. Map V block 38.

Turnabout: 1545 W. Broadway (732-8115). As mentioned with their other location previously in this tour, consignment stock here is top-quality. Open Monday to Thursday and Saturday 10 to 6; Friday 10 to 7; and Sunday noon to 5. Map V block 38.

Tokyo Fashions: 1549 W. Broadway (733-3823). This store focusses on imported women's fashions from Japan -- for the smaller figure. There are also sweaters and they do expert alterations. All goods were very Japanese-looking. Open Monday to Friday 10 to 6; and Saturday 10 to 5. Map V block 38.

NOTES:

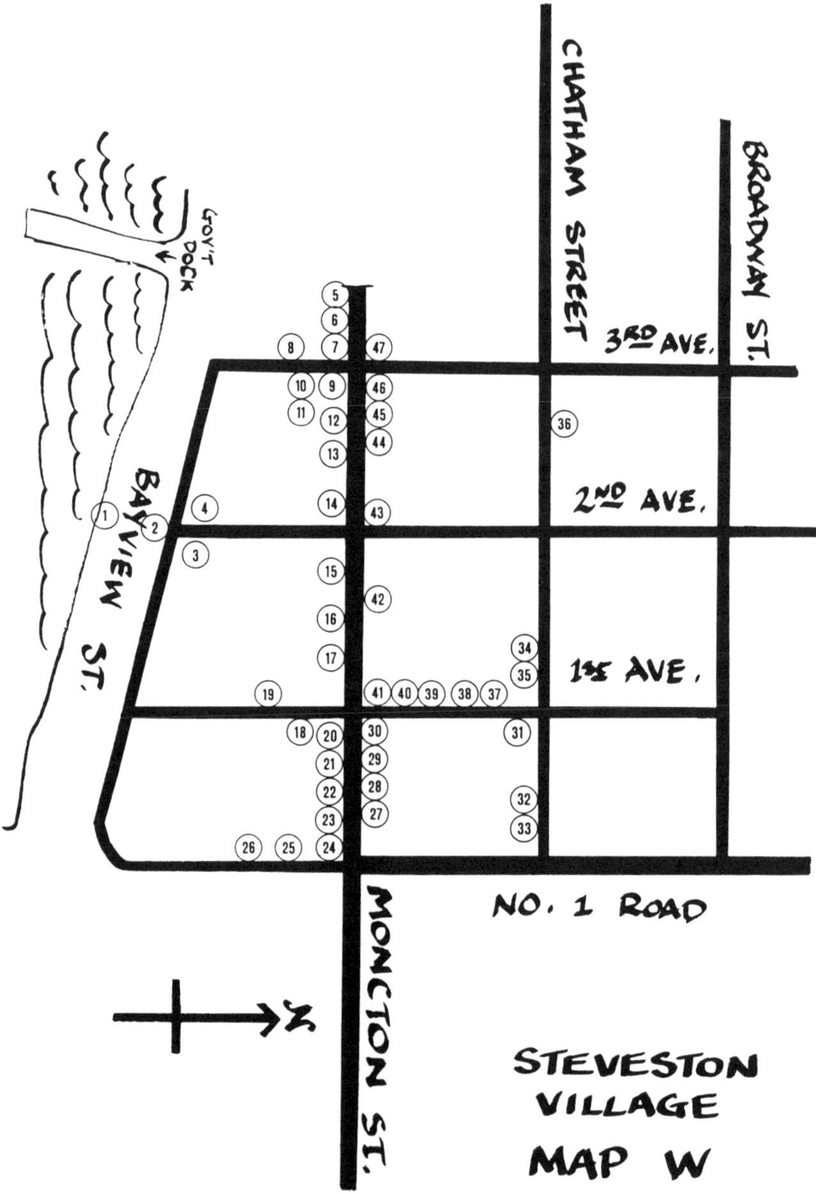
CHATHAM STREET
BROADWAY ST.
GOV'T DOCK
3RD AVE.
2ND AVE.
1ST AVE.
BAYVIEW ST.
NO. 1 ROAD
MONCTON ST.
N
STEVESTON VILLAGE
MAP W

Steveston

Interesting and unusual items in a charming setting

This is a mini-tour, taking about two hours. We wrote it up as a *walking tour,* but it's quite possible to drive the tour route, or dart from shop to shop on a misty day, too.

Find Steveston by driving south through Richmond or by driving Highway 99 South and taking the Steveston Hwy. exit westbound. If you're heading through Richmond southbound on No. 3 Road, you'll come to Steveston Highway much past Lansdowne and Richmond Square malls. The last major street before Steveston Hwy. is Williams. It's a right turn (westbound) onto Steveston Highway. Turn left at No. 1 Road and you'll soon see signs indicating Steveston Village.

If driving up from the U.S., take the Peace Portal crossing (at Blaine) and follow Hwy. 99 North right through Surrey and across Delta and through the Deas Tunnel (also know as George Massey Tunnel). Very soon after the tunnel crossing, exit to Steveston Hwy. westbound, which will take you right into Steveston. Watch for signs directing you into Steveston Village after you pass Number 2 Road.

The main roads we'll tour are Chatham, Moncton and Bayview.

Steveston Docks: at the foot of Moncton. The Government dock is now closed to the public, so if you're in the market for fresh fish, you can now buy it a couple of blocks east, at the foot of 2nd Ave. We found prices fairly competitive with in-town markets, but of course, the fish is fresher here. Map W circle 1.

Steveston Landing: 3800 Bayview. This commercial shopping development was at one time controversial with local residents. Since its completion, however, the townsfolk seem happy with it, because it blends in so well with the overall character of Steveston. Among the shops are: Orange Gal: This is full of trendy sportswear, at #101 (271-3935); Lulu Island Designs: #119 (275-LULU). Here you'll find artsy T-shirts, sweats and wonderful local art; and Steveston Landing Fish Co.: #102 (275-4746). There's a good fresh fish market here. Most shops at Steveston Landing are open Monday to Saturday 10 to 6; and Sunday 1 to 5. Map W circle 2.

Bayview Quay: 12240 2nd Ave (at Bayview). Among the choices: Horizon Ladies Wear, Caribbean Expression, Gifts Galore, Quay Reflections, Brims to Ewe, Yarns of Steveston, Aquatic Adventures, and Jewel of Steveston. Most shops are open Monday to Friday 10 am to 9 pm; and Sunday 10 to 6. Map W circle 3.

The Sleigh's Tea House: 3711 Bayview (275-5188). This is a quaint rest stop with its own name woven into the lace cafe curtains at the windows. They also do special Fawlty Towers evenings from time to time. Hours are: Monday to Saturday 11 to 9. Map W circle 4.

High Impact Watersports: 3400 Moncton (272-FOOT). This place sells wetsuits, boards, T's and water ski magazines. Hours of operation are Tuesday to Friday noon to 6 pm; Saturday 10 to 5; closed Monday and Sunday. Map W circle 5.

Steveston Fish Shoppe: 3420 Moncton (277-3135). Here you'll find good prices on fresh fish. Open seven days 10 am to 5 pm. Map W circle 6.

Richmond Danish Bakery: 2420B Moncton (277-7520). This local treasure has been operating from this location since 1957. Muffins could be on special at just 50 cents each. A note in the window points out: "Hans can't get out of bed early on Sunday, so everything for sale on Sunday was baked Saturday!" Other offerings include cookies, rosettes and bavarian creams. Hours are Tuesday to Thursday 9 to 5:30; Friday 9 to 8; Saturday 8:30 to 6; and Sunday 10 to 5. Map W circle 7.

Riverside Gallery: 3480D Moncton (274-1414). This place is tucked away in the back, selling paintings, prints and glass floats — all wonderful. Open seven days 10 to 5. Map W circle 8.

The Steveston Bookstore: 3480 Moncton (274-3604) This shop focusses on marine books, with topics ranging from boat repair, rigging, how-to-assess boats, live-aboards, marine life, singlehanded sailing, cruising, knots, and fishing, to cookbooks and titles for kids. Both new and used books are offered. Hours are Monday to Friday 10 to 6; and weekends 10:30 to 6. Map W circle 9.

Prime Arts & Crafts: #4, 3500 Moncton, #4 (no listing). They sell good teak figures and hangings, among other objets d'art. Hours are Tuesday to Thursday 11:30 to 5:30; Friday 11:30 to 6; and weekends 11 to 5; and closed Mondays. Map W circle 10.

Gulf of Georgia Gallery: 3500 Moncton, #5 (271-3883). Here they sell high-quality fine art. Hours are Tuesday to Sunday 11 to 5; and closed Monday. Map W circle 11.

Jeans 2: 3500 Moncton (271-2992). This place features casual wear, T's, tops and more. Hours are Monday to Thursday 10 to 5:30; Friday and Saturday 10 to 6; and Sunday 11 to 5:30; or they'll stay open later if you call ahead. Map W circle 12.

Sara's Old-Fashioned Ice Cream: 3500 Moncton (271-6507). They sell clean ice cream buckets with lids for just 3 for a dollar. Ice cream is good value, too. Hours vary (longer in summer months). Map W circle 13.

Steveston Marine & Hardware: 3560 Moncton (277-7031). This is one of the best hardware stores in the entire lower mainland! Established in 1941, this is as much a tour down memory lane as a shopping destination. The store's agents bid for antique brass fittings (carried in an upstairs department with the ship fittings) at auctions worldwide. Goods in that department include deck lights, portholes from dimantled ships, spotlights, clocks, barometers and brass hinges. The regular hardware items downstairs include hand tools, power tools, paint, marine hoses and ropes, aircraft wire, automotive gear and a vast selection of single screws, bolts and other small items. Hours are Monday to Thursday and Saturday 8:30 to 6; Friday 8:30 to 8; and Sunday 10 to 5. Map W circle 14.

Marty's Antiques & Giftware: 100, 3580 Moncton (271-5637). Here they offer good quality but reasonably-priced antiques. They also buy old hockey and baseball cards. Hours are Monday to Thursday and weekends 10 to 5; and Friday 10 to 8. Map W circle 15.

Name-Dropper Boutique: 140, 3580 Moncton (274-2432). This is one of our old-favourite women's consignment shops. Open seven days 11 to 5. Map W circle 16.

Nikaido Gifts: 3640 Moncton (271-5637). This boutique sells an array of fine Japanese gift items, many unusual or unique. Hours are Monday to Saturday 10 to 5; and Sunday noon to 4. Map W circle 17.

Country Mouse Arts & Craft Shop: 3760 Moncton (272-2458). This nice little gift shop carries items from all over B.C., such as pottery, handpainted silk, jewellery, glassworks, handmade greeting cards, framed prints and more. Hours are Monday to Saturday 10 to 5; and Sunday noon to 5. Map W circle 18.

On your way past 1st, note the mural on the building at 12191 1st Ave. (map W circle 19), depicting a lighthouse.

Moncton Street Natural Foods Market: 3760 Moncton (274-3447). They offer gourmet coffee, vitamins, herbs, fresh pasta and a gourmet salad bar. Hours are (usually) Monday to Saturday 10 to 6; and Sunday noon to 5. Map W circle 20.

Beetles Fitness & Leisure Wear: 3760 Moncton (277-4528). It tells all in its name, and is open Monday to Saturday 10 to 4; and Sunday noon to 4. Map W circle 21.

Richmond General Hospital Auxiliary Thrift Shop: 3920 Moncton (271-1551). This is another of our time-tested favourites, selling good quality bric-a-brac and clothing at low, low prices. Hours are Monday to Saturday 10 to 3; and closed Sunday. Map W circle 22.

The Sandpiper: 3980 Moncton (271-3833). This one sells unisex casual clothing. Hours are Tuesday to Friday noon to 4:30; Saturday 11 to 5; Sunday 1 to 4; and closed Monday. Map W circle 23.

Fraser Mart: 3980A Moncton (277-1311). And here they sell a variety of hard-to-find Japanese foods and wares. Open seven days 9 to "7-ish". Map W circle 24.

The Kite Emporium: 12231 1st Ave. (272-0673). Around the corner from Fraser Mart, there's a nice collection of kites and kite string sold right alongside lottery tickets. Hours are Monday to Saturday 9 to 5; and closed Sundays. Map W circle 25.

Steveston Heritage Market: 12251 1st Ave. Here's a charming collection of shops and services housed in what used to be Easthope Engines, a company which converted sailing vessels to motorized ones on this site for 90 years. It was developed as a heritage revitalization project a few years ago, and today showcases a number of businesses including: Red Barn Antiques (275-7766), Jimm's Cafe (277-1037), Seas on Shore (271-5822), Simply Irresistable (275-1352), Steveston Sandwich House & Deli (275-9397), Steveston Bakery (271-3656—day old bread is half-price), Heringer's Market (274-6328 — also sells Murchie's coffee and tea), and a good produce shop, Sea Coast Market (271-4386). Hours are generally Monday to Saturday 10 to 5; and Sunday 10 to 4. Map W circle 26.

Now, double back to Moncton:

Feline's Gifts: 120, 3911 Moncton (277-0122). This shop sells table and bed lines in Battenberg lace, gorgeous fish platters, frames, gifts, and of course, stuffed calico fabric cats of every description. Visa is accepted. Hours are Monday to Saturday 10 to 5; and Sunday noon to 5. Map W circle 27.

L & L Discount Sales: 3851 Moncton (274-3713). This place, with its friendly manager, Mandy, offers half price day-old bread, 10 percent off Tuesdays for Seniors and healthy discounts on all kinds of household wares and bric-a-brac. Hours are Monday to Friday 9:30 to 5; Saturday 10 to 5:30; and Sunday noon to 5:30. Map W circle 29.

Budget Appliance Centre: 3831 Moncton (271-8891). This is one of the few places in the lower mainland to buy freight-damaged appliances, but they don't always have them in stock, so call ahead. Their regular appliance stock is priced to compete with cross-border shopping, so be sure to include them in your hunt for price comparisons. Open Monday to Saturday 9 to 5:30. Map W circle 30.

Sunbeams Boutique: 140, 12000 1st Ave. (275-9878). This little shop sells children's clothing and accessories galore. Hours are Monday noon to 5; Tuesday to Saturday 10 to 5; and Sunday 10 to 4. Map W circle 31.

Steveston Trading Post: 12071 1st Ave. (272-5272). Here you'll find every manner of household item sold on consignment. Hours are Monday to Saturday 10 to 5; and closed Sunday. Map W circle 32.

Clothes Encounters: 1, 3891 Chatham (271-0310). This is a good consignment shop featuring newborn to trendy teen sizes and maternity wear. Hours are Tuesday to Saturday 10:30 to 5. Map W circle 33.

Nibbles Bakery: 110, 12031 1st Ave. (275-7620) This bakeshop is right at the southwest corner of Chatham and 1st. They offer a "Healthy Happy Hour" special Monday to Saturday from 4 to 5 pm where all baked goods are half-price! Regular hours are Monday to Friday 8:30 to 5:30; Saturday 9 to 5; and closed Sundays; but often open on holidays, so call ahead. Map W circle 34.

Pearce's Pies and Pastries: 125, 3800 Chatham (no phone). Find this one back around the corner. It's busy on weekends, but quiet during the week when Barbara Pearce bakes her famous goodies. You can drop in with your own pie plate and Barbara will custom-bake to your requirements. There's no phone, so drop in to order. Hours are Monday to Friday 11 to 5:30; Saturday 10:30 to 6; and Sunday 1 to 4:30. Map W circle 35.

Serendipity's Backyard: 110, 3631 Chatham (275-1683). This is a new metaphysical bookstore and giftshop offering a growing selection of books, tapes, crystals, jewellery and incense — all in a comfortable, peaceful atmosphere. Open Tuesday to Thursday 10 to 5:30; Friday noon to 7; Saturday 10 to 5; and Sunday 1 to 5. Map W circle 36.

Steveston General Store: 4, 1389 Chatham (272-5039). This long-established Steveston store sells furniture, paintings and carpets.

Hours are Monday to Saturday 10 to 5; and closed Sunday. Map W circle 37.

Thrifty Baby: 12071 1st Ave. (272-2924). This has long been a great consignment store, originally on Moncton, but now on 1st. You'll find lots of clothing to children's size 14 and many like-new toys. Hours are Monday to Saturday 10 to 5. Map W circle 38.

Daisies Boutique: 12131 1st Ave. (271-9402). This is yet another fine consignment shop (this time for women's clothes). Hours are Monday to Saturday 10 to 5; and closed Sunday. Map W circle 39.

British Home Store: 12151 1st Ave. (274-2261). Not to be confused with the original of the same name, Steveston's version features a little tea room and a number of imported biscuits and teas. Open Monday to Saturday 11 to 6; and Sunday 1 to 5. Map W circle 40.

Steveston Museum and Post Office: 3811 Moncton (271-6868). This is worth a visit—it was featured in big-time films (you'll see autographed photos of stars on the walls) and offers a modest display of Steveston relics. Best of all, there's a free tour pamphlet of the area. Hours are Monday to Saturday 9:30 to 5; closed Sunday; and closed for lunch from 1 to 1:30 daily. Map W circle 41.

Pacific Net & Twine Company: 3731 Moncton (274-7238). This store sells fishing supplies and offers a glimpse of the Steveston of yesteryear. Hours are Monday to Saturday 9 to 5; and closed Sunday. Map W circle 42.

Nikka Industries: 3551 Moncton (271-6332). Here is another business echoing Steveston's fishing history. You'll find professional fishing tackle, marine hardware, paint and rope, safety equipment and quality rainwear. Hours are Monday to Friday 8:30 to 5; Saturday 9 to 4; and Sunday 10 to 4. Map W circle 43.

Bare Basics Lingerie Boutique: 110, 3511 Moncton (271-5330). This shop sells rather high quality (but fancy) underthings for m'lady. Hours are Monday to Saturday 10 to 5:30; and Sunday noon to 4. Map W circle 44.

Season's Gifts and Accessories: 3471 Moncton (241-0663). This place offers unusual giftware and novelties. Hours are Monday to Saturday 10 to 5:30; and Sunday noon to 5. Map W circle 45.

Memories Maternity & Bridal on Consignment: 3471 Moncton (272-2939). Once again, the name almost tells it all, but no matter what you imagine, you can't possibly be ready for the myriad sewing notions, fabrics, flowers, beading, findings and knitting wool and patterns you'll find here. This is one of only two bridal consignment shops in the entire lower mainland, and the only one we know of which cleverly combines maternity with matrimony — though we know many individuals who have done so privately! Hours are Tuesday to Saturday 10 to 5; and Sunday noon to 5. Closed some Sundays during the summer, so plan ahead. Map W circle 46.

From The Heart: 100, 3400 Moncton (241-2622). This relative newcomer to the area sells fresh and freeze-dried flowers and floral arrangements and gifts for every occasion. Open seven days 10 to 6. Map W circle 47.

Now if you're hungry after all this gallavanting about, why not drop into the Steveston Cannery Cafe at 3711 Moncton (272-1222) for a bowl of Gary's Boston-style clam chowder, and Judy's famous deep dish apple pie? Show them this copy of the Serious Shopper's Guide to Vancouver, and they'll buy you (and any friends dining with you) a cup of coffee or tea to go with your meal.

Another great restaurant is the Steveston Seafood House, 3951 Moncton (271-5252) open daily for dinner.

For more casual chow, drop in to Pajo's fish and chips (best in the region) at the foot of Second, on the water, open daily from Easter until Thanksgiving. Cod or halibut is served in newspaper the old-fashioned way!

If you take this shopping jaunt during early summer, be sure to cruise by the raspberry U-picks on No. 2 Road on the way home. If you drive back via Steveston Hwy., on a clear day you can see Mt. Baker perfectly between No. 4 and No. 5 Road, off in the distant southeast.

NOTES:

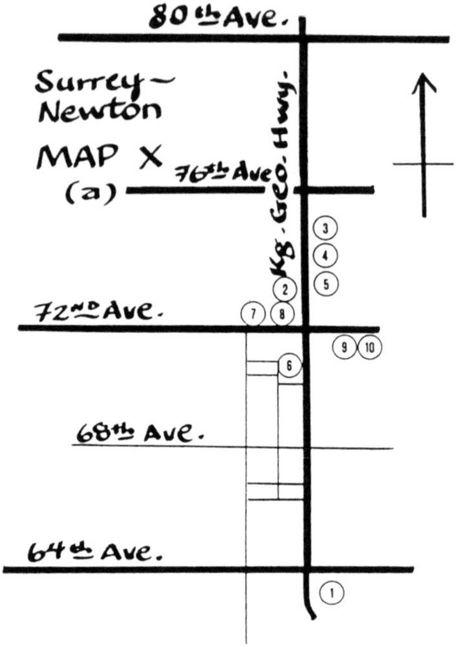
80th Ave.
Surrey ~ Newton
MAP X
(a)
76th Ave.
Kg. Geo. Hwy.
72nd Ave.
68th Ave.
64th Ave.
1
2
3
4
5
6
7
8
9
10

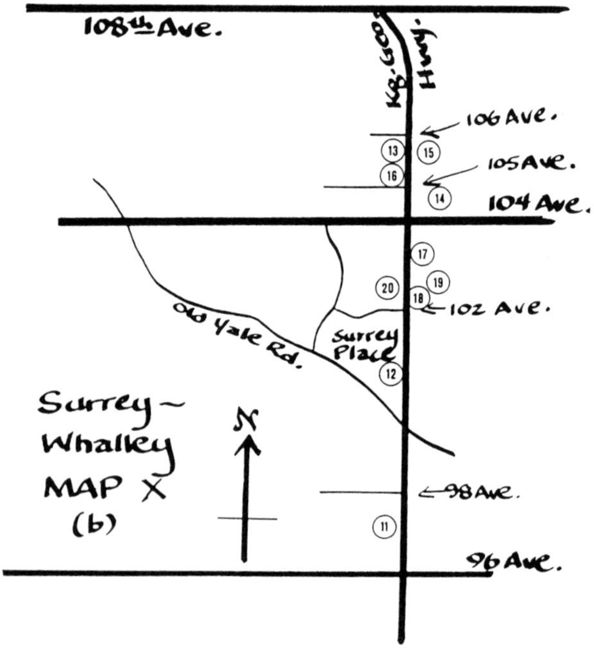
108th Ave.
Kg. Geo. Hwy.
106 Ave.
105 Ave.
104 Ave.
102 Ave.
Old Yale Rd.
Surrey Place
Surrey ~ Whalley
MAP X
(b)
N
98 Ave.
96 Ave.
11
12
13
14
15
16
17
18
19
20

Surrey: Newton, Whalley and the Guildford area

Strip-malls galore

This is a medium-sized tour of two to three hours, because the stops are so spread out. For this reason, we do not recommend public transit.

Parking in the strip malls is easy at any time.

Reach the central area we explore along the King George Highway by crossing the Pattullo Bridge from New West into Surrey and continuing south. From Richmond, Highway 10 crosses King George just south of the Surrey Public Market. The Ladner Trunk Road also leads into the area from Delta and Ladner.

From the U.S. border, take Hwy. 99A (north), which is actually King George Highway itself.

Surrey is more than we expected for scenery, but bargains required some "cherry-picking": one here, one there. There are grand vistas, unspoiled rivers, vast stretches of bucolic farmland, treed ravines and lovely homes. And we hear that Whalley is destined to become the second-biggest metropolis in B.C., so see this unspoiled beauty while you can! But first, Newton:

<u>Surrey Public Market:</u> 6400 King George Highway. What was originally a roller rink has now been transformed into a very basic but nice farmers' market. See public markets section for details.

<u>Tiiu's Tobacco and Treats:</u> 6400 King George Hwy. (594-3393). Owner Ted Lyne stocks an impressive number of foreign and domestic newspapers and magazines in this shop in the Market, including (from the U.K.) the Sunday Times, the Mirror, the Express, News of the World, Manchester Guardian, Sunday Telegraph, the Observer, the Mail and the Times' Literary Supplement. You'll also find the Seattle Times and many German magazines. People come from far and wide to pick up their favourite reading material. Open seven days 10 to 6. Map X circle 1.

<u>Costco:</u> 7423 King George Hwy (596-7348). A positive boon to those who are members and require good, cheap, new appliances and even tires and footstuffs. Most items must be bought in large quantities. Call ahead to inquire about membership, if you're interested. Open Monday to Friday 11 to 8:30 (tire shop Monday to Friday 11 to 7); Saturday 9:30 to 6; and Sunday 11 to 5. Wholesale members have extended hours. Map X circle 2.

Real Canadian Superstore: 7550 King George Hwy. (439-4400). Aggressive marketing and some truly unique high-grade food products you can't find elsewhere are creating a devoted following for this low-frills format mega-market. Fighting for parking and long queues to the cashiers are among the drawbacks, but as we said, many (ourselves included) are loyal Superstore shoppers. Open seven days 9 a.m. to 10 p.m. Map X circle 3.

Hutch: 410, 7488 King George Hwy. (596-7175). The original factory location for the jeans manufacturers is long gone from Venables and Clark, but this one carries on the tradition of factory-direct pricing for casual clothing for the family. Open Monday to Wednesday 9 :30 to 5:30; Thurday and Friday 9:30 to 8; Saturday 9:30 to 5:30; and Sunday noon to 4. Map X circle 4.

Factory Outlet for Fashion: 320, 7488 King George Hwy. (599-8355). The name pretty much says it all. They sell women's fashions at a discount. Open Monday to Saturday 9:30 to 5:30; and Sunday noon to 5. Map X circle 5.

Crazy Benny's New & Used Sporting Goods: 7093 King George Hwy. in Newton Square (594-9911). Bargain time for sportsters, plus skate sharpening. Open Monday to Wednesday 9:30 to 6; Thursday to Saturday 9:30 to 7; and Sunday 10:30 to 4. Map X circle 6.

Weston's In-Store Bakery: 101, 7093 King George Hwy. in Newton Square (597-4163). Discount prices on loaves of bread are found here. Open Monday to Wednesday 10 to 7; Thursday and Friday 10 to 8; Saturday 9 to 6; and Sunday 10 to 6. Map X circle 6.

Bev's Discount Stationery: 13393 72nd Ave. (597-2141). Their everyday price on a legal size, four drawer, full-depth file cabinet with reinforced lock is about $100 less than we've seen a similar unit almost anywhere. Hours are Monday to Saturday 10 to 5:30. Map X circle 7.

Reflections on Plates: 13389 72nd Ave. (596-2434). Collectors will find their "best" plates here. Open Monday to Thursday and Saturday 10 to 5:30; and Friday 10 to 6. Map X circle 8.

Newton Wave Pool: 13730 72nd Ave. (594-7873). Not a shopping spot but what a place to visit with kids in tow! Remember to bring bathing suits if you plan a dip, and call ahead to be sure a birthday party hasn't booked the huge place full. Map X circle 9.

Lovers Fish & Chips: 9, 13767 72nd Ave. in Somerset Square (590-2216). Locals tipped us to this place, considered the area's best. Hours are Monday to Thursday and Saturday 11:30 to 7:30; Friday 11:30 to 8:30; Sunday 3:30 to 7:30; and open an extra half hour for take-out. Map X circle 10.

Now entering Whalley:

Revenue Canada: 9755 King George Hwy. We included this point of interest in case you want to stop in and make a clean breast of it or pay your next-year's taxes early. You may have always wondered where those guys you quibble with on the phone in April are ensconced: Here it is. Map X circle 11.

Surrey Place: 102 Ave. and King George Hwy. This modern shopping mall is anchored by Zeller's, The Bay and Fairweather. Details are in our malls section. Map X circle 12.

Gold N'Guns: 10671 King George Hwy. (581-3240). We joke that they'll never experience a hold-up here, but aside from the firearms, they do have a good selection (and competitive pricing on) gold, especially gold chains. Open Monday to Saturday 10 to 5. Map X circle 13.

Fanny's Fabrics: 10560 King George Hwy. (584-2929). Yet another location of this big yard goods chain. Healthy discounts are always available on bolts of fabric along the back wall. Open Monday to Friday 9:30 to 9; Saturday 9 to 5:30; and Sunday noon to 5. Map X circle 14.

Value Village: 10642 King George Hwy. (588-5225). Here's another Value Village worth popping into. Some proceeds from this supermarket-sized thrift store go to local charities. Open Monday to Friday 9 to 9; Saturday 9 to 6; and Sunday 10 to 6. Map X circle 15.

Kid's World Warehouse Store: 10653 King George Hwy. (584-9574). This is the main warehouse operation for the Kid's World stores, with bargains in every manner of children's furniture, toys and clothing. Here's a tip: phone ahead to ask when new stock is being shelved, because those who get there first find the best deals. They also have a pamphlet with discounts -- it's annoying to use, but if persist, you can find bargains of 40 to 60 percent off. Hours are Monday to Wednesday and Saturday 10 to 6; Thursday and Friday 10 to 8; and Sunday noon to 5. Map X circle 16.

London Drugs: 10348 King George Hwy. (520-9008). The usual wonderful selection of modestly-discounted cosmetics, housewares and pharmaceuticals are here, plus their steady policy on discounting books and magazines. And did we mention their great sale prices and coupon books for added savings? Hours are Monday to Saturday 9 a.m. to 10 p.m.; and Sunday 10 to 8. Map X circle 17.

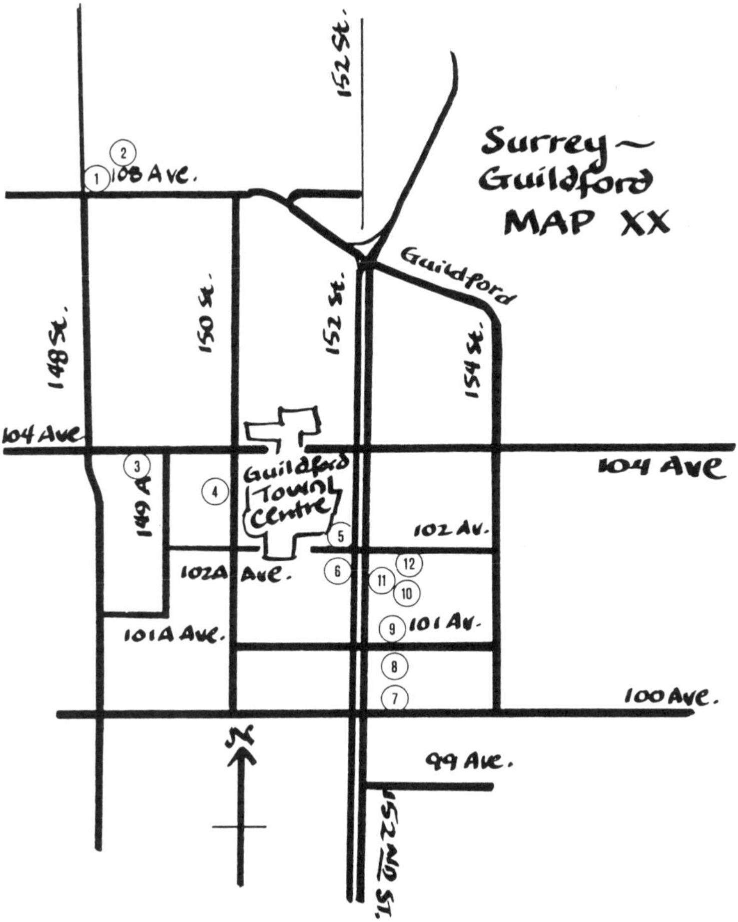
Surrey~
Guildford
MAP XX
108 Ave.
104 Ave
104 Ave
102 Av.
102A Ave.
101 Av.
101A Ave.
100 Ave.
99 Ave.
148 St.
150 St.
152 St.
152 St.
154 St.
149 A
152ND St.
Guildford
Guildford Town Centre
N
1
2
3
4
5
6
7
8
9
10
11
12

K-Mart: 13665 102nd St. (581-5466). This is an easy-access location of K-Mart, with lots of free parking and the usual lower-end family clothing choices. Open Monday to Saturday 9:30 to 9; and Sunday 11 to 5. Map X circle 18.

Save-on Foods: 10312 King George Hwy. (588-7500). Another mega-store that easy to get into -- and they are very competitive in price because there are competitors nearby. Open seven days 8 a.m. to midnight. Map X circle 19.

Safeway Superstore: 10355 King George Hwy. (584-7811). As we said -- proximity breeds discounts: both stores match lowest prices to keep customers from "shopping across the street". Hours here are also seven days 8 a.m. to midnight. Map X circle 20.

And on to Guildford for bargain shopping in the mall area:

The Bay Clearance Centre: 14885 108th Ave. (589-1149). Included here are men's, women's and children's clothing and shoes. Not the place for a quick stop (lots of stuff is jumbled together on tables), you'll need time to paw through the heaps. Fashions are sorted by colour rather than size. All items are excess stock from the B.C. and Alberta stores and all are marked down by 50 percent when they arrive and given one of a number of coloured tags. Each Tuesday a different colour is further discounted by 25 or 50 percent additional and every Thursday one colour tag is reduced by 75 percent more. Usually the 75 percent off items are grouped on a special clearance rack in each department. Hours are Monday to Wednesday and Saturday 9:30 to 5:30; Thursday and Friday 9:30 to 9; and Sunday noon to 5. Map XX circle 1.

Toys Plus More: 14887 108th Ave. (588-6700). This is one of our favourite sources for birthday loot bags and stocking stuffers: There's an entire row of small items. Generally the stock is all toys (many from previous fads) but sometimes they carry kids' clothing and shoes, too. This location stores their excess stock above the boxes of sale items so it feels more closed-in than the Burnaby store. Open Monday, Tuesday and Saturday 9:30 to 6; Wednesday to Friday 9:30 to 9; and Sunday 10 to 6. Map XX circle 2.

C & M Sports Ltd.: 14904 104th Ave. (584-3006); Repairs and parts: 584-3030). We aren't sure about this entry, but we had to include it because it's so one-of-a-kind. They buy, sell, trade, repair and consign rifles, shotguns and handguns for sportsmen and target practice. All repairs are by gunsmith Cliff Jahn. You set your price on consigned items (which make up 50 percent of their stock) and they add just 20 percent. Hours are Tuesday to Thursday and Saturday 10 to 5; and Friday 10 to 8. Map XX circle 3.

Expanding Images: 10385 150th St. (583-6430). Everything for the pregnant woman may be rented from one week to six months. The price tags carry both the selling prices and the cost of renting for various periods of time. They sell pants, shorts, bathing suits and rent dresses, suits, blouses and skirts. There's a clearance rack with some new items and some previous rentals. They also have a Vancouver store near City Hall. Gift certificates are also available -- the perfect solution for pregnant friends. Open Monday to Saturday 11 to 5; and Sunday noon to 5. Map XX circle 4.

Woodwynn: 10191 152nd St. (584-1018). The usual discounted linens, housewares and clothing. Open Monday, Tuesday and Saturday 9 to 5:30; Wednesday to Friday 9 to 9; and Sunday noon to 5. Map XX circle 5.

Canadian Tire: 15190 101st Ave. (421-9379). Another source of housewares, sporting goods and camping supplies. Open Monday to Friday 9 to 9; Saturday 9 to 6; and Sunday 10 to 5; Map XX circle 6.

Jewellery Clearance: 105, 15277 100 Ave. (589-1115). They carry a line of children's 10K gold jewellery, adult sizes of gold and silver, diamonds and they claim to have cheaper prices on everything. There's a buzzer system to let you into the store. Hours are Monday to Friday 9:30 to 9; Saturday 9:30 to 6; and Sunday 11 to 5. Map XX circle 7.

Sport Mart: 132, 15280 101st Ave. (582-1133). Discounts on all kinds of sports clothing and equipment are available here everyday. Open Monday to Wednesday and Saturday 9 to 6; Thursday and Friday 9 to 9; and Sunday 11 to 5. Map XX circle 8.

Nevada Bob's Discount Golf & Tennis: 1, 15285 101st Ave. (589-4311). Their policy is that they will not knowingly be undersold and that their manager will match any competitor's price. Open Monday, Tuesday and Saturday 9 to 6; Thursday and Friday 9 to 9; and Sunday 1 to 5. Map XX circle 9.

TJ's Kiddies Korner: 1, 15285 101st Ave. (584-8020). They offer a price-match guarantee which will meet any competitor's advertised price. They also have a specially-priced parents' starter set including crib, sheets, dresser, change table and car seat for about $700. Open Monday to Thursday and Saturday 10 to 5:30; Friday 10 to 9; and Sunday noon to 5. Map XX circle 10.

Phoenix Used Books: 10202 152nd St. (584-7684). They buy, sell and trade books and carry a good selection of new-looking paperbacks for 5 to 12 year olds at used prices (hard-to-find in most used book stores).

There's a floor-to-ceiling, well-organized collection. Open Monday to Saturday 10 to 5; and Sunday noon to 5. Map XX circle 11.

Big n'Tall Shop: 15240 102A Ave. (585-1022). Designed for the large man, this one is not bargain-priced but they do have a mailing list to notified interested customers of their sales, when prices are quite reasonable. Open Monday to Thursday and Saturday 9 to 5:30; and Friday 9 to 9. Map XX circle 12.

NOTES:

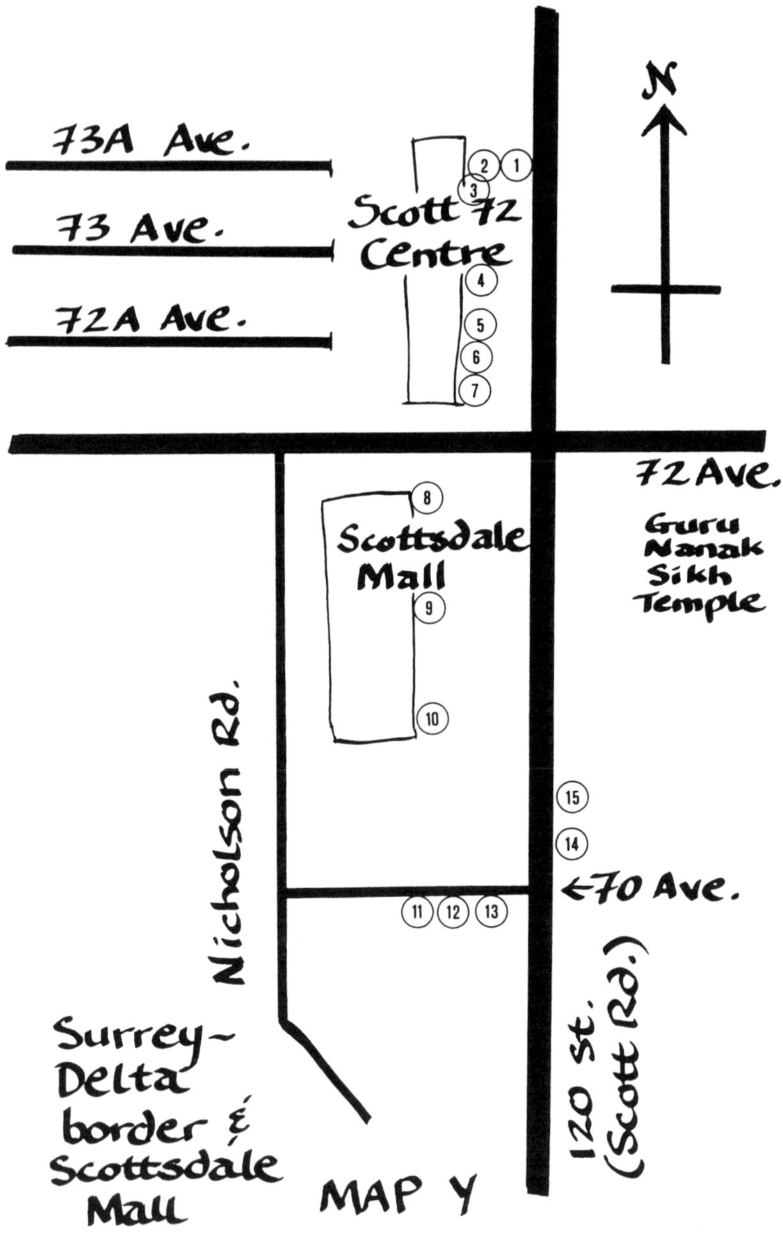
N
73A Ave.
73 Ave.
72A Ave.
Scott 72 Centre
1
2
3
4
5
6
7
72 Ave.
Guru Nanak Sikh Temple
Scottsdale Mall
8
9
10
Nicholson Rd.
15
14
←70 Ave.
11
12
13
120 St. (Scott Rd.)
Surrey-Delta border & Scottsdale Mall
MAP Y

Surrey-Delta

Along the Sur-Del border on Scott Road

This is a medium sized tour which should take only 2 to 3 hours to complete. Many of the stops are among the 55 stores in Scottsdale Mall. The main mall anchors are Zeller's and Field's. Otherwise, we have selected only those with unique or hard-to-find items for inclusion. Each of the mall stops is open "mall hours", unless otherwise stated in the listings. Scottsdale Mall hours are Monday, Tuesday and Saturday 9:30 to 5; Wednesday to Friday 9:30 to 9:30; and Sunday noon to 5. Location is 7143 120th St.

Scott Road is the dividing line between Surrey and Delta. Scott Road is also known as 120th .

The area may be reached from Vancouver by driving through New West and across the Pattullo Bridge. Take the Scott Road exit (the first after the bridge) and follow it to about 73rd Ave. to begin the tour.

From the U.S., take either Hwy. 99 north until it intercepts Scott Road (120th), or follow King George Hwy. (99A) north past Surrey Public Market to 64th Ave. and take 64th west (left) to Scott Road. In either of these cases, follow Scott Road north to 73rd Ave. Scottsdale Mall will be on your left at 72nd, but the tour begins one block past that.

By public transit, bus #391 goes directly from the end of the SkyTrain (at Scott Road Station) to Scottsdale Mall.

With the proliferation of strip malls and mall lots, there is no trouble parking in the area, at virtually any time of the day.

<u>Phulkari Emporium:</u> 7349 120th St. (599-5564). This East Indian store sells sari fabric, bangles, Punjabi-style custom-made silk suits for women and offers a good number of Indian music tapes. Open seven days 10 to 8. Map Y circle 1.

<u>Scott 72 Supermarket:</u> 7347B 120th St. (584-8288). An Indian supermarket, this one sells bulk spices and grain, Indian-style cookware, fresh produce, cashews and unusual items like mango juice crystals, all in a very neat and tidy environment which smells delicious! Labels on the more exotic cans and packages are not in English and some of the label art is ornate and gorgeous. Open Monday to Friday 9 to 9; Saturday 9:30 to 8; and Sunday 10 to 6. Map Y circle 2.

London Drugs: 7315 120th St. (520-9017). The usual computers, electronics and cosmetic departments are featured here, with a larger selection of seasonal specialties than in many of their stores. Books and magazines are 10 percent off and the chain frequently offers coupon book specials, even on the already-sale-priced merchandise. Open Monday to Saturday 9 to 10; and Sunday 10 to 8. Map Y circle 3.

Lumberland: 7313 120th St. (591-9926). Senior's Day highlights every Tuesday and Wednesday with 10 percent off their everyday stock of paint, plumbling, electrical and other home repair items. There are usually seasonal specials, such as patio furniture in the summer, inside repair tools in the cooler months, and naturally a giant warehouse of lumber and finishing touches. Open Monday to Friday 9 to 9; Saturday 9 to 6; and Sunday 10 to 5. Map Y circle 4.

Dots Discount Ladies Wear: 7273 120th St. (596-2990). This location of the discount women's fashions chain features lots of changing rooms and again, their policy of "lowest prices in Canada or its yours free". Garments tend to be organized by label rather than size, which is handy for status-seekers, not so great for shoppers in a hurry. Also, they have less children's clothing than at their Richmond location, for instance. Hours are Monday to Friday 10 to 9; Saturday 10 to 5:30; and Sunday 11 to 5. Map Y circle 5.

Fun Under $5: 7229 120th St. (599-4211). One of our favourites, this place does what its name implies, with plenty of goofy novelties, accessories and seasonal items — many well under the $5 ceiling. We found more toys and clothing and less housewares at this location than at others. Open Monday, Tuesday and Saturday 9:30 to 6; Wednesday to Friday 9:30 to 9; and Sunday noon to 5. Map Y circle 6.

Workwear World: 7225 120th St. (590-3839). The usual Workwear assortment of boots, jeans, shirts, hard hats, overalls and down vests reinforce their reputation as outfitters for the outdoor worker. Good values. Open Monday to Friday 9:30 to 9; Saturday 9:30 to 5:30; and Sunday noon to 5. Map Y circle 7.

Zellers: 7155 120th St. (596-9561). They offer "Club Z" cards for bonus savings and advertise themselves as the place "where the lowest price is the law". We don't know about that but ad wars with Woolco net the consumer even greater savings, as the conflict escalates to include prices! Focus is on family clothing, housewares, toys and "sizes plus for the big man and woman". Open Monday to Saturday 9:30 to 9:30; and Sunday 11 to 5. Map Y circle 8 (Scottsdale Mall).

Christopher's: Scottsdale Mall (590-3636). Very high-end goods are assembled here including gifts items, hand-blown glass, china, brass and five-foot tall fabric palm trees. There's a good mark-down section at the back. Map Y circle 9.

For Seasons: Scottsdale Mall (590-2534). This is an interesting source for designer-type women's clothing at reasonable prices. Open Monday and Tuesday 9:30 to 5:30; Wednesday to Friday 9:30 to 9; Saturday 9:30 to 5; and Sunday noon to 5. Map Y circle 9.

Just Kid'n Children's Wear: Scottsdale Mall (596-6959). Amass $300 on the bonus card they offer here and you'll get $30 off your next purchase. Clothing is size 6 months to 10/12. Kids' styles, made by a local manufacturer (like "Please Mum") are good buys. Map Y circle 9.

Fashion Addition: Scottsdale Mall (599-9916). Here large sizes in women's designer fashions run 14 to 24+, with labels like Leslie Fay, Jones New York and Casual Isle in the foreground. Map Y circle 9.

Showoff: Scottsdale Mall (594-1854). We were correct in guessing this is the new name for an old favourite of ours — the wonderful discounter called Francine's. They sell generic types of women's labels — not big-name designers but the clothing is very hip, very current and very inexpensive. They advertise "the lowest prices in Canada and U.S.A." and offer to beat the competition with a 10 percent margin, "guaranteed". If after you've bought the garment they reduce the same item's price within seven days of your original purchase, they'll happily refund the difference, so keep your sales slip. Map Y circle 9.

Oriental Imports: Scottsdale Mall (596-3222). Here we liked the stuffed animals, dolls, brassware, Chinese embroidered items and other gift items. Map Y circle 9.

Pacific Cotton: Scottsdale Mall (596-6993). They are proud of the fact that most of their stock is Canadian-made. Most of it is nice, casual clothing for women. Map Y circle 9.

Vitamin Discount Stores: Scottsdale Mall (597-1176). We've always gotten good value for the money at these stores. If you bring in a current membership card from any fitness club, you receive an additional saving of 10 percent. Map Y circle 9.

Black Bond Books: Scottsdale Mall (596-1541). Anne has always been partial to this particular location of Black Bond. There's a good discount table with book values, too. Map Y circle 9.

California Code: Scottsdale Mall (596-3203). Trendy fashions and California hip stuff is the mode here in both men's and women's styles. Map Y circle 9.

Field's: Scottsdale Mall (596-2737). Seniors' Day is the last Monday of every month, when 15 percent is taken off everything. This is a small store with footwear and family clothing at low prices. Map Y circle 9.

Suzanne's: Scottsdale Mall (590-5288). The stock here reminds us of our much-lamented Pirjo Liisa, which closed its Vancouver operations last year. There's Jantzen, Alia, Tan Jay and Snazzie, with something always on sale in women's clothing. Map Y circle 9.

Coach's Choice: Scottsdale Mall (597-9711). Here they're known as outfitters for the serious sports fan. They sell professional team hats (football, baseball, hockey), logo pins, jackets, T-shirts and baseball shirts, all emblazoned with your favourite team's ID. Map Y circle 9.

Save-on Foods & Drugs: 7015 120th St. (596-2944). In the bulk food section you can refill your own pop bottles. There are fresh flowers galore in the plant section, which is called "flowers Galore". Books, as always, are 10 percent off and in the store there's a little snack bar called Granny's Muffins with such eat-there bargains as a salad bar for $2.99 per pound. Open seven days 8 a.m. to midnight. Map Y circle 10.

Foots Sports Collectibles & Comics: 102, 6950 Nicholson (599-4142). The emphasis here is on comics and games, rather than sports cards, but there are cards by the packet, Dungeons and Dragons paraphrenalia, supplies and games, comic-related collectables and a bulletin board for gamers to get together. Hours are Monday and Saturday 10 to 5; Tuesday 10 to 6; Wednesday and Thursday 10 to 7; Friday 10 to 5:30; and Sunday 11 to 5. Map Y circle 11.

Sowing Seeds Christian Supplies: 105, 6950 Nicholson (597-5171). This store carries books, gift items, cards and extensive children's book section. Open Monday to Thursday and Saturday 9:30 to 5:30; Friday 9:30 to 6; and naturally, closed Sunday. Map Y circle 12.

Limber's Active Wear: 106A 6464 Nicholson (594-6464). Dance, skate and active wear is sold here. There are dance supplies galore, shoes, tights and aerobic wear. The windows are covered in posters announcing dance events. Open Monday to Thursday and Saturday 10 to 5:30; Friday 10 to 8; and Sunday noon to 4. Map Y circle 13.

East West Market: 104, 7028 120th St. (584-2117). Here you can buy bulk spices, grains, nuts, housewares, and such unusual items as frozen goat meat and Indian newspapers. Open Monday and Saturday 9 to 7; Tuesday 9 to 7:30; Wednesday and Thursday 9 to 8; Friday 9 to 8:30; and Sunday 10 to 7. Map Y circle 14.

<u>The East-West Collection:</u> 106, 7028 120th St. (590-8861). This shop sells fabrics, notions, accessories, a large selection of ready-made clothes, embroidered and beaded saree-lengths and loads of costume jewellery. Open Monday to Saturday 10 to 7; and Sunday 11 to 6. Map Y circle 15.

NOTES:

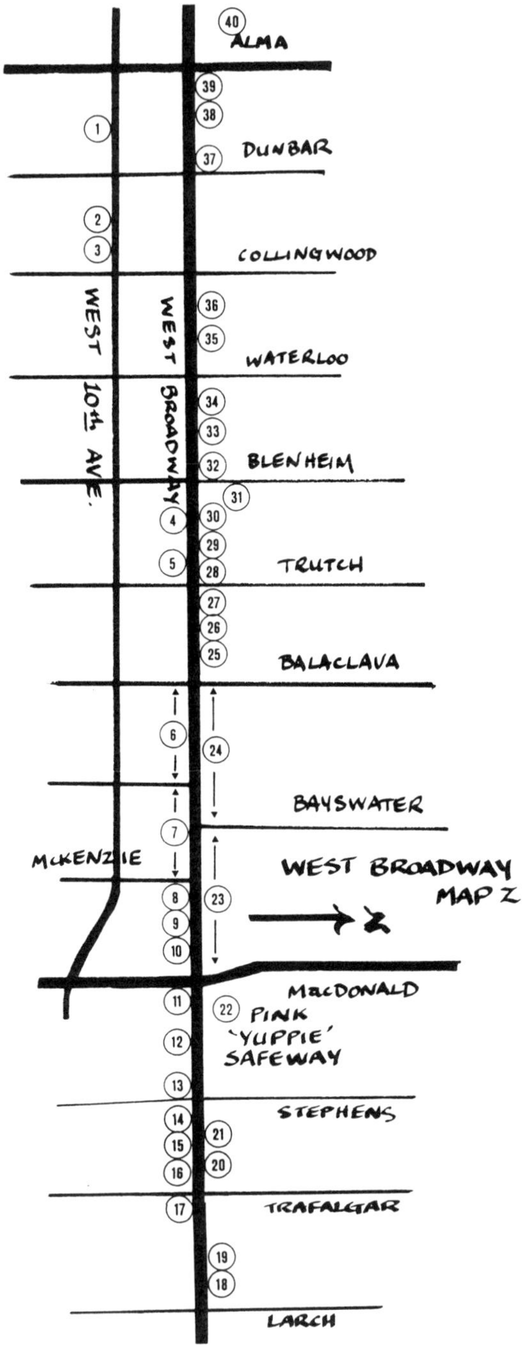

ALMA
DUNBAR
COLLINGWOOD
WATERLOO
BLENHEIM
TRUTCH
BALACLAVA
BAYSWATER
McKENZIE
MacDONALD
STEPHENS
TRAFALGAR
LARCH
WEST 10th AVE.
WEST BROADWAY
WEST BROADWAY
MAP Z
Z
PINK
'YUPPIE'
SAFEWAY
1
2
3
4
5
6
7
8
9
10
11
12
13
14
15
16
17
18
19
20
21
22
23
24
25
26
27
28
29
30
31
32
33
34
35
36
37
38
39
40

West Broadway

Macdonald to Alma

Eclectic and fascinating — bargains, too!

This is a major tour, for which you should plan all day — or a minimum of 4 to 5 hours if you want to try to see everything.

Generally speaking, parking is easy along most of West Broadway, except during morning and afternoon rush hours, when most areas restrict street parking. At other times of the day, metered parking is available on a first-come, first-served basis. Once you get west of about Macdonald, free street parking is available all day — even during rush hours. Side streets in this area offer some other parking options and the odd store will offer free, off-street parking.

Broadway is one of the main east-west thoroughfares in Vancouver, running into the city from the east as an extension of the Lougheed Highway, and more or less dribbling out at the western end at Alma, where it becomes 9th Avenue for a few short blocks. Broadway is, in fact, 9th Avenue, although no local would be caught dead calling it that. This inside info, however, will help visitors plot it in their minds between (naturally enough) 10th and 8th.

Of all the tours in this book, West Broadway was probably the most challenging for us. We left it until the very last minute to update it, so it would be as current as possible. In these days of tight money, businesses came and went over the three year period we researched our tours, and Broadway was no exception. That's another reason why we urge readers to call ahead to the places that most interest them, and avoid disappointment.

In the hip/funk Broadway and Larch area you'll find our rest-stop, the very "in", 24-hour eatery, Benny's Bagels. Further west, Broadway offers a potpourri of trendy import fashion shops and an area west of Macdonald dominated by Vancouver's Greek community, with an abundance of inexpensive produce shops, Greek markets and specialty items.

Driving north from the U.S., simply take Highway 99 north until you cross the Oak Street Bridge, and stick to Oak right on down to Broadway. For shopping in the South Granville area, please see our South Granville tour, and also refer to our general guide for furniture shopping in the lower mainland on page 203.

To reach the beginning of our tour, turn left (west) at Oak Street and proceed to MacDonald.

S.P.C.A. Thrift Store: 3626 West Broadway (736-4136). A typical thrift store, this one (in its new quarters) carries a good selection of sporting goods, garden tools, household items and some clothing. We've found it a good source for weird novelty items like the giant cartoon-y plaster statue of a clothed piggy we gave out as a "prize" at our book launch for Cheap Eats! Our only beef with the place is that prices are not marked on anything, so you get the sneaking suspicion that if you're well-dressed, the prcie is higher. In any case, everything's negotiable, and proceeds do go to a good cause. Another, newer location is on Clark Drive near Venables. Open seven days 10 to 6. Map Z circle 1.

Antiques on Broadway: 3476 West Broadway (732-1916). Really more of a second-hand store, if you dig you might find something antique. We saw an old stained glass window (cheap) and several rooms crammed with interesting stuff — the upper shelves are laden with goodies. Open Monday to Saturday 10 to 5. Map Z circle 2.

Agora Food Co-op: 3410 West Broadway (733-3505). This is a good source for bulk food and fresh produce. There's a children's play area, too. Seniors receive a discount on Tuesday, Wednesday and Sunday. You'll see different, "organic"-looking brands than in the supermarket. Open Monday to Fridau 10 to 7; and weekends 10 to 6. Map Z circle 3.

Blockbuster Video: 3298 West Broadway (732-4734). Bargains here include previously-viewed laser discs at $29.88 and used videos from $8.88. Open seven days, 10 to midnight. Map Z circle 4.

Yee & Co: 3252 West Broadway (739-9733). This tiny store sells women's clothing (some with their own label). Look for the large good-luck Japanese cat behind the cash desk. Open Tuesday to Saturday 11 to 6; and Sunday 1 to 6. Map Z circle 5.

Nicole Adrienne: 3064 West Broadway (734-2422). On the former site of Marc Downs, this place also sells women's clothing and the promo items are in brown boxes with prices ranging from $5 to $10. Weekly specials are posted on a sign out front. Open Monday to Wednesday and Saturday 10 to 6; Thursday and Friday 10 to 7; and Sunday noon to 5. Map Z block 6.

Grand Prix Hobby Supplies: 3038 West Broadway (733-7114). The size of this store was cut to half last year, but they still seem to have all the original stock of model kits, craft supplies, balsa wood, decorations, glass stain — you name it. Hours are Monday to Saturday 9 to 5:30. Map Z block 6.

Margaret Gabriel Book Sellers: 3036 West Broadway (738-BOOK). Here you'll find used, and rare books in a bright and clean-looking used bookstore. They sell coffee at a bargain 50 cents a cup (to sip while browsing) so there's naturally a no-rush atmosphere. They will seek out-of-print books for you and they also have a monthly promotion of a gift certificate draw. Open Monday to Wednesday and Friday to Sunday 11 to 6; and Thursday 11 to 9. Map Z block 6.

Latern Lighting: 3024 West Broadway (734-1518). They claim to sell "Canada's largest stock of lampshades" in a small (but tightly-packed) store. They also carry light fittings, and replacement crystals for chandeliers. Hours are Monday to Saturday 9 to 5:30. Map Z block 6.

Shoe Warehouse: 3010 West Broadway (738-1843). Their claim is "brand names always at least 25% off). Stock consists of men's women's and children's shoes and boots (and lots of casual shoes and runners). Lorraine likes the stock because it is different from what the other discounters carry, but Anne admits she's never found anything to buy here! Open Monday, Tuesday and Saturday 10 to 6; Wednesday and Thursday 10 to 7; Friday 10 to 9; and Sunday noon to 5. Map Z block 6.

The Toybox: 3002 West Broadway (738-4322). All the usual high-quality lines like Lego and Biro are stocked here (at the corner of Carnarvon St.), plus Ravenburger games and puzzles, very expensive-looking stuffed animals and wonderful puppets. They have those sweet Czech cone puppets which are always a hit. There's also a good quality book selection and loads of stocking-stuffers and party favours. Anne finds The Toybox a reliable source for kids' birthday gifts, even at the last minute. Open Monday to Thursday and Saturday 9:30 to 6; and Friday 9:30 to 7. Map Z block 6.

Peach Ave. Clothing: 2970 West Broadway (739-8355). This is a good place for casual clothing ("for skinny bods only", says Lorraine) for women. There are baseball shirts, jeans, casual dresses and Yes brand items. Hours are Monday to Saturday 10 to 6; and Sunday noon to 5. Map Z block 7.

Parthenon Super Market: 2968 West Broadway (733-4191). This wonderful-smelling Greek deli-market is full of homous, tabouli salad, dolmades, bulk Feta cheese, plump marinated olives and Mediterranean specialty foods. This is where Anne buys her Greek almond syrup to make steamed almond milk at home for a fraction of what it costs in a local coffee bar. Open Monday to Thursday and Saturday 9:30 to 7:30; Friday 9:30 to 8; and Sunday 10 to 6. Map Z block 7.

Johnny's Wax-Pax: 2934 West Broadway (739-0488). Still riding the crest of the collecting wave, this small store sells packaged trading cards, sports and film paraphrenalia (Batman, Star Trek, etc.), posters, and some old cards in protective cases. Open Tuesday to Friday 11 to 7; Saturday 10 to 6; and Sunday noon to 5:30. Map Z block 7.

Peregrine Books: 2932 West Broadway (738-6523). This fine bookstore sells mainly new volumes and has a substantial section on women's studies. There's a used section at the back of the store and a bargain table at the front. Hours are Monday to Saturday 10 to 6; and Sunday 1 to 6. Map Z block 7.

Lens & Shutter: 2902 West Broadway (736-5676). A local success story, this place rose to become the largest photo store in Western Canada, selling film, cameras, accessories and processing at bargain rates. They've settled into the mainstream now, with a Pro-room for professionals and frequent guest workshops from famous names in the business. They do a big mail order business, too. Open Monday to Thursday and Saturday 9:3o to 6; and Friday 9:30 to 9. Map Z block 7.

Ben's Stationery: 2906 West Broadway (732-5888). A highlight here is Amundson cards, which have a picture of several different kinds of sport fish with herbs and a recipe for cooking that particular fish inside the card — perfect for the sports fisherman on your birthday list. There are also school and stationery supplies and both postage and rubber stamps. Open Monday to Saturday 9:30 to 5:30. Map Z block 7.

Over the Moon Chocolates: 2868 West Broadway (737-0880). This wonderful place for those of us with unstoppable sweet tooths won the Province People's Pick for top chocolate. Open seven days 11 to 11. Map Z circle 8.

Broadway Brewing Company: 2860 West Broadway (736-4801). Their self-confessed Sunday policy is: "Open on cold or rainy days 12 to 5. On sunny days see you at the beach". Here's the place for supplies for making your own brewski at bargain rates. Beer winds up costing you $3.39 to $7.60 per dozen and wine runs $1.54 to $3.96 per finished bottle. Both brewing supplies and juice for making wine are packaged in boxes, so at first glance it looks like a wine shop, but it's definitely do-it-yourself and save. Open Tuesday to Friday 10 to 7; Saturday 10 to 6; and Sunday according to the weather, as above. Map Z circle 9.

Hang-Ups: 2858 West Broadway (736-8510). This is one of Anne's favourite charity thrift shops. It's run by Canadian Mental Health and ALL the proceeds go to them, as staff is entirely volunteer. It's a typical thrift shop with men's, women's and children's clothing, accessories and shoes, plus books and a few housewares. Open Monday to Saturday 10 to 5. Map Z circle 10.

CLOSED

<u>The Neat Shop:</u> 2790 West Broadway (73[illegible]) [illegible]is cute gift shop sells cards, gift bags, Disne[illegible] [illegible] cards and the ubiquitous Tro[illegible] [illegible], Thursday and Friday 11 to 7; [illegible] 11 to 5:30; Saturday 10 to 6; and Sunday no[illegible] 5. [illegible] Z circle 11.

<u>Flutterby's Lingerie & Hosiery:</u> 2778 West Broadway (731-8194). Lingerie and hosiery take the spotlight here. Some items are sexy, some strictly utilitarian. Open Monday to Friday 10 to 6; Saturday 10 to 5:30; and Sunday noon to 5. Map Z circle 12.

<u>Serena Fashions:</u> 2700 Broadway (733-7332). This large corner store (at Stephens St.) sells women's designer clothing, plus some lovely fashions under their own label. Others such as Mr. Jax are featured in colourful, attractive displays. Open Monday to Thursday 10 to 6; Friday 10 to 7; Saturday 9:30 to 5:30; and Sunday noon to 5. Map Z circle 13.

<u>Pink Peppercorn:</u> 2686 West Broadway (736-4213). This is the lower mainland's only cookbook store - and what a selection they have! The summer "pink elephant" sale reduces many of their fine cookbooks from 10 to 50 percent. Open Monday to Saturday 10 to 5:30. Map Z circle 14.

<u>Heart & Soul:</u> 2680 West Broadway (736-7767). Here's our favourite source of candles, incense, healing crystals and the like, all for far lower prices than we've found elsewhere. Hours are Monday to Saturday 10 to 6; and Sunday 11 to 5. Map Z circle 15.

<u>Have-to-Have More Clothes:</u> 2612 West Broadway (738-1115). This trendy women's clothing store holds great clearance sales. Otherwise, their prices are still pretty reasonable. Hours are Monday to Saturday 10 to 6; and Sunday noon to 5. Map Z circle 16.

<u>Kitsilano Natural Food Store:</u> 2582 West Broadway (734-1822). Just to show we haven't given up our Westcoast hippie roots, this place continues to thrive. Upstairs is one of Vancouver's best vegetarian restaurants, Woodlands. In the store are health foods, bulk grains, legumes, nuts, butters, and seeds, vitamins, juice extractors, and the like. Hours are Monday to Thursday 9 to 8; Friday 9 to 9; Saturday 9 to 6:30 and Sunday 10 to 6. Map Z circle 17.

Benny's Bagels: 2503 West Broadway (736-4686). This incredibly hip 24-hour cafe and bakery is the designated rest-stop in our West Broadway tour. Just bring in your copy of The Serious Shopper's Guide, show it to your server when you order, and owners Michael and Colin will honour their offer of a free beverage for the person carrying this book (along with a free beverage for each of the friends shopping with that person), when you each order a meal. Their offer is good up to an including December 31, 1993. Open seven days, 24 hours. Map Z circle 18.

Old House & Home: 2507 West Broadway (731-2515). Right next to Benny's is this wonderful source of movie and TV props, which as the sign proclaims is "open to the public". There are all kinds of fascinating treasures and "junque" to paw through. Hours vary, but since they always have their @#%&*!! answering machine on, we find it impossible to call ahead for exact times. Map Z circle 19.

The Travel Bug: 2667 West Broadway (737-1122). Another unique entry, this is one of the few total-service travel boutiques in town, selling travel guides, passport cases, travel security aids and every device and gadget you could think of to make your life on the road comfortable, convenient and secure. The owner is well-travelled and very knowledgeable and happy to give you advice when you need it. Open Monday to Wednesday and Saturday 10 to 6; Thursday and Friday 10 to 8; and Sunday noon to 5. Map Z circle 20.

Banyen Books/Banyen Sound: 2671/2669 West Broadway (732-7912/737-8858). These side-by-side stores are the heart of the new age and personal growth movements in Vancouver. In fact, people come in and write from miles around, since many of their books and records simply can't be found elsewhere in Canada. Take a deep, cleansing breath and mellow out before entering. Open Monday to Friday 10 to 9; Saturday 10 to 6; and Sunday 11 to 6. Map Z circle 21.

Safeway: 2733 West Broadway (732-5226). Say "the yuppie Safeway" and everyone knows you mean this pink and stone one, at Broadway and Macdonald. It's Anne's favourite, next to the one in City Square at 12th and Cambie. Great produce, neat displays, happy cashiers, free, easy-access parking under cover (entrance off Macdonald) and easy-to-find products make this really user-friendly. Open the usual seven days 8 to midnight. Map Z circle 22.

Broadway Shoe Salon: 2809 West Broadway (731-1410). Focussing mainly on comfortable lines like Birkenstock, Keds and Clinic brands, this place offers shoe repair as well as stock in men's, women's and children's sizes. Open Monday to Thursday and Saturday 9 to 6; Friday 9 to 8; and Sunday noon to 5. Map Z block 23.

Sequels: 2813 West Broadway (731-7247). This place, formerly a consignment store, now sells new clothing only, but at discount prices. There are lovely accessories, too. Bins of clothing are cleared out at $5 or $10 as well. Open Monday to Saturday 10 to 6; and Sunday noon to 4. Map Z block 23.

Pacific Park: 2821 West Broadway (732-3998). Newly opened in the summer of 1992, this places sells "quality clothing at wholesale prices" — men's, women's and children's sizes in silks and cottons are featured. Last time we stopped by, we found a cute cow-patterned girl's dress and reasonably-priced hand-knit sweaters from Hong Kong. Hours are Monday to Saturday 10 to 6; and Sunday noon to 5. Map Z block 23.

Salvation Army Thrift Store: 2841 West Broadway (734-1824). Our costume-collecting friend Marilyn Rapanos favours this shop for its wigs and seredipity finds. Their "better class of junk" according to another friend, includes clothing, books and some furniture. Some of the most tantalizing window items are held back until the date on the window sign, so you're guaranteed to be drawn back again. Seniors get an additional 10 percent saving on the 30th of each month. Open Monday to Saturday 9 to 5. Map Z block 23.

Blackberry Books: 2855 West Broadway (739-8116). Good quality books are well-displayed in this nicely-carpeted, attractive store. Also available are clever cards. Open seven days 9 to 9. Map Z block 23.

Regis Framing: 2857 West Broadway (732-1444). This place is famous for fine framing — and most work can be accomplished on a same-day basis. They also sell posters and art prints galore. Open Monday to Thursday 10 to 6; Friday 10 to 9; Saturday 10 to 5; and Sunday noon to 4. Map Z block 23.

Current Fashion: 2887 West Broadway (733-3466). This shop is located on the site of the old Frugal's store, which had the longest going-out-of-business sale we can remember! Under brand new management and with a new name, this is now a place for knock-off copies of famous designers like Armani and Mr. Jax, recreated by local designers for far less than you'd expect to pay. Women's fashions are marketed under the Cha Cha label. Open Monday to Wednesday and Friday 10:30 to 5:30; Thursday 10:30 to 8:30; Saturday 10 to 6; and Sunday noon to 4. Map Z block 23.

Stars on Broadway: 2905 West Broadway (732-7662). Women's clothing is the highlight here with labels like Almost Heaven, Mexx and Leslie Fay. There's always a sale rack at the back. Last time we visited, there was a 25 percent sale — off everything in the store! Open Monday to Thursday 10 to 6; Friday 10 to 8; Saturday 10 to 5:30; and Sunday noon to 5. Map Z block 23.

Mark James: 2941 West Broadway (734-2381). This is the chi-chi men's shop where Equity magazine chief Michael Campbell finesses his wardrobe accessories on Boxing Day. The store also sells itself as "official clothiers of the Vancouver Canucks", but we're not sure if that's a plus or minus. Does Pavel Bure shop here or what? Anyway, the labels and quality are all top-notch, there's everything from business attire to casual and sports apparel in a beautiful, trendy and spacious store, topped by fascinating window displays which change regularly. 'Round the corner is their sister-operation, a great, bouncy restaurant called Fiasco. Store hours are Monday to Thursday and Saturday 10 to 6; Friday 10 to 9; and Sunday 11:30 to 5:30. Map Z block 23.

Please Mum: 2951 West Broadway (732-4574). This is where all the Yuppie-puppies we know are dressed, in expensive (albeit gorgeous) designer clothing for kiddies. Sizes fitted are 3 months to 14 years. Open Monday to Thursday and Saturday 9:30 to 6; Friday 9:30 to 8; and Sunday noon to 5. Map Z block 24.

Sunda Fashion: 2953 West Broadway (738-8986). The stock here is mainly Oriental import clothing for women, in their own Sunda brand and others. There are T-shirts, blouses and accessories. Open Monday 12:30 to 5:30; and Tuesday to Sunday 11 to 5:30. Map Z block 24.

YES: 2955 West Broadway (736-4484). This trendy men's and women's clothing store always has a sales rack outside. Their sales are excellent. Look for Mexx and Esprit lines here, plus other casual wear. Hours are Monday to Wednesday and Saturday 10 to 6; Thursday and Friday 10 to 9; and Sunday noon to 5. Map Z block 24.

Eugenia's Boutique: 2957 West Broadway (734-1176). They create their own line of cotton-lycra clothing, such as tops, dresses and leggings. They also stock other brands and sell everything from T-shirts to beaded gowns! Hours are Monday to Wednesday 11 to 6; and Thursday to Saturday 10 to 7:30. Map Z block 24.

Finn's Clothing: 3031 West Broadway (732-3831). This is where all the private school boys buy their "other" clothes. It's fine men's clothing, suits, jeans, Hathaway shirts, golf shirts and Tommy Hilfiger attire. It's casual, classy and classic — less trendy and more conservative than Mark James. Open Monday to Thursday 9:30 to 6; Friday 9:30 to 7; and Saturday 9 to 5:30. Map Z block 24.

Clothestime: 3025 West Broadway (736-9998). Fine ladies' clothing — especially designer lines — is sold here at a discount. Last time in we found London Fog coats and clothing well discounted. In fact, London Fog items are always discounted here. It's not a rock-bottom bargain place, but there are some good deals in classic styles. Open Monday to Thursday 10 to 7; Friday 10 to 7; and Saturday 10 to 5:30. Map Z block 24.

Majolika's Import: 3065 West Broadway (733-1621). This is one of Anne's favourite gift stores — always something unique and inexpensive that "looks like more". There are candles, cards, tea cosies, linens, housewares, and, as we said, gifts. Open Monday to Saturday 10 to 6. Map Z block 24.

Vancouver Kidsbooks: 3083 West Broadway (738-5335). Owner Phyllis Simon is a former children's librarian, so when she set her mind to creating a source for great books for kids, she did a bang-up job! Simon has two children of her own, and is a gifted public speaker. The store runs all kinds of readings and children's programs, too. They sell cards as well as books. Hours are Monday to Saturday 10 to 6; and Sunday noon to 5. Map Z block 24.

Kid's Expressions: 3095 West Broadway (737-1588). Here you'll discover kids' clothing from Oshkosh, Giggles and other good, everyday lines. They also operate as a Sears catalogue agent for parcel pickup for orders. Regular clothing stock runs from sizes newborn to 14. Open Monday to Thursday 10 to 5:30; and Friday and Saturday 10 to 6. Map Z block 24.

Hollywood Theatre: 3123 West Broadway (738-3211). A local landmark, this movie house shows recent-release movies in double-bills for just $2.25 (Monday) and $3.25 (any other day of the week). Seniors, children and handicapped pay $2.50 every day. Movies change weekly. Call their number for a recorded message to find out what's on if you plan to be in this area in the evenings. Most showings are at 7:30 and 9:30 p.m. Map Z circle 25.

Best Quality Produce: 3151 West Broadway (732-7088). The folks who run this place offer good prices, friendly service and some unique Chinese specialty condiments we've never seen elsewhere. There is also a selection of fresh pasta, some salsas and cheeses. They were runners-up in a recent Province poll for best fruit markets. Open Monday to Friday 9 to 7; Friday 9 to 9; and Sunday 9 to 6. Map Z circle 26.

Great Wall of China Collectibles: 3175 West Broadway (736-4115). This is not a china import store, but they do have several walls of collector plates, porcelain-head dolls, and locally-made jewellery including lovely hand-painted porcelain. Open Tuesday to Thursday and Saturday 10 to 5; and Friday 10 to 8. Map Z circle 27.

Broadway Records & Tapes: 3207 West Broadway (736-1281). A large and varied selection of used records, new and used CDs and tapes is offered here. The store has been around for ages - obviously since before CDs were invented! Open Monday to Thursday and Saturday 10 to 6; Friday 10 to 9; and Sunday noon to 5. Map Z circle 28.

West Coast Books: 3209 West Broadway (732-6311). This place specializes in used and out-of-print books. It's an attractive store, and well-planned for the browser. We coveted the (not for sale) apartment-shaped umbrella stand at the entrance. Hours are Monday to Friday 10 to 9; and Saturday and Sunday 10 to 6. Map Z circle 29.

Broadway Produce: 3287 West Broadway (734-5112). Surely some of the lowest produce prices (and best quality) in town are to be found in this otherwise undistinguished store. We couldn't find it ourselves till a friend pointed it out. Everyday prices are lower than most and sale prices positively outstanding. There are also some cheeses, Avalon bottled milk, East Indian spices and canned goods. Open Saturday to Thursday 8 to 7; and Friday from 8 to 8. Map Z circle 30.

Off-Broadway Designer Consignment: 2490 Blenheim (739-0483). Right around the corner from Broadway Produce, this darling little shop sells really high quality women's and children's "previously-owned" garments. Open Monday to Saturday 10 to 5:30; and Sunday noon to 4. Map Z circle 31.

Ed's Linens: 3301 West Broadway (731-2700). A smaller version of the giant store in Richmond, this one at Broadway and Blenheim offers the same low, discount prices on kitchen linens, bed linens, and bath items. Open Monday to Wednesday and Saturday 9:30 to 5:30; Thursday and Friday 9:30 to 9; and Sunday noon to 5. Map Z circle 32.

Shiraz Carpets: 3343 West Broadway (731-2488). They stock (and naturally, sell) stacks of fine carpets in silks and wools. They claim to "beat any advertised price or it's yours free". Open Monday to Saturday 10:30 to 6. Map Z circle 33.

Community Sports: 3355 West Broadway (733-1612). Book distributor extraordinaire, Allan MacDougall loves the sales here, and so do we. Aside from their regular stock of sports equipment for every sport, they always have a sale rack, and something on special. Get on their mailing list when you stop by for advance notice of special seasonal sales. Open Monday to Wednesday and weekends 9:30 to 6; and Thursday and Friday 9:30 to 9. Map Z circle 34.

The Clay Zone: 3427 West Broadway (731-9474). A local potter has her studio in the rear, plus the work of four other potters is showcases in this pleasant shop. They also sell paintings, cards and jewellery — all locally made, of course. Open Tuesday to Saturday 11 to 6. Map Z circle 35.

Wine Art Sales: 3429 West Broadway (731-4726). All the supplies the home wine-maker or brewer would ever require are available here, plus lots of free advice. Open Tuesday to Saturday 9:30 to 5:30. Map Z circle 36.

Canada West Antiques: 3607 West Broadway (733-3213). The focus here is on antique Canadian pine, country furniture, quilts, hooked rugs and folk art. Contemporary pieces and decor accents are designed to be compatible with the older furniture. There's a good deal of authentic stock from Ontario, Quebec and the Maritimes, of better quality than most container loads brought in from Ireland and other pine sources. Stock is — for the most part — expensive, but well worth it in quality. Hours are Monday to Saturday 10:30 to 5:30; and Sunday 1 to 4:30. Map Z circle 37.

Wally's Folly: 3639 West Broadway (736-5848). Judy Walchuk put her singing career on the back burner to follow another dream, and she has succeeded in creating "Vancouver's only world-famous functional art lamp shade shop". Every creation is completely hand-made with brocade, lace, beaded fringe, silk flowers and antique findings that Judy has personally scoured from sources world-wide. She is indeed a master-craftsperson! Her lampshades grace the homes of the rich and famous, such as Kurt Russell and Goldie Hawn (she had many of them custom-made for their Aspen home), Mark Harmon and Pam Dawber, Shelley Duvall, the Pointer Sisters, Bruce Springsteen (though we don't know if Juliana ended up with them after the divorce), Bernadette Peters, and Henry Mancini, among many others.

Judy also had a professional video produced to demonstrate for those who want to attempt to make their own shades, how it is done - and the video takes you step by step through a beginner's lampshade which looks just gorgeous when it's done.

Shop hours are Tuesday to Saturday noon to 5, though Judy will take appointments for custom work at other times. Map Z circle 38.

Lukila's Recycled Clothing: 3649 West Broadway (732-6407). The name is somewhat misleading, because this is NOT a consignment store, but they do sell "previously-owned" women's clothing and some apparel for men and children. There are also some nice shoes, hats and purses. Open Monday to Wednesday 11 to 5:30; Thursday and Friday 11 to 7; Saturday 10 to 5:30; and Sunday 12:30 to 5. Map Z circle 39.

True Confections: #6, 3701 West Broadway (222-8489). For those of you who are a little peckish after all that shopping, here's a treat. Right across Alma (where Harpo's Chicken used to be), there's a newish location of Vancouver's best late-night dessert spot. Come to think of it, it's open pretty long hours in the daytime, too. The cakes, cheesecakes and pies are to DIE for! Hours are Monday to Thursday 4 p.m. to midnight; Friday 4 p.m. to 2 a.m.; Saturday 1 p.m to 2 a.m.; and Sunday 1 p.m. to midnight. Map Z circle 40.

ADDENDUM:

African Market: 2665 West Broadway (732-7480). Anne's daughter Becky couldn't believe we overlooked this great source of hand-woven fabric purses, hats, and beads and decorations, so we had to add it in. There's a second location at 2258 West 4th. Hours *really* vary: when we called to verify open hours, a husky voice told us "We are going with the sun", which seems to mean open from about 11 to 6 and some weekends, so you'd be well advised to call ahead.

NOTES:

West Van — Ambleside

A different world

This is a medium-sized tour which should take about 3 to 4 hours if you want to take in everything.

Ambleside is the heart of West Vancouver, and a shopping area that has remained virtually unchanged over the past twenty years. Shop owners are friendly and unpretentious — except that they can't help but let you know how privileged they feel to be living not just in glorious British Columbia, but in Wonderful West Van. That's okay, because we feel just a twinge of jealousy — and then we remember that the reason we're not living there is because WE CAN'T HASSLE THE BRIDGE!

To get to the area, you do indeed have the cross "the bridge" — that being The Lions Gate Bridge, of course. People driving from Vancouver will generally head northbound on Georgia which goes directly onto the bridge (careful to avoid the right lane which draws you into a pleasant but long journey around Stanley Park).

Alternately, you can cross from East Vancouver to the north shore via the Second Narrows Bridge and take the highway right to the Taylor Way exit, then travel west along Marine Drive in West Van to start the tour.

U.S. visitors will find the simplest route is to use the Aldergrove border crossing into Canada and head straight north on Highway 13 (264th St). until it intersects with TransCanada 1. From there, you travel Highway 1 west right across the Port Mann Bridge into Coquitlam and stay on the highway clear across the Second Narrows and into North (and subsequently West) Vancouver.

Another method from the U.S. is to cross at Douglas (Blaine), take the King George Highway north and cross the Pattullo Bridge into New Westminster, then follow the signs toward Burnaby and Coquitlam. You'll want to get onto Columbia St. in New West, which becomes North Road and takes you onto Highway 1.

Parking in the Ambleside area is generally easy right on the street, or a few stores (like the Safeway) have an off-street lot reserved for their customers' convenience.

By public transit from Vancouver, take the #250 (Horseshoe Bay/ Dundarave/Vancouver) bus north on Georgia St.

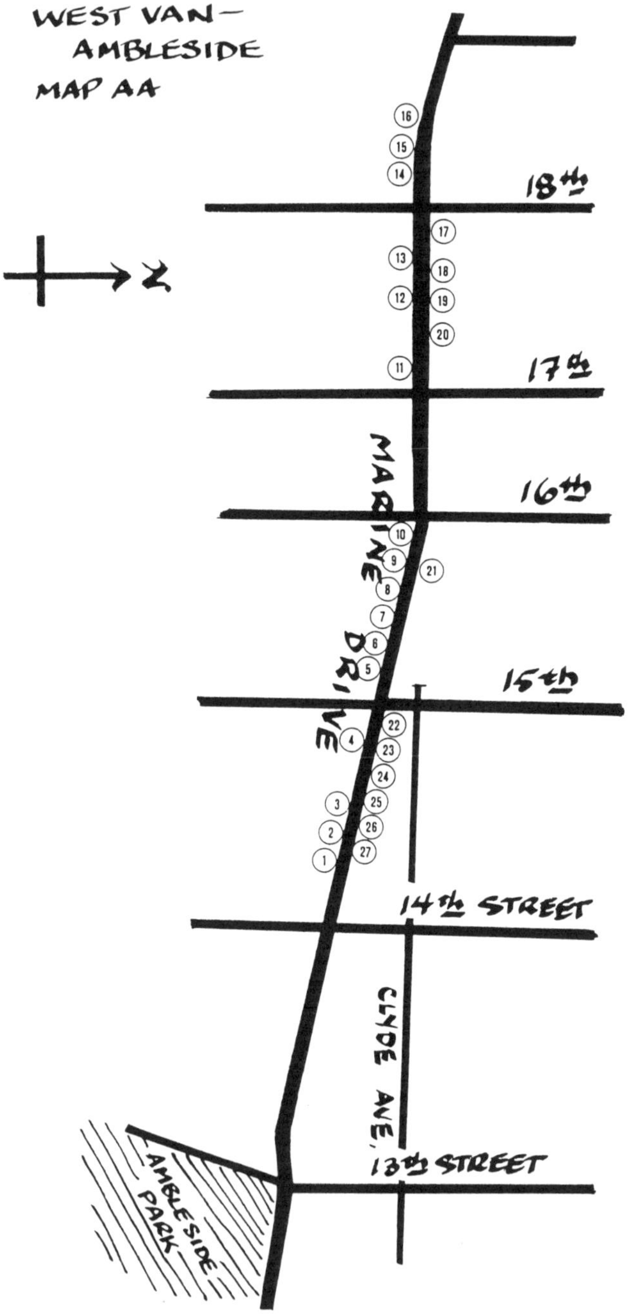
WEST VAN—
AMBLESIDE
MAP AA
N
18th
17th
16th
15th
14th STREET
13th STREET
MARINE DRIVE
CLYDE AVE.
AMBLESIDE PARK
1
2
3
4
5
6
7
8
9
10
11
12
13
14
15
16
17
18
19
20
21
22
23
24
25
26
27

Superstar Athletic Footwear: 1454 Marine (926-4612). As expected, this store sells shoes for sports, but they also stock jackets, aerobic wear, sweat suits and the like. Open Monday to Wednesday 10 to 6; Thursday and Friday 10 to 8; and Saturday 9:30 to 5:30. Map AA circle 1.

The Avant Gardener: 1460 Marine (926-8784). This is where to go for those hard-to-find gardening items. It's is famous far and wide. Outside at the curb is a stuffed figure they call "Rosemary" which is surrounded by plants and inside there are herbs, topiary animals, bulbs and of course plants. The upstairs salon has a brass whale-shaped weathervane and a gardeners' exchange board for ads. They also sell cards and gifts for green-thumbers and other garden-related items. Open Monday to Friday 10 to 6; and Saturday 9:30 to 5:30. Map AA circle 2.

Boutique Pia: 1462 Marine (922-3610). Lorraine's comment: "I didn't know you could still buy velour!". This shop is a little stuffy and conservative for our tastes, but a good source of casual clothing for the mature woman. Open Monday to Saturday 10 to 5. Map AA circle 3.

Leslie Jane: 1480 Marine (922-8612). You'll spot the flower-bordered windows and the chalk board info right away. We decided we'd dub this "old world charm"-type clothing, plus some lovely giftware. Many of the pieces could almost be vintage. Hours are Tuesday to Friday 10 to 8; Saturday 10 to 6; and Sunday noon to 5. Map AA circle 4.

Juilliard Antiques: 1512 Marine (926-0809). This tiny shop sells Persian miniatures and a stock of Mid-Eastern furniture, all quite ornate. Open Tuesday to Saturday noon to 5. Map AA circle 5.

Ceramic Centre: 1516 Marine (926-2448). Rough-hewn shelves hold pottery here and Persian carpets grace the floors and walls. There are beautiful weavings, larger-than-life lamp bases and — hold onto your hat — a mark-down corner with great discounts. Open Monday to Saturday 9:30 to 6. Map AA circle 6.

Antiques and Old Lace: 1530 Marine (922-3282). Aptly named, this place carries antique clothing (some reproduction, but very convincing), old lace, china, vintage silver, and collectors' thimbles. We couldn't help but visualize those two dotty old ladies from Arsenic and Old Lace in this milieu. Open Monday to Saturday 10 to 5:30. Map AA circle 7.

Japanese Accents Kiku: 1532 Marine (925-2584). A staircase that lead to nowhere in this one-storey shop justifies itself by acting as a display support for small items. The stock includes china, tableware, screens, kimonos and ceremonial items from Japan. Open Monday to Saturday 10 to 5; Map AA circle 8.

Town & Village Shop: 1534 Marine (922-2220). Wondrous goods are sold here including Portmeiron china, and Anne's treasured WMF stainless flatware from Germany (so hard to find in Western Canada), plus gifts, tableware, Medici cards and even some opulently-illustrated children's books. Hours are Monday to Saturday 10 to 5:30. Map AA circle 9.

West Van Furniture Sales: 1582 Marine (926-0307). This place sells a very good assortment of new and used furniture, but the highlight for us was owner Don's frog collection. Apparently it started with a set of frogs that arrived as part of an estate they bought years ago, and now it's grown until it fills and entire wall in the store! Hours are Monday to Saturday 9 to 5:30. Map AA circle 10.

Lion's Mark Antiques: 1730 Marine (926-7710). The focus here is on silver and china, all attractively-displayed around the perimeter of the store. In the middle there are a few pieces of nice furniture. Open Tuesday to Saturday 10 to 5. Map AA circle 11.

West Van Collectors Shop: 1744 Marine (926-4010). This place is a treasure-trove of jewellery, objets d'art, sterling silver, paintings and cabinets full of silver and ornaments. The charming owner will stay open a little later "if it's an emergency". Regular hours are Monday to Saturday 10 to 5. Map AA circle 12.

Simpson Home Hardware: 1750 Marine (922-4138). Though the windows look very upmarket, inside it's the same familiar, homey atmosphere one expects from a hardware store replete with housewares, hardware, bulk nails and so on. Open Monday to Friday 8:30 to 6; Saturday 8:30 to 5:30; and Sunday noon to 5. Map AA circle 13.

Windsor Meats: 1810 Marine (926-1440). You can't miss the sides of beef in the window. Inside there's our famous Saltspring Island lamb, family-size or individual steak and kidney pies, and free-range chicken. Hours are Monday to Thursday and Saturday 9 to 5:30; and Friday 9 to 6. Map AA circle 14.

Bernard Callebaut Chocolaterie: 1836 Marine (925-3080). Yes, this is the genuine article: Real Belgian chocolate, plus ice cream bars in flavours like milk-ginger, almond and pistachio. Open Monday to Saturday 10 to 6. Map AA circle 15.

Kid & Kaboodle: 1850 Marine (922-8829). Basic elements in boys' and girls' wear in sizes from newborn to 6x are carried here. There's a nice little play area, too. Hours are Monday to Saturday 10 to 5. Map AA circle 16.

Jackee's Homecraft Gallery: 1761 Marine (926-5711). Countrified wood items, pottery, fabric arts and hooked rugs mainly created by local artisans and artists fill this store. Open Monday to Saturday 10 to 5. Map AA circle 17.

Neat Things: 1765 Marine (926-9512). This studio and gallery of handmade jewellery also gives classes for young people, novices and experienced artisans. Seasonal classes (like "Christmas bows") are slotted in for cooler months. There are also classes in working with titanium and niobium, two colourful metals which are good even for those sensitive to earring posts in anything other than pure gold. AS for the silver pieces for sale, "if it looks like silver, it's sterling". There's also fine pottery and silver and gold enamelled jewellery. Find it down a tiny alleyway at this address. Open Tuesday to Saturday 10 to 5. Map AA circle 18.

Wildflower: 1757 Marine (925-3237). A talented florist here creates wreaths decorated with dried flowers, centrepieces and other distinctive arrangements. The artificial flowers that look exactly like dried ones are actually fabric which has been heated till it attains the look. Prices are reasonable. When we stopped in, a dried rose bouquet was just $7. Open Monday to Saturday 9 to 5:30. Map AA circle 19.

Guild House Antiques: 1731 Marine (926-6272). Massive pieces of furniture and a collection reminiscent of the Explorers' Club (as in Around the World in 80 Days) highlight this stop. Antiques from everywhere mingle with polar bear skins, an Indian mask, antique kimono, Highland dress uniform and museum-quality pieces for every serious collector. Parking is available at the rear. Hours are Monday to Saturday 10 to 5. Map AA circle 20.

Sunmark Stationery: 1543 Marine (922-3442). A good selection of stationery, cards and party supplies are offered here. Open Monday to Saturday 9 to 6. Map AA circle 21.

Swiss Sportshaus: 490 15th St. (922-9107). They are closed during the summer months, but otherwise stock a big selection of winter sports attire, ski equipment and clothing. A signboard out front announced specials. Open Monday to Friday 9:30 to 6; and Saturday 9:30 to 5:30. Map AA circle 22.

Huguette's: 1489 Marine (925-2710). Very classy (and classic) European imports in women's clothing are the focus here, highlighted by the

Basler label. Open Monday to Saturday 10 to 5; and Sunday noon to 5. Map AA circle 23.

Hall of Fame Sports Cards: 120, 1425 Marine (922-1529). Here you can buy, sell or trade sportscards, new and old. Posters and magazines round out the sports-theme stock. Open Monday to Thursday noon to 6; Friday noon to 8; Saturday 10 to 6; and Sunday 11 to 5. Map AA circle 24.

Ambleside Toys 'n Hobbies: 1425 Marine (922-3512). This store is virtually packed with stock: Books, toys and model supplies and kits. Hours are Monday to Saturday 9:30 to 5:30; and Sunday noon to 4. Map AA circle 25.

The Bookstall in Ambleside: 1425 Clyde 9(26-2425). Books, books, everywhere — on the shelves, on the floor, plus there's a lifetime worth of National Geo's. This is a very fine used book store. Open Monday to Friday 9:30 to 5:30; Saturday 10 to 6; and Sunday 1 to 5. Map AA circle 26.

Bijan Specialty Foods: 1451 Clyde (925-1055). This place specializes in Mid-East and Mediterranean foods and condiments. They also carry bulk rice, olives and cheese, etc. Ice cream cones there are $1.25. Open Monday to Saturday 9 to 7; and Sunday 10 to 6. Map AA circle 27.

NOTES:

West Van — Dundarave

Bargains and consignment aplenty

This is a small tour, which can be completed in one to two hours.

To reach the area, follow directions for West Van — Ambleside (previous tour), and continue along Marine Drive to 24th St.

By public transit from Vancouver, take the #250 (Horseshoe Bay / Dundarave / Vancouver) bus north on Georgia St.

Street parking in Dundarave can be difficult, but side streets sometimes yield spots and Stong's has a large parking lot for the use of their customers.

Stong's Market: 2491 Marine (926-7384). This is a full-line grocery store with lots of fresh produce and good value in the meat department. It's sister store is in Dunbar. Each store has a good reputation locally. Open Monday to Wednesday 9 to 7; Thursday and Friday 9 to 9; and Saturday 6 to 6. Map BB circle 1.

Treasure Chest Antiques: 2465 Marine (922-4848). This store offers copper, glass, china, collectables and antique furniture with a liberal sprinkling of Oriental carpets. Open Tuesday to Saturday 10 to 5:30; and Sunday noon to 4. Map BB circle 2.

B.J.'s Fashions: 2463 Marine (926-0712). Here you'll discover high-end (and gorgeous) women's apparel and shoes. Last visit, Lorriane found Inuit-style parkas and an Egyptian motif sweater that she adored. Hours are Monday to Saturday 9:30 to 5:30; and Sunday noon to 5. Map BB circle 3.

Boutique Exchange: 2461 Marine (922-6414). Next to B.J.'s there's a small staircase leading up to the Boutique Exchange, where you'll find high-quality women's consignment clothing. They have a loyal following, for good reason. Open Tuesday to Saturday 10 to 5. Map BB circle 4.

The Kensington Shop: 2447 Marine (922-0655). Related to Treasure Chest Antiques, this store recently moved to the rear of this location with entrances from the lane and the street. Antique pine furniture, much of it from Ireland, is nicely displayed and decorated with small brass accents and china. Open Tuesday to Saturday 10 to 5; and Sunday noon to 5. Map BB circle 5.

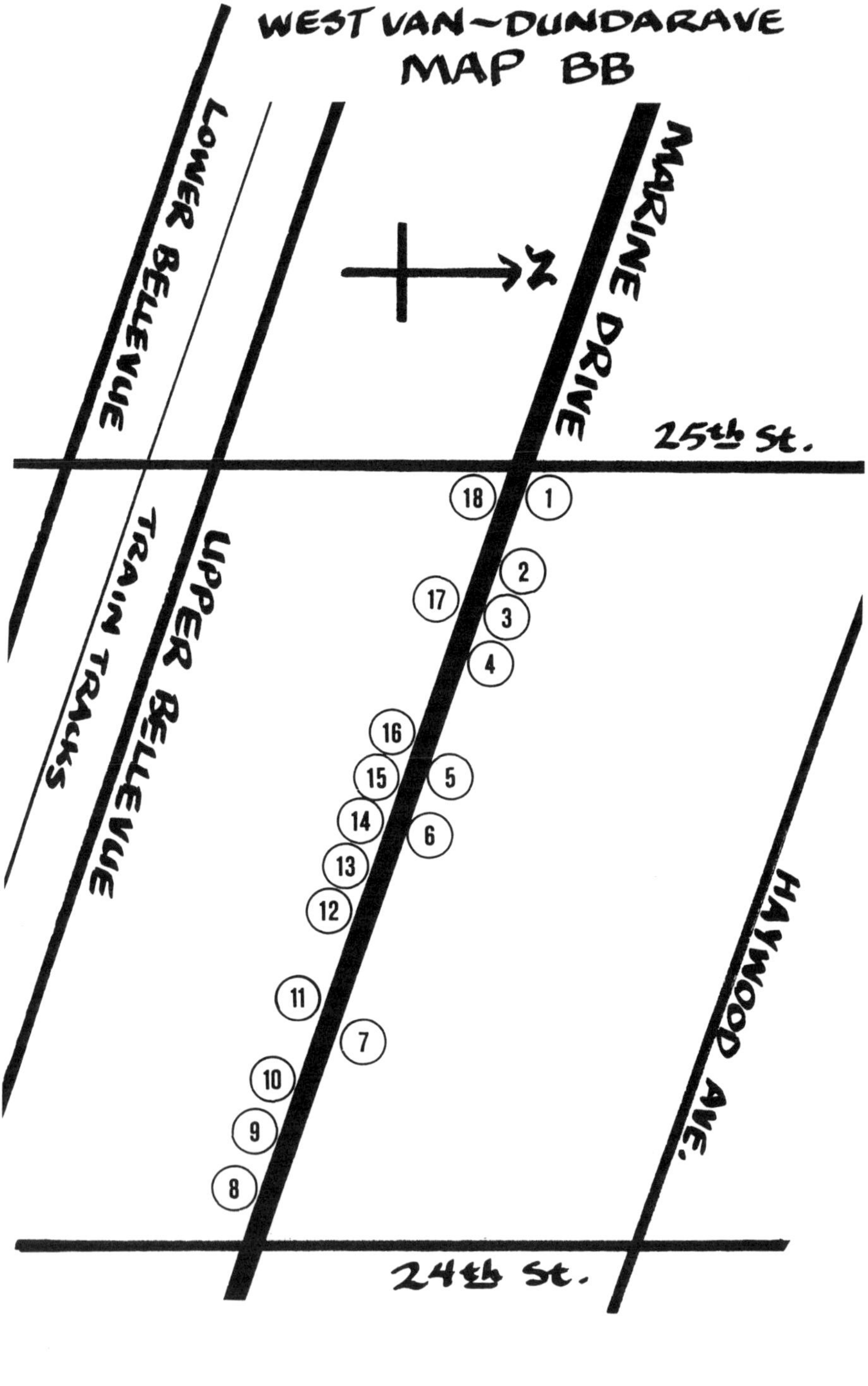
WEST VAN~DUNDARAVE
MAP BB
LOWER BELLEVUE
MARINE DRIVE
N
25th St.
TRAIN TRACKS
UPPER BELLEVUE
HAYWOOD AVE.
24th St.
1
2
3
4
5
6
7
8
9
10
11
12
13
14
15
16
17
18

Encore Fashion Boutique: 2445 Marine (922-2020). Women's consignment clothing as well as fashion accessories are located on the main floor of the shop, while children's and maternity wear are upstairs. Their standards are high and many items are like new. They have a long-standing reputation. Hours are Monday to Saturday 10 to 5. Map BB circle 6.

Casual Elegance Fashion Boutique: 2419 Marine (925-1254). Silk, wool, cotton and other natural fibre clothing are featured in this store — self-described as "for discriminating taste". Stock is mainly separates. Hours are Monday to Saturday 10 to 5; and Sunday noon to 5. Map BB circle 7.

Fashion Fair: 2404 Marine (926-3521). This is the newest and smallest of the consignment stores in this area (though it's been there a long time). In addition to women's clothing there are shoes, purses, books and bric-a-brac. Their display technique is somewhat haphazard. Open Tuesday to Saturday 10 to 4. Map BB circle 8.

Cottonental: 2416 Marine (925-0800). Featuring the Morati label, this local chain store carries all-cotton, women's casual clothing. Hours are Monday to Saturday 9:30 to 5:30. Map BB circle 9.

Bohemia Antiques: 2424 Marine (922-6020). This store is deceptively larger than it appears at first glance, as it winds around into several rooms behind the sales desk. They showcase a large collection of china, silver and collectables displayed on the antique furniture that makes up the backbone of their stock. We admired the collection of small silver snuff boxes in the window on our last visit. Open Monday to Saturday 10 to 5. Map BB circle 10.

The Studio Shop: 2436 Marine (925-1985). This place has an intriguing selection of giftware ranging from cards and kitchenware to locally-made felt hats and handknitted children's sweaters. We decided that they had lots of neat stuff — and that having only a few of each type of item made every offering seem more unique and special. We particularly liked the Ninja turtle sweaters at $50. Hours are Monday to Saturday 9:30 to 5:30. Map BB circle 11.

The Thread Bear: 2440 Marine (922-0308). Lorraine offered: "This is the kind of store that I want to have when I grow up!" There are quilt fabrics and supplies, home decorator fabrics, patterns and fabric for the most incredible stuffed bears and other animals we've ever seen, and inspiring samples already made up to inspire you. Our favourite was the cow dressed as a milkman. They also offer classes in quilting, jointed teddy bears, paper embossing and much more. A newsletter listing the classes is available in the store, or you may pick it up when they venture out to an annual show, like the Teddy Bear and Doll Show. Store hours are Monday to Saturday 9:30 to 5:30; and Sunday noon to 5. Map BB circle 12.

Alpine Meadows: 2444 Marine (922-1413). This is not a very large store, but what there is of it is crammed with every imaginable item required by the serious or recreational runner: Shorts, shoes, shirts and more. The staff seems particularly knowledgeable. A bulletin board in the store carries notices of up-coming running events. Open Monday to Saturday 10 to 6. Map BB circle 13.

Dundarave Bakery: 2454 Marine (922-7533). Here we found fresh pastries and yummies, homemade-looking pies, bread and Cornish pasties, which we taste-tested and found almost as good as the ones we tried in Cornwall! Open Monday to Saturday 9 to 5:30. Map BB circle 14.

The Cherry Tree: 2458 Marine (925-1650). Large stuffed animals lounge at the entrance, leading you to this sweet gift shop with its cards, glassware and pottery — all interesting, quality stock. Hours are Monday to Saturday 10 to 5:30. Map BB circle 15.

Amber Bookshop: 2460A Marine (926-1133). This shop is located downstairs (signs on the sidewalk direct you down), and French doors open out into the street behind. They offer a good children's collection, attractive book displays and a worthwhile selection of local interest volumes, including our own Cheap Eats! Hours are Monday to Saturday 9:30 to 5:30. Map BB circle 16.

Pebbles Children's Wear: 2468 Marine (922-0613). Rather rich for our pocketbooks, this place does carry sizes newborn to size 16 (boys' and girls') in such distinguished labels as Mexx, Vuarnet and Ocean Pacific. Open Monday to Saturday 10 to 5:30; and Sunday 11 to 5. Map BB circle 18.

Capers: 2496 Marine (925-3316). Mention West Van dining and everyone in the know says "Capers". When Lorraine last visited, they were giving out samples of organically-raised corn — the best she ever tasted! The coffee bar offers cappuccino and espresso, as well as wheat grass juice and carrot juice. They sell a large selection of fresh organically-grown produce that looks perfect. There's also a full line of organic packaged goods. They have pretty much pioneered the notion of healthy, fresh westcoast-style foods in the lower mainland and continue that tradition seven days a week from 8 a.m. to 7 p.m. Map BB circle 19.

White Rock

Country charm and bargains

This is a major tour for which you should allow between four and five hours, if you hope to take in every stop.

North Bluff Road is the dividing point between South Surrey and White Rock.

White Rock may be reached simply by following Hwy. 99 South directly to the two main turnoffs for White Rock (clearly marked exits from the highway), or, for American visitors, White Rock is the first community north of the border crossing at Douglas (Peace Arch).

It is a long journey to White Rock via public transit, but it can be accomplished, right from downtown Vancouver. Take the #351 / Crescent Beach bus on Howe St. (at Pender) direct (it runs every half hour days, hourly in the evening), or take the SkyTrain to 22nd St. Station in New West, and then transfer to the #353 / Ocean Park bus into White Rock. The latter bus runs only during the daytime. Either route will take you about an hour.

For those who fancy a Kerrisdale-type shopping experience (high quality goods and matching prices), find Windsor Square, a new shopping mall complex with store fronts facing onto 152nd between 20th and 19th Avenues.

Generally speaking, the nicest items are to be found in shops at the crest of the hill, with quality declining with the grade of the road. Many places offer Seniors' discounts.

Street parking in White Rock is generally easy on weekdays.

Black Bond Books: 15142 North Bluff (538-2211). This quality bookstore has been in White Rock as long as we can remember. Outside, there's a sale rack and markdown tables inside sometimes offer values as much as 70 percent off list. A good selection of current favourites, too. Open Monday to Saturday 9:30 to 5:30. Map CC circle 1.

By the Crate Warehouse Outlets: 15136 North Bluff (536-0488). A strange combination of goods is offered here (mainly clothing), including sportswear and T-shirts, but also encompassing table bases and decorating supplies, toys and accessories -- AND -- a cappuccino bar! Hours are Monday to Thursday and Saturday 9 to 5:30; Friday 9 to 8. Map CC circle 2.

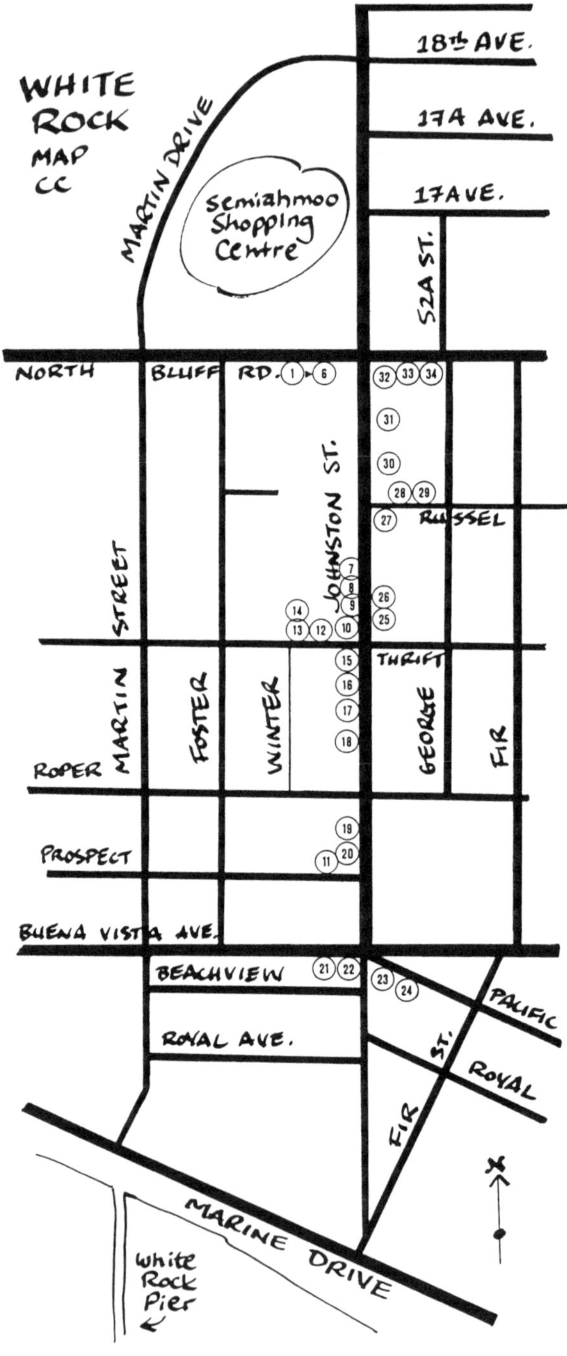
WHITE ROCK MAP CC
18th AVE.
17A AVE.
17 AVE.
MARTIN DRIVE
Semiahmoo Shopping Centre
52A ST.
NORTH BLUFF RD.
JOHNSTON ST.
RUSSEL
MARTIN STREET
THRIFT
FOSTER
WINTER
GEORGE
FIR
ROPER
PROSPECT
BUENA VISTA AVE.
BEACHVIEW
PACIFIC
ROYAL AVE.
ROYAL
FIR ST.
MARINE DRIVE
White Rock Pier
N
1
6
7
8
9
10
11
12
13
14
15
16
17
18
19
20
21
22
23
24
25
26
27
28
29
30
31
32
33
34

Ocean Pacific Lighting: 101-1645 140th (538-3511). Here's a good place for lamps and fixtures, open Monday to Thursday 9 to 5:30; Friday 9 to 8; and Saturday 9 to 5. Map CC circle 3.

Buns Master: 1534 Foster (538-2277). Typical Buns Master assortment of fresh breads, rolls, cookies, pizza bases, cheese sticks, cinnamon buns, pies and even bagels. The shop is downstairs from street level. Open seven days 8 to 6. Map CC circle 4.

La Boutique 2: 1544 Foster (531-1125). Anne has had a lot of reader commentary (all favourable) about this consignment store, which features really nice shoes, clothing and accessories, but unfortunately, as one reader pointed out "it smells like a thrift shop!" Open Monday and Wednesday to Saturday 11 to 5; closed Tuesday. Map CC circle 5.

The Gallery Art Supplies: 1556 Foster (531-8226). This art supplier also sells prints, pottery, framing and some fine photos and original water colours. Hours are Monday to Friday 9 to 6; and Saturday 9 to 5. Map CC circle 6.

Little Folks Shop: 1483 Johnston (538-0698). Here's a fine source for distinctive children's wear, from infant to size 16. Open Monday to Thursday and Saturday 9:30 to 5:30; and Friday 9 to 9. Map CC circle 7.

White Rose Book Store: 1481 Johnston (531-7353). This store specializes in old, new and rare books. Unfortunately, items in the fine display of Indian artifacts are not for sale. Open Monday to Saturday 10 to 5:30. Map CC circle 8.

Touches: 1479 Johnston (531-3142). Aptly named, this shop combines decorator touches with the finest bed, bath, table and kitchen linens, quilts and gift items. Hours are Monday to Saturday 9:30 to 5:30. Map CC circle 9.

The Jumping Bean Coffee & Gifts: 1461 Johnston (535-1199). A store for every taste, this one sells chocolates by Daniel from Le Chocolat Belge, a wide assortment of gift mugs, gourmet coffee and cards and stationery. Tuesdays, seniors get a 10 percent discount. Open Monday to Saturday 9 to 6. Map CC circle 10.

Peace Arch Hospital Superfluity Shop: 15167 Prospect (no phone). Many consider this the best thrift shop in the lower mainland, and our White Rock connections, Rick and Betty Forchuk enthusiastically agree! Hours are Tuesday to Friday 10:30 to 3; and Saturday 10:30 to 2. Map CC circle 11.

Feathers Ladies Wear: 1457B Johnston (531-6988). A traditional ladies' wear shop, this one spotlights lots of Alta and Mr. Leonard separates and suits. Open Monday to Saturday 9:30 to 5:30. Map CC circle 12.

Beads Galore: 1457 Johnston (536-5400). Beads, findings, semi-precious stones and classes highlight this stop in Hillcrest Mall. Create your own jewellery and save. Hours are Monday to Saturday 10:30 to 5:30. Map CC circle 13.

Hillcrest Bakery: 1421 Johnston (531-1750). At the rear of Hillcrest mini-mall you'll find fresh muffins, baked goods and a diet loaf at only $1.10. The great smell of fresh baking is free! Open Monday to Friday 8:30 to 6; and Saturday 8:30 to 5. Map CC circle 14.

The Thrift Shop: 1383 Johnston (531-5464). Mostly clothing here, partitioned off from Ray's Barber's (at the back) are great bargains. You can fill a bag for $5! Hours are Monday to Friday 8:30 to 5:30; Saturday 8 to 5. Map CC circle 15.

Country Sun Natural Foods: 1377 Johnston (531-1112). Natural foods, books on health, bulk food and organic produce are featured here, plus (or should we say 'minus'?) there's a ten percent discount on vitamins. Open Monday to Saturday 9 to 5:30. Map CC circle 16.

Rochelle's Needlecraft: 1367 Johnston (536-6211). Here you'll find needlecraft supplies, kits, floss and wool and custom framing. Open Tuesday to Saturday 10 to 5. Map CC circle 17.

Salvation Army Thrift Shop: 1335 Johnston (531-6494). The usual assortment of bric-a-brac and discards are here -- plus some great finds, if you're persistent. They advertise "big discounts on furniture" and their pricing policy seems to bear that slogan out. The store is modest for a Sally Ann, but sometimes full of great items. Open Monday to Saturday 9 to 5. Map CC circle 18.

Kidazzles: 1253 Johnston (531-7931). This is a great consignment store showcasing children's and maternity wear (some new items made by cottage industry in the neighbourhood), plus much-needed maternity rentals. Some of the new items are well marked-down at intervals, so watch for their sales. Hours are Monday to Wednesday 9 to 5; Thursday and Friday 9 to 9; Saturday 10 to 6; and Sunday noon to 4. Map CC circle 19.

The Livingroom Store: 1233 Johnston (536-3545). Run by the White Rock Christian Fellowship, this shop sells clothing, housewares, books and some new crafts at low prices. Open Monday to Saturday 10 to 3. Map CC circle 20.

The Attic: 15182 Buenavista (531-1135). They buy, sell and consign furniture, antiques and collectibles here. Hours are Monday to Wednesday 9:30 to 5:30; and Thursday to Saturday 9:30 to 5. Map CC circle 21.

Cash 2 U Liquidations Inc.: 1195 Johnston (536-4000). In this low-overhead atmosphere at Johnston and Buena Vista, you'll find toys, party supplies, giftware, odds'n'sods -- all very bargain basement, since goods are often in or on top of their shipping boxes. It's one of broadcaster and TV expert Rick Forchuk's favourite haunts. Forchuk and his wife Betty have discovered estate sale merchandise and many great "finds". Open Monday to Saturday 9:30 to 5. Map CC circle 22.

Shaw's Feed & Seed: 15242 Pacific (537-3040). Spot the garden gnomes and pink flamingoes in the window and you've come to the right place! Here you'll find gardening and supplies galore. Hours are Monday to Saturday 9 to 5:30. Map CC circle 23.

White Rock Bread Box: 15228 Pacific (531-3116). This small and cosy shop looks like nothing so much as an old-timey country store, with its produce out in the covered back porch, cold meats, cheeses, bread and other baked goods, tarts and fresh sandwiches for sale. They've been a fixture in the neighbourhood for over 14 years. Open Monday to Saturday 9 to 5. Map CC circle 24.

Bamboos: 1456 Johnston Rd. (531-7697). Here's a good place for rattan, wicker and country crafts, silk plants, candles and many Asian imports. Open Monday to Saturday 10 to 5. Map CC circle 25.

Silly Sisters' Clothesline: 1468 Johnston (538-4475). The whimsical name belies a charming store featuring mainly women's (but also some children's and men's) clothing and accessories, alongside a full cappuccino bar selling 'capps' for only one dollar. When we visited, they were hosting a 'silly sale', with serious price reductions. Hours are Monday to Thursday and Saturday 9:30 to 6; Friday 9:30 to 8; and Sunday noon to 5. Map CC circle 26.

The Country Wreath: 15232 Russell (531-2232). This shop is a real charmer (one of our favourites), with its gorgeous country-style wreaths, country crafts and accent pieces for gift giving or self-indulgence. Open Monday to Saturday 9:30 to 5. Map CC circle 27.

Inside Story Fashions: 15239 Russell (536-2848). A double-wide store with an exclusive and European feel about it, this one sells women's designer clothing, shoes and accessories. Open Monday to Saturday 10 to 5:30. Map CC circle 28.

Irmengard's Fashions & Millinery: 15221 Russell (531-3617). Upmarket and mature fashions are the key here, with White Stag and London Fog among the women's labels we saw. There are some nice hats, too. Open Monday to Friday 9:30 to 5:30; and Saturday from 9:30 to 5. Map CC circle 29.

Casablanca Imports: 1542 Johnston (538-2053). Another lovely store with European imports such as Priani from Italy, this one sells designer clothing and accessories for women. Hours are Monday to Saturday 10 to 5:30 (hours vary here, so it might be wise to call ahead). Map CC circle 30.

Laura's Fashion Fabrics: 1552 Johnston (531-3293). A good source for fabric, sewing machines, supplies and notions, this one is open Monday to Saturday 9:30 to 5:30. Map CC circle 31.

Sunflyer Gift Gallery: 15216 North Bluff (535-1545). A nicely set-out store, this one sells local carvings, gift items, pottery, stained glass and candles. Hours are Monday to Saturday 10 to 5:30. Map CC circle 32.

Collector's Gallery: 15222 North Bluff (538-7216). Here's our choice for the serious collector: collectors' plates, giftwares, and an interesting assortment of limited edition ceramic animal heads. Open Monday to Friday 9:30 to 5:30; and Saturday 9:30 to 5. Map CC circle 33.

Cheri's, of Course: 15226 North Bluff (538-2255). Stylish and contemporary, the women's fashions here are available in sizes 4 to 18. Many are designer labels, and run the gamut from office clothing to formal. Open Monday to Saturday 10 to 5:30. Map CC circle 34.

Whitby's Bookstore & Coffeehouse: 14837/14829 Marine Dr. (536-3711, 536-3713). This place topped the Province poll for new age shops. It sells books, tapes, calendars, crystals and art and rents video tapes. In the coffee house next door to the shop, there are wonderfully nutritious foods and specialty coffees. According to Province reader and White Rock resident Barbara Underwood, owner Lynette Wilson "has encouraged local people to think of the location as their personal retreat. There are various activities offering anyone interested an opportunity to enhance their lifestyle through personal growth...Tai Chi, Yoga, course of miracles, etc." Store open Monday to Friday 10 to 9; weekends 10 to 5:30; Coffee house open Monday to Friday 8 a.m. to 10 p.m.; and weekends 8 a.m. to 5:30 p.m. Map CC circle 35.

Yaletown

"Insider" fashions and furniture

This is a small tour taking about two hours to complete. It might be fun to visit for the morning, ending your tour by dropping into our rest-stop, Johni's Bistro, for a quick lunch.

Stops in this area are close together, so you can walk the entire tour area in the time we've alloted.

"Yaletown" is a seedy area rapidly on its way up. In fact, my industrial real estate pal, Don Vassos, who runs CB Financial (one of our largest commercial and industrial real estate firms), claims that this is the new "in" area of the '90s.

Commercial buildings have been upgraded and filled with trendy businesses, artists' studios and residential lofts, and the building "in-fill" has been primarily posh residential condo high-rises, bringing to the area an urbane, active and well-heeled population quite different from only five years ago.

Many of the Yaletown buildings hide fine furniture treasures, fabrics and decorating accents you will have to see to believe! Vancouver's reputation for interior design today rivals that of New York, Paris, Milan, Rome and Chicago! These Yaletown businesses are wholesalers, but they blatantly sell to the public -- you and me, that is.

This is a serendipity area -- Mainland, for example, has a number of buildings other than the Showmart that house clothing agents -- it is not unusual to find hand-lettered signs spontaneously stuck up on a post or on a sandwich board on the street announcing a sample sale. Hottest times for these sales are November/December and May/June, following market week in New York, L.A. and in the Vancouver Showmart Building. Stock must be quickly flipped over at those times to make room for the new season's styles.

For furniture, if you work with a decorator, shop with him or her, as they can often get an additional discount and thereby reduce the fees they would normally get entirely from you. The crossroads of Yaletown are Hamilton and Davie, encompassing Homer, Mainland and even as far as Beatty. *The SkyTrain stop at B.C. Place is just a couple of blocks away, and many Vancouver buses (including the Greyhound terminal) service the area, as well.*

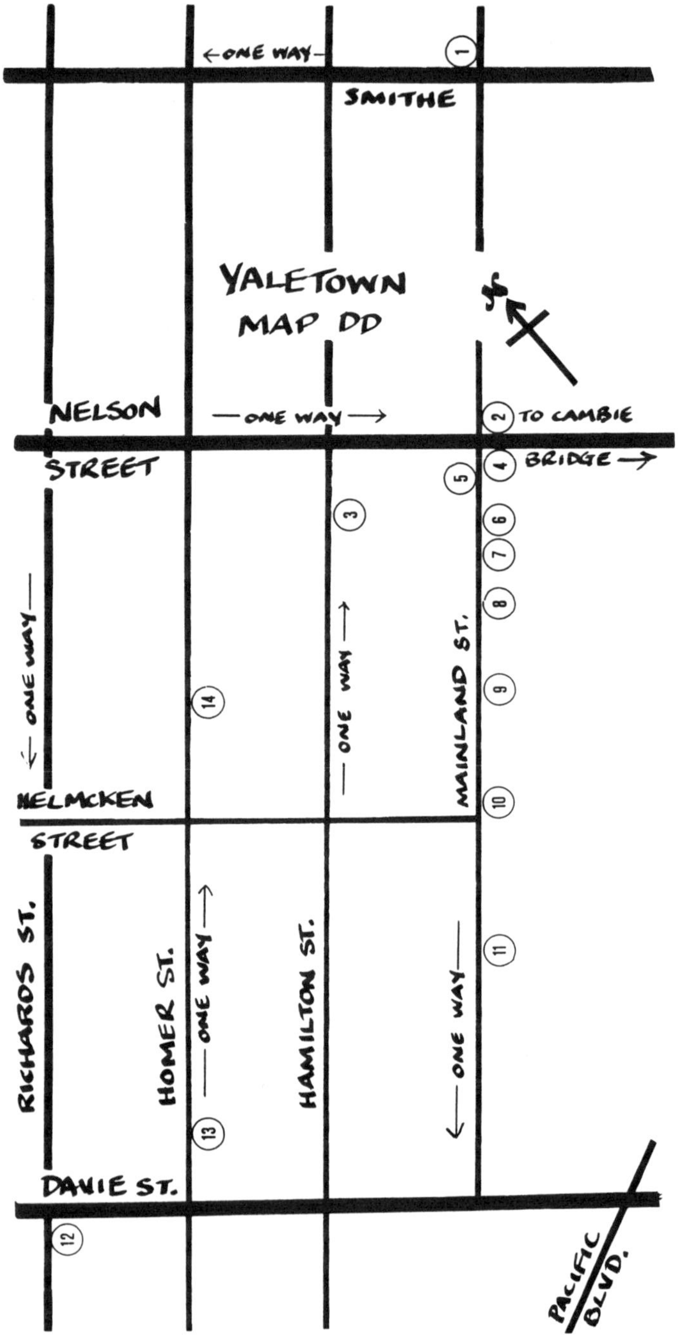

← ONE WAY
SMITHE
YALETOWN
MAP DD
NELSON
STREET
— ONE WAY →
TO CAMBIE
BRIDGE →
← ONE WAY —
— ONE WAY →
MAINLAND ST.
HELMCKEN
STREET
RICHARDS ST.
HOMER ST.
— ONE WAY →
HAMILTON ST.
← ONE WAY —
DAVIE ST.
PACIFIC
BLVD.
1
2
3
4
5
6
7
8
9
10
11
12
13
14

To reach Yaletown from the U.S., drive right into Vancouver via Highway 99 South and eventually you'll cross the Oak Street Bridge into the city. Follow Oak right down to West Broadway, turn left (west), and the next major intersection is Granville. At the street BEFORE Granville (Hemlock), turn right and follow the signs onto the Granville Street Bridge. This takes you into the downtown area. As you exit the Bridge, keep to the right and take the Seymour Street exit (first possible right), watch for cars entering your lane from the right at the end of the next block (Drake) stay in the right lane. Turn right at the following corner onto Davie and you're on the outskirts of Yaletown.

Yaletown showrooms are mainly open from 9 to 5 (or 6) weekdays only.

Metered parking is available on the street. Don't be fooled by apparently-available diagonal parking in front of the loading docks on Mainland -- this is private parking and illegally-parked cars do get regularly (and promptly) ticketed.

Among the furniture showrooms and fashion outlets in the Yaletown area are:

<u>Moratti:</u> 883 Hamilton (688-0431). They have periodic sales -- sometimes at this location, and sometimes in a hotel suite rented for that purpose (ask to be put on their phone-out list). The focus is on clothing: Casual and lots of cottons. Map DD circle 1.

<u>Showmart Building:</u> 910 Mainland. This building is technically closed to the general public, but a notice board a half flight up from the main door announces sales events. Note: Do not disturb offices unless a sale sign is posted at the door! Open Monday to Friday (wholesale hours vary) only. Map DD circle 2.

<u>Yaletown Interiors:</u> 1004 to 1020 Hamilton (669-7544). The focus here is on fine home furnishings, leather upholstered furniture, lamps and objets d'art. Open Monday to Saturday 9:30 to 6; and Sunday 11 to 5. Map DD circle 3.

<u>The Sample Room:</u> 1000 Mainland (662-7626). Johni De Groot began this enterprise as the first outlet of its kind in the old Showmart building and graduated to wonderful expanded premises a few years ago. The operation keeps expanding, in fact, as Johni adds on with bistro, bar and bakery to make the experience of shopping there even more user-friendly than it already was! This is where all the visiting movie stars shop for bargains, because it was long ago discovered by local filmmakers and show biz types.

Agents and manufacturers basically wouldn't dream of selling to anyone else -- turnover here is rapid. The Sample Room takes a tiny slice of a commission and delivers the goods to grateful consumers at savings of 35 to 50 percent off retail -- or even less. Many are one-of-a-kind samples, all in sample sizes and all first-quality.

Johni also sells a luxury line of leather garments at what must be the lowest prices (for high-quality, that is) in Canada. Open Monday and Tuesday 9 to 5; Wednesday 9 to 8; Thursday and Friday 9 to 10; Saturday 9 to 9; and Sunday 11 to 6. Map DD circle 4.

Johni's Bistro is our designated rest stop on this tour. When you're shopping Yaletown and you need some sustenance, stop in to Johni's and remember to bring in your copy of The Serious Shopper's Guide. Show it to your server when you order, and you and your shopping companions will receive a two-for-one deal on your entrees. If two of you are shopping, one entree is free (same for three people -- one dines free), and if four of you dine together, TWO receive their meals free. Map DD circle 4.

Shoes by Folio: 1005 Mainland (689-7110). Owned by the Sample Room, this place sells shoes, purses, jewellery, and boots by famous name designers, at modest discounts. This is where Anne bought her show-stopping Anne Klein thigh-high boots for a fraction of their price in L.A.! Many of the styles are unique in Vancouver. Besides the famous name brands, they carry their own Folio line. Open Monday to Wednesday and Saturday 10 to 6; Thursday and Friday 10 to 8; and Sunday 11 to 5. Map DD circle 5.

Roche-Bobois: 1010 Mainland (669-5443). Certainly the shining star among furniture shops in Vancouver, people come from far and wide to visit Roche-Bobois and drool over their magnificent array of leading-edge super-designed furniture. And why not? Branches of the international chain are in Palm Beach, Madrid, London and Brussels, so their reputation stretches round the globe. It's furniture to die for -- high, high end, but gorgeous, all displayed in magazine-quality, inspirational groupings. Open Monday to Saturday 9:30 to 5:30. Map DD circle 6.

Bathscape Inc.: 1010B Mainland (688-8180). Maybe this IS where you'll find everything but the kitchen sink. Actually, they sell everything for the bathroom AND the bathroom sink! Included in the selection are towels, fixtures and accessories of every kind. Open Monday to Friday 9 to 5:30; and Saturday 10 to 5. Map DD circle 7.

Signature Interiors: 1028 Mainland (662-7100). Leather furniture and antique reproductions take centre-stage here, where we saw a four-poster bead with a leather bedspread. Open Monday to Friday 9 to 5; Saturday 10 to 4; and Sunday noon to 4. Map DD circle 8.

Ideal Interiors: 1036 Mainland (685-4207). Here we found objets d'art, classy furniture and even a mink bedspread! Open Monday to Friday 9:30 to 5; Saturday 10 to 5; and Sunday noon to 4. Map DD circle 9.

J. Collins: 1080 Mainland (685-8414) This well-established furniture house sells brass, china and accent pieces as well as their quality furniture. Open Monday to Saturday 9 to 5; and Sunday noon to 5. Map DD circle 10.

Showcase Kitchens: 1126 Mainland (684-6824). This is a great place for ideas. Open Monday to Friday 9 to 5; and Saturday 10 to 4. Map DD circle 11.

Wearhouse Warehouse: 590 Davie (681-5552). We're glad we got to include a few fashions stops in this furniture tour, because the finds are such bargains. This place always has sale racks at the back of the store, and everything else is discounted price anyway. Among the lines are Esprit, Mexx and Almost Heaven. There are some larger-sizes, though most of the stock tends to be medium-range sizes in women's and children's fashions. There are lots of samples, so those of us who can wear a sample size do well. Lorraine found one sample so fresh from the designer it even had a note pinned to it saying "try this again with a yoke"! Open Monday to Friday 10 to 5:30; Saturday 10 to 5; and Sunday noon to 5. Map DD circle 12.

Jana & Co. Imports: 1190 Homer (688-3657). We've been going to Jana sales for ages, but it still seems to be a well-kept secret. Not anymore! This import house has sweaters made in the Orient to their own specifications under the Maggie label and always has a room full of samples and ends of lines at greatly-reduced prices. Open Monday to Friday 8:30 to 5. Map DD circle 13.

Wall to Wall Kids Clothing: 1062 Homer (687-7517). This place sells goods from manufacturers of kids clothing (like Please Mum), and while they do hold periodic sales, the factory has a sales area open during the week everyday. Open Monday to Friday 10 to 4:30. Map DD circle 14.

NOTES:

Antiques, Used Furniture and Chatchkahs

Parts of the lower mainland abound with fabulous antiques, Canadiana, collectables and wonderful junk you can't imagine that anyone else would throw out. But as the old saying goes: One person's trash is another's treasure. And so it goes.

A few particular crossroads are particularly fertile hunting ground. Please also refer to our area tours of Lower Lonsdale, Almadene, Langley, Steveston and Cloverdale.

Other areas are worth checking out: Fort Langley (Anne's personal fave), Main Street north and south of about 27th Avenue (actually, we like this area lots, too), West 4th Avenue near Alma (also go to *Sellution* at 2765 West 4th, a favourite haunt of cookbook author Kasey Wilson), and Gastown (go see Anne's friend Del at *Windsor Antique Furniture & Restoration* who brought her favourite swivel office chair back from the dead).

It's a good idea to check out the auction listings in the daily newspapers, and we find the local weeklies good tip-sheets for thrift sales, antique sales and estate sales in areas we don't usually visit.

Garage sales yield some amazing finds (if you know what to look for) and Anne personally saw a woman cart away an 80-year-old solid oak shoeshine table which opened up to reveal a little metal footrest with all the original shoeshine stuff still snuggled underneath — for a measly four bucks! Don't be seduced into assuming that the Shaughnessy garage sales are the best one, either. We've yet to discover a single well-priced "find" there.

The best sales tend to be in the slightly nouveau riche pockets of Dunbar, Kerrisdale and South Granville or in the British Properties in West Van. Some of the newspaper claims in ads for these sales are somewhat overblown — we find it better to drive around and spontaneously look for signs on boulevards and main intersections.

Periodic collectors' sales are well advertised and offer great variety, if few bargains.

Before heading out, it's a good idea to do some reading. We've found a number of informative books on antiques at *Book Warehouse,* and of course, there's a great current selection on Canadiana and Canadian antiques at the library.

Asian Restaurants

This section really has nothing to do with shopping, but we thought if you are visiting from another area, you might enjoy some of the vast choices among Asian cooking styles available in Vancouver. Here are the main areas:

Chinatown: Vancouver's Chinatown is second only in size to San Francisco's in all of North America. Obviously, the choices here are many, but they're mainly in the Cantonese style, or else they are soup houses or noodle shops. There are many bun shops (our favourite is *Loong Foong* on Keefer) with a small seating area in the rear and low, low prices for food.

Crossroads for Vancouver's Chinatown are Main and Pender, with the area branching into many streets and sidestreets beyond. *By public transit, take the #22 north on Burrard or the #19 east on Pender.*

Mount Pleasant/Kingsway: Just a drive down Kingsway from about 7th Avenue southward, or a tour of Fraser Street from the Kingsway junction (where 16th Ave. would be) reveals many choices: Vietnamese, Japanese, Korean, Thai, Malaysian, Cambodian, Sri Lankan, East Indian (especially near 41st and Main or Fraser), Indonesian, and of course versions of Chinese like Mandarin, Cantonese, Szechuan, and Hot Pot. The word for soup in some of these places is Pho, which is often in the name of the restaurant. In addition, there are many Asian seafood restaurants where freshness is the key word.

By public transit, the Fraser #8 runs up to Fraser from Hastings and Granville, and the #19 Metrotown runs to Kingsway from Granville and Pender.

Richmond: Elsewhere in this text, we'd alluded to the Asian influence in this area. In fact, the new Aberdeen Centre is like nothing so much as our memories of Aberdeen near Hong Kong. Aberdeen Centre is anchored by the now-famous *Top Gun Restaurant*, as well as a Chinese cafe and a Japanese restaurant.

Aberdeen Centre is located near Cambie Road and No. 3 Road, not far from the airport.

Park Road in Richmond Centre is loaded with Chinese restaurants, including another *Top Gun* and many other versions of Asian food. It's up near the newly-revamped and expanded Richmond Centre Mall. *To get there by public transit from Vancouver, take the #401, #403 or #406 on Howe Street.*

Then, there's the strip mall just north of Lansdowne (look northward from the doorway of *Woodwynn*, in fact, and you're looking right at it), which among other Asian restaurants features the incredible *Mongolie Grill*—what an experience (and good food, too). *For public transit, take the #403 or #406 from Howe, downtown.*

Japantown: This is near Oppenheimer Park on Powell a few blocks east of Main. It isn't a very nice area after dark, but there is a great food bargain to be had in the *Japanese Deli House* (all you can eat sushi for a set price), and many Japanese food stores worth browsing in during the day. By public transit, The #4 Powell or the #8 Davie bus will take you into the area from downtown.

Carpets, Rugs and Carpeting

This is another consumer area where you should be well-informed before you head out.

We've learned a number of things about area carpeting. One is: have it delivered. Another is: don't try to lay it yourself unless you're VERY handy and very confident. It's a bear of a job!

In the rug department, many, many claims are made about a rug's value, and very, very few of these are bona fine. So, go to a reputable dealer. Bone up on rug lore before heading out. And if you must buy at auction, really examine the goods at the previewing before getting swept away with auction fever.

Among the best areas for large-area carpeting are Bridgeport Road (We like *Bridgeport Carpets* the best) near No. 5 Road in Richmond; Terminal Avenue in downtown eastside Vancouver; and parts of Vancouver's Clark Drive near Grant and Gravely. You can virtually drive from store to store to comparison shop, and most have remnants cut from larger installations for a good discount off the original price.

For fine carpets, most of the action is in the South Granville area, near Granville and West Broadway, and again, you can visit from shop to shop in a matter of half an hour. There are also some fine carpet dealers in the downtown area, and some good dealers on Marine Drive in North Van.

Fresh Fruit

This section encompasses everything from fruit right off the farm to good, bulk discounters in town. If you want real values, however, you'll have to drive into the Okanagan or at least up the Fraser Valley to Sardis and Mission. Here are a few areas closer to home:

Fruit Stands: Among the best areas for fruit stands are along No. 5 Road, Steveston Highway and Cambie Road in Richmond. As the weather warms up, these little businesses spring to attention. To take advantage of this shopping adventure, you'll really have to drive.

Another good area is along Marine Drive (not Marine Way) in Burnaby, where you'll find our "fave" *Hop On Farms*, along with three or four others, all selling farm-fresh produce and fruit.

Along Hwy. 10 (Westminster Highway) from Richmond to New West there are literally dozens of U-picks and fruit stands, in season.

Further out in the Valley, you'll start seeing signs for U-picks and fruit stands from TransCanada 1. Prices are very low, especially at U-picks. Some require that you call ahead and bring your own ice cream buckets. Check daily newspapers in the classifieds for details from June to September.

Public Markets: Some of these are tourist attractions and we were certainly among the early ones who said they'd never work (we were wrong!), but there's also a good variety of produce trucked right in on the farmer's truck that morning. Most of these markets work in a manner that dictates that many of the "good" locations in the market are leased by year-round tenants, and then there are lesser locations where tables are set up and rented on a weekly or seasonal basis. The prices are usually better (and the produce fresher) at the latter.

Among the active markets are:

Bridgepoint Market: This relatively-new development sits on the water in Richmond. *You can see it as you near the end of the Oak Street Bridge, entering Richmond.* See our "malls" section for details.

Granville Island Public Market: (666-5784). The award-winning development is the biggest of our indoor markets, and very crowded on weekends. *By transit, take the #50 south from Granville Mall.* Open Tuesday to Sunday 9 to 6; closed Monday.

Lonsdale Quay Public Market: It's at 123 Carrie Cates Court in North Van (985-6261) — and you can *take the SeaBus* right there from downtown Vancouver. Everything from fashions to gifts and fresh produce is displayed in clean, wide-open aisles. There's a special area just for children, too. Open Monday to Thursday and weekends 9:30 to 6:30; Friday 9:30 to 9.

Robson Public Market: 1610 Robson (at Cardero, 682-2733). This market combines local artisans, fresh baking, gourmet foods, specialty wines, fish-mongers and the ambience of an open-air market all under a vaulted glass atrium. *Take the #3 Robson from Granville Mall.* Open seven days 9 to 9.

Surrey Public Market: *Take the SkyTrain to Scott Road station and transfer to #321 bus.* Open Tuesday to Sunday 10 to 6; closed Monday.

Westminster Quay Public Market: There's free two-hour parking out front; see the New West tour for highlights. *By transit, take the SkyTrain to the New Westminster station.* Open Monday to Thursday and weekends 9:30 to 6:30; Friday 9:30 to 8.

White Rock Public Market: This quaint market overlooks Semiahmoo Bay. *SkyTrain takes you to 22nd St. Station; transfer to #353 bus.* Open longer hours in the summer.

Other places for fresh produce: A number of places just east of the "yuppie" Safeway at Broadway and MacDonald (notably *Broadway Produce* at 3287 West Broadway, and *Best Quality Produce* at 3151 West Broadway) sell remarkably fresh and inexpensive produce and do such a booming business that they can afford to always have something reduced even further!

Try *Kea Market* on Broadway near Main and *Wellcome Market* on Kingsway.

We also like *South Arm Farmer's Market* for cheap year-round prices and *Richmond Country Farms* for amazingly cheap corn on the cob in summer — each is on Steveston Hwy.

Then there's *Sunrise Market* down in Japantown at 300 Powell where the chefs all used to go at dawn to fight over the freshest produce as it was unloaded from the trucks (now they mostly go to Granville Island because of its proximity to downtown).

Shopping for Furniture

Rather than give you specific tours in this section, we've decided that a better strategy is to tell you the best general areas, when to shop, and how to get there. You'll quickly discover that stores in these areas are almost side by side, so these are the ideal places for comparison shopping, buy-it-all-in-a-day, and filling in the finishing touches on a project or room.

High End:

By far the best high end areas are South Granville and Yaletown.

To reach South Granville from the U.S., drive right into Vancouver via Highway 99 South and eventually you'll cross the Oak Street Bridge into the city. Follow Oak right down to West Broadway, turn left (west), and the next major intersection is Granville.

To reach Yaletown, follow the same directions, only at the street BEFORE Granville (Hemlock), turn right and follow the signs onto the Granville Street Bridge. This takes you into the downtown area. As you exit the Bridge, keep to the right and take the Seymour Street exit (first possible right), watch for cars entering your lane from the right at the end of the next block (Drake) stay in the right lane. Turn right at the following corner onto Davie and you're on the outskirts of Yaletown.

For South Granville and Yaletown stores, please see our full tours elsewhere starting on pages 127 and 193 respectively.

If you work with a decorator, shop with him or her, as they can often get an additional discount and thereby reduce the fees they would normally get entirely from you. The crossroads of Yaletown are Hamilton and Davie, encompassing Homer, Mainland and even as far as Beatty.

Yaletown showrooms are mainly open from 9 to 5 (or 6) weekdays only. Please read the Yaletown tour and call ahead to any shops that interest you.

Bargain Basement:

The best areas for el-cheapo furniture are along Main Street (see our section on antiques and used items for details), on Clark Drive between Grant and Venables (including the new outlet for the *SPCA Thrift shop* and *Low Price Furniture* nearby), around the corner on Venables near Commercial (our favourite name: *B & E Liquidators*), and a few really cheap stores near No. 3 Road and Alderbridge in Richmond.

There are a few clear-out places on Grandview Highway (the extension of East 12th Ave. in Vancouver) near the border to Burnaby (*Grantree Clearance Centre, Stacy's Warehouse,* etc.). Otherwise, Kingsway is a good place to look, as it abounds with liquidators, thrift stores and discounters. There are a few really excellent places in the two blocks around Fraser and Broadway in Vancouver, too.

Don't forget the locations of *Value Village* on Victoria Drive at 49th Ave., and also at Hastings, just west of Victoria and the *Salvation Army's* main branch at 12th Avenue and Sophia, just west of Main.

Mid-range:

In this category, we include the knock-down, grow-with-your-family type of furnishings that *Ikea* just about wrote the book on: Ikea, on Sweden Way, just west of the Richmond end of the Knight Street Bridge (if driving from Vancouver, exit at Bridgeport Road, as if going to the airport) is the obvious place to start -- it's as "user friendly" as they get! We never pass the place without checking to see what's in Ikea's "as-is" section.

Nearby, and all along Bridgeport, for that matter, you'll find Ikea imitators, oak specialists and places for children's furniture. Follow Bridgeport all the way to No. 3 Road (and on No. 3 around Lansdowne) for the total picture. West of No. 3 Road you'll also find *Stacy's* (beware of the high-powered salesmen!) and if you get even closer to the airport, you see *Segal's Furniture*, which is generally very fashionable and well-made.

North Van's Marine Drive is fairly good for mid-range furniture, particularly near Fell and Pemberton.

Richmond and North Van furniture stores are usually open longer hours than their Vancouver counterparts, often from 9:30 or 10 until 6 weekdays (Thursdays and Fridays to 9), 10 to 5:30 Saturdays, and noon to 4 or 5 Sundays. Again, these open-times are generalizations, so please call your favoured destination in advance.

Malls and Shopping Centres of the Lower Mainland

Many of the lower mainland's shopping malls are on handy transit routes, though if you're planning on packing around lots of shopping bags you might prefer to drive and take advantage of handy free parking at most of the malls located outside of downtown Vancouver itself. We've included directions, where they might prove helpful, and a brief overview of the types of stores you might expect to find at each.

Most of these malls would be welcome additions to nearby shopping tours in this edition, if you have the time for add-ons. Almost without exception, they include fine restaurants (or at the very least—quality fast food outlets). Public amenities such as clean restrooms are available, and many offer child-minding, play areas and rest areas (for grown-ups and little ones alike). Most malls are fully-accessible to the handicapped, and almost all of the larger department stores offer Mothers' Room facilities for the convenience of nursing moms and diaper-changing. To be sure if the mall you plan to visit meets your special requirements, please call ahead -- we've given administration office numbers for each, where available.

Note that hours may vary seasonally: many extend shopping hours before Christmas. Boxing Day sales (December 26, for American citizens not familiar with our Canadian holiday) inspire huge line-ups of bargain-hungry shoppers. Some places not generally open on Mondays will open if that day of the week is a public holiday -- and some close unexpectedly, so it's best to know what's what (or rather -- when's when).

Common "bankers'" holidays are New Year's Day (Jan. 1), Chinese New Year (second new moon of the western calendar year — in Chinatown, of course), Easter and Passover (usually in mid- April), Victoria Day (third Monday in May), Canada Day (July 1), B.C. Day (first Monday in August), Labour Day (first Monday in September), Thanksgiving Day (different in Canada, this is celebrated on the second Monday in October), Remembrance Day (in Eastern Canada, it's common to continue with business as usual; in B.C. this is usually a public holiday: Nov. 11), Christmas Day and Boxing Day (as above). Some stores are closed on these holidays, others are open with special sales events.

Ethnic areas have their own special days: Epiphany—Jan. 6 (Russian & Ukranian), Robbie Burns Day (Scots), St. Patrick's Day (Irish), St. Jean Baptiste Day (French), Guy Fawkes Day (English), and so on.

Aberdeen Centre:

(273-1234)

If this isn't like a mini-Hong Kong, we don't know what is. In fact, we've seen some of these same stores in Admiralty Centre and Pacific Place in Hong Kong. The main anchors are not stores at all, but a Chinese restaurant (very popular with the locals for dim sum) and bowling lanes, each called *Top Gun*. There's a movie house called the *Golden Princess Theatre* (279-9366). There are places for Chinese herbs and dried foods, typical Chinese toy and novelty stores and all the shops that will make you think of Aberdeen and the floating junk that took you to Jumbo Restaurant through the fog drifting in from Victoria Harbour. Find it at 130, 4400 Hazelbridge Way, near Cambie Road and No. 3 Road in Richmond, or *take the #407 bus from the Marpole loop in south Vancouver*. Mall hours are Sunday to Wednesday 11 to 7:30; and Thursday to Saturday 11 to 9:30.

Arbutus Village Square:

(732-4255)

Always one of the trendier westside malls, this one's main attraction is a very fine Safeway. There's also a *Duthie's Books, The Knit & Stitch Shoppe, Purdy's Chocolates, Woolly Gift Shoppe* and *Van den Bosch Patisserie & Bakery*. The whole place was redone recently with a glass atrium and marble decor closing in what used to be a rain-soaked open area in the winter. It's between King Edward and West 33rd Ave. at 4255 Arbutus, of course. *To reach it by bus take the #14 south on Granville Mall.* Mall hours are Monday to Wednesday and Saturday 10 to 6; Thursday and Friday 10 to 9; and Sunday noon to 5.

Bentall Centre Mall:

(661-5656)

Almost lost in the blur of downtown activity, this mall boasts 50 shops selling deli and ethnic food, chocolates, books, eyewear, clothing and jewellery. It's located at 595 Burrard at Dunsmuir, *just a few moment's walk from the Vancouver Trade & Convention Centre. From other areas, take the #1 or #22 bus which go right past it.* Open Monday to Friday usually 9:30 to 10 to 5:30.

Brentwood Mall:

(298-7314)

We have always liked Brentwood Mall for bargains. The main anchor is Eatons. Find it at 4567 Lougheed at Willingdon. *By public transit, take the #151 or #152 on Hastings or the #120 on Pender. Each ends at the bus loop right on site at the mall.* The mall itself looks like a circus tent from a distance. Inside you'll find *Zellers, Ingledew's Shoe Clearance Centre, Suzanne's* — high fashion at mark-down prices, *Pennington's* (large sizes), *Randy River, Reitman's, Shoppers Drug*

Mart and *Toys and Wheels,* among others. Hours are: Monday and Tuesday 10 to 6; Wednesday to Friday 10 to 9; Saturday 9:30 to 5:30 and Sunday noon to 5.

Bridgepoint Market:
(273-8500)
This largely undiscovered market and shopping concourse offers indoor and outdoor (patio) dining, a children's playground, and interesting "specialty" shopping, such as the unique and fabulous *Gourmet Away* (the best "Thai sauce" you'll ever try, plus incredible peanut butter brownies and reasonable catering, 276- 0355). Another place we like there is *Prickles and Palms Creations* — five foot tall "soft sculpture" cactuses and unusual ceramics and silk flowers. The Market is at 8811 River Road, Richmond, but *you must pretty well reach it by car* (there is ample free parking). The Fraser River tour goes from here to New West Quay. Open seven days 9 to 6.

Capilano Mall:
(980-8561)
This large mall at 935 Marine Dr., North Van is anchored by *Sears, Shoppers Drug Mart,* and *Coles, the Book People.* There is also a *Cotton Ginny, Fabricland, Grand and Toy and Le Chateau,* plus more. *By public transit, take the SkyBus to Lonsdale Quay and transfer to the #239 bus.* Hours are Monday to Wenesday 10 to 5:30; Thursday and Friday 10 to 9; Saturday 9:30 to 5:30; and Sunday noon to 5.

Champlain Mall:
(438-3308)
This revamped mall features *Zellers, SuperValu, Peoples Drug Mart, Purdy's* and *Grandma Lee's Bake Shop,* at 3200 East 54th Ave. *To get there by transit, take the SkyTrain to either Joyce Station or 29th Ave. Station and tranfer to the #26 bus which goes right to Champlain Mall.* Hours are Mounday, Tuesday and Saturday 9:30 to 5:30; Wednesday to Friday 9:30 to 9; and Sunday noon to 5.

City Square:
(876-5102)
Two stone heritage structures (the old "Normal School" buildings) were incorporated into the design of this mall located across from Vancouver's distinctive art deco period City Hall at 555 West 12th Ave. Convenient underground parking is free for the first two hours.

Chief anchor is a luxury *Safeway* store, and upstairs are temporary hawkers with all manner of funky hand-made goods, as well as unique stores like (for men) *The Windsor Knot* and *The Men's Club,* (for sweet-toothers) *Sweet William's Dessert Shop* and *Roxy Chocolate* (yum!), and stores such as *Black's Cameras, Daniadown* and *Fashion Addition. Public transit users should take the #15 bus south on Burrard.* Hours are Monday to Wednesday 10 to 6; Thursday and Friday 10 to 9; Saturday 9:30 to 6; and Sunday noon to 5 (except for Safeway which is open seven days 8 a.m. to midnight).

Columbia Square:
(521-3304)
This mall development is anchored by a big *London Drugs* and an *IGA* store. Most of the tenants are restaurants and medical or dental offices, so hours vary dramatically. Many match London Drugs'(520-9003) hours, of course: Monday to Saturday 9 am to 10 pm; and Sunday 11 to 8. *Find it within walking distance of the SkyTrain's Columbia Station.*

Coquitlam Centre:
(464-1414)
Province reader Jacquie Ponsart swears that Coquitlam Centre's *Darlings Ice Cream Parlour* (464-6531) is "the best real Italian ice cream I have ever experienced!!'

Coquitlam Centre, at 2929 Barnet Hwy., Coquitlam, is the showpiece of lower mainland malls, with sweeping views, many- tiered atriums and beautiful scupture and art throughout mall concourses. Its main anchors are *Woodward's, Eatons, Shoppers Drug Mart* and *The Bay.* It also offers other amenities, such as a child-minding service and food fair. Some special shops are: *Aunt Bob's Old-Fashion Cinnamon Rolls* (like the ones at the P.N.E.), *Birks Jewellers, The Body Shop, Coles, Fairweather, The Home Team* (team T's and sweats), *Ingledew's* (a wonderful selection of high-fashion shoes), *Ronson's Shoes* (many choices for hard-to-fit feet), *W.H. Smith books*, and one of our favourites, *The Sock Drawer.*

To reach Coquitlam Centre by bus, catch the #160 (eastbound on Hastings) at Hastings and Granville. It goes right there, but the trip will take at least one hour, more in heavy traffic. Open hours are Monday, Tuesday and Saturday 9:30 to 5:30; Wednesday to Friday 9:30 to 9; and Sunday 11:30 to 5.

Crossroads Shopping Centre:
(872-0999)
For some reason, this area seems always to get overlooked and we can't understand why. There's free parking (underground, off 8th Ave., and in the small courtyard area off Broadway), there are some good stores, and it certainly is at the crossroads: just west of Cambie on the north side of Broadway. We modestly hope mentioning it in this book helps.

The main anchor is *Dots Discount Ladies Wear* (874-2454), but there's also a liquor branch, a location of *Las Vegas Discount Golf and Tennis,* and *Renatta Wig and Hair Boutique,* one of the few places in the lower mainland that will rent some of its wigs prior to Hallowe'en (872-1844). Dots maintains the longest open hours (Monday to Wednesday and Saturday 9:30 to 5:30; Thursday and Friday 9:30 to 9; and Sunday noon to 5), but some of the other Crossroads stores are open late, as well.

To reach the area by public transit, take the #17 Oak bus from Robson, Pender or Cambie across the Cambie bridge and get off the bus at Broadway.

<u>Eaton Centre Metrotown:</u>
(438-4715)
This has to be our favourite mall, and the one that we find most user-friendly: It's chock full of amenities, such as kiddie rides in many passageways (and an old fashioned, instant photo booth inside the Central Avenue entrance near *Eatons*), and that wonderful Dancing With Your Shadow wall in the food fair (free high-tech entertainment where kids and adults alike are irresistably drawn into spontaneous performance).

Eaton Centre Metrotown is the home of Western Canada's only *Brettons* store (a scaled-down version of Seattle's delightful Nordstrom), *Brussels Chocolates, The Candy Factory, Japan Camera Centre* (where the photo for this book was taken), *Cookies by George, Real Canadian Super Store* and of course, *Eatons.* We like *Kim-John Gifts & China* for top-quality, bargain-priced tableware (call 431-7822 if you're after a special pattern), *RSVP* stationers for writing supplies, funny cards and novelties, and *Tall Girl* ladies wear, because we're tall-ish. There's free parking on site, much of it conveniently under cover.

All roads lead to Metrotown (in this case, all buses, and the SkyTrain), or you can take the #19 bus east on Pender and end up at 4700 Kingsway, Burnaby, too. Mall hours are Monday, Tuesday and Saturday 9:30 to 5:30; Wednesday to Friday 9:30 to 9; and Sunday noon to 5.

<u>Gastown:</u>
(Gastown Business Improvement Society: 683-5650)
This touristy shopping area pinpoints the birthplace (or rebirth) of Vancouver after a devastating fire leveled the city in 1886. Today its distinctive Victorian architecture is protected by heritage legislation, and the cobbled street is lined with funky boutiques and fashionable shops and restaurants. Of interest is the Steam Clock at Cambie and Water Streets, and courtyards or shopping promenades like The Mews, The Courtyard, Le Magazine. Maple Tree Square and The

Landing — the last is described more fully elsewhere in this section.

To reach the area, take the SkyTrain to Waterfront Station or the #50 bus north on Granville Mall. You can also take the #1 bus north on Burrard, or Gastown is a four-minute walk from the Vancouver Visitor and Convention Centre and the Pan Pacific or Waterfront Hotels.

Granville Island: (666-5784). This adventure in shopping is unlike any you'll ever take. You'll find yourself surrounded with water views, bobbing fishing boats and pleasure craft and happy faces on relaxed locals who realize daily how lucky they are to live in close proximity to this wonderful public amenity. The Granville Street and Burrard Street bridges pass overhead and the Cambie Street bridge is visible off to the east. It's a very pleasant place to shop and browse.

Shops are mostly converted shipping warehouses, or newly-constructed replicas in keeping with the seafront style of Granville Island. Buildings which house retail operations must also conform to the image, and rugged, weathered signs proclaim The Net Loft (featuring the amazing *Beadworks* shop, the fabricpainting and dyeing fabrics and fashions of *Maiwa Handprints* and 12 other businesses representing arts and crafts, native art, kitchen ware, books and gifts), *Crystal Ark, Kids Only Market* (see below) and the glorious *South China Seas Trading Company* (expensive but worth it and Kay's expert advice and recipes are free). Granville Island shops are generally open daily from 10 to 6, but many are closed Mondays. *To reach the area by public transit, take the #50 bus south on Granville Mall.*

Guildford Town Centre:
(584-4890)
This large mall at 104th Ave. and 152nd St. in Surrey is anchored by *Woodward's, Eatons, Zellers, London Drugs* and a *Woodwynn* across the parking lot -- not actually in the mall. Mall shops include the *Canucks' Winning Spirit* retail store (T's and sweats from league teams in hockey, baseball, football, etc., plus the Card Doctor for free advice on sportscard collecting), *Benetton, Cotton Ginny, Hans Christian Toys, House of Knives* (one of our favourites), *W.H. Smith books, the Sony Store* and a range of movie theatres. *To reach Guildford, take the SkyTrain to Scott Road station and transfer to the #320 or #330 bus.* Mall hours are Monday, Tuesday and Saturday 9:30 to 5:30; Wednesday to Friday 9:30 to 9; and Sunday noon to 5.

Harbour Centre Mall:
(689-7304)
Located directly across from the SkyTrain Waterfront station and SeaBus terminal, this mall at 555 West Hastings seems well-located

to take advantage of the tourist trade. Hours are Monday to Saturday 10 to 6.

Kensington Square Shopping Centre:
(294-1410)
Over 30 convenient shops are grouped at 423 Grove, Burnaby (near East Hastings and Kensington), including one of our personal favourites, a great discount kid's store called *Toys Plus More.* There's also a big *Safeway* and a *Shoppers Drug Mart. Reach it by transit by taking the #10 or #14 bus from Granville Mall and transferring to the #135 bus.* Hours are Monday to Wednesday and Saturday 9:30 to 5:30; and Thursday and Friday 9:30 to 9.

Kids Only Market:
(689-8447)
As the name implies, everything at 1496 Cartwright, Granville Island is geared to kids. Among those stores represented are *The Everything Wet Store, The Games People* and *Kaboodles.* Down the block at 1508 Anderson are *Over the Rainbow Drop-in Programs* (683-2624). Market hours are Monday to Thursday 10 to 6; Friday and Saturday 10 to 9; and Sunday noon to 6.

Kingsgate Shopping Centre:
(879-0144)
This Mt. Pleasant neighbourhood shopping mall is anchored by an *IGA* upstairs and a *Shoppers Drug Mart* in the main promenade. Parking outside or under cover is usually easy. Highlights include *Aqua Terra Pets,* which is worth knowing about because it's one of the few lower mainland pet shops where bird, fish and reptile owners can purchase live crickets for their pets on a Sunday. There's also a fairly well-stocked liquor branch and *Workwear World,* all at 370 East Broadway at Main. *By public transit, the #9 Broadway bus stops right at the mall.* Mall hours vary — generally they are Monday to Wednesday and Saturday 9:30 to 6; Thursday and Friday 9:30 to 9; and some stores are open Sunday 11 to 5.

The Landing:
(687-1144)
The posh shops at this revitalized heritage building at 375 Water Street mark the Gateway to historic Gastown. Vancouver's most "current" restaurant, *Cheyna* (688-4800) opened there recently. Among the special stores are the pricey but luxurious *Van Unen & Co., Polo Ralph Lauren* (ditto), the gourmet foods and tabletop fashions of *Lightheart & Company* and the whimsical children's fashions of *Miki House.* There's also an outlet for candy shop extraordinaire *Tout Sweet* and our favourite spot for burgers and chili, *Sodas Diner.* Shops are

open Monday to Saturday 10 to 6; and Sunday noon to 5. *To get there, follow directions for Gastown —just a short stroll from the Vancouver Visitors and Convention Bureau.*

Lansdowne Park Shopping Centre:
(270-1344)
Another of our favourites, the appeal here is free parking and spacious, uncrowded and trendy shops. Among the anchor stores are *Woodward's, Eatons, Woodwynn, Birks and Fairweather's.* We also like *the House of Knives, Knights of Bath* (bath boutique), *Ming Wo* (great kitchenware and gadgets), *Simply Sox & Lingerie,* and the new *Winning Spirit* outlet of the Vancouver Canucks for sports clothing from all kinds of teams and expert advice from the peripatetic "Card Doctor". Hours are Monday, Tuesday and Saturday 9:30 to 5:30; Wednesday to Friday 9:30 to 9; and Sunday noon to 5. *To get there by transit take the #403 or #406 bus on Howe St.*

Lonsdale Quay Market:
(985-6261)
The SeaBus takes you right to the door, or cross the Lion's Gate Bridge and head toward Lonsdale (east) and south to Esplanade. The actual address is 123 Carrie Cates Court, North Van. You'll find lot of parking in a lot out front. Inside, there's a ballroom upstairs in the mall, plus a whole little area concentrated with children's stores. Aside from those attractions, there are shops like *Au Chocolat, FACES* (a discount non-branded, but excellent cosmetics line you can't buy anywhere else), *Nautical But Nice, Miriam's Ice Cream, the North Shore Wine Cellar, Beadworks, Duso's* (the last two similar to their outlets at Granville Island) and *The Sock Exchange.* Mall hours are Monday to Thursday and weekends 9:30 to 6:30; and Friday 9:30 to 9.

Lougheed Mall:
(421-3434)
Newly updated, this mall stands at 9855 Austin in Burnaby and is anchored by *The Bay* and *Woolco.* Over 185 shops and services include the wonderful *Kim-John Gifts & China, W.H. Smith books, the Bombay Company,* and *Coles books. To get there by transit, take the SkyTrain to Columbia Station and transfer to the #147 ot #148 bus.* Open Monday and Tuesday 10 to 6; Wednesday to Friday 10 to 9; Saturday 9:30 to 5:30; and Sunday noon to 5.

Lynn Valley Centre:
(980-9354)
This neighbourhood mall at 1199 Lynn Valley Road, North Van, is anchored by *Stong's, Zellers* and *Shoppers Drug Mart.* There is also a *Workwear World, Creative Kidstuff Toys, Kidz Biz, Lynn Valley Knit*

& Stitch Shop, and a favourite bookstore, *Reader's Retreat. By public transit take the SeaBus to Lonsdale Quay and transfer to the #229 bus which goes right to Lynn Valley.* Mall hours: Monday to Wednesday and Saturday 10 to 6; Thursday and Friday 10 to 9; and Sunday noon to 5.

Metrotown Centre:
(438-2444)
Over 180 shops and services are located at Metrotown Centre, including anchors *Woodward's, The Bay,* and *Sears.* One of our favourite locations of *Book Warehouse* is here, too, along with the Canucks' retail operation (though they sell sports togs from many more than just *our* hockey team), *Winning Spirit.* This mall houses the only remaining lower mainland location of *Bennie's Shoes* (437-8896), a place which carries footwear for the hard to fit — especially teeny-tiny sizes. *Metrotown is right on the SkyTrain line* at 4800 Kingsway, Burnaby, open Monday, Tuesday and Saturday 9:30 to 5:30; Wednesday to Friday 9:30 to 9; and Sunday noon to 5.

Oakridge Shopping Centre:
(261-2511)
Probably the most upmarket and popular lower mainland mall is smack dab in the middle of the affluent westside at 650 West 41st Avenue, between Oak and Cambie. *Woodward's* dominates, with its own multi-facted department store, a fine *Woodward's Book Store,* and yet another separate crafts store.

Oakridge is also the home of Canada's first location of *Abercrombie & Fitch* plus *Crabtree & Evelyn, Tout Sweet, Perks* (executive playthings and elegant travel accessories), *RSVP* (unique stationery and novelties), *Marks & Sparks* (we mean Spencer, of course), *Purdy's, Roots, The Sox Clinic, Ports International, Wear Else* (a wonderfully-hip store for working women), *Ingledew's, Esprit at the Next Exit, La Vie En Rose* (naughty but extravagant lingerie), *Bowring's* (high end gifts), *Birks* (a particularly nice version of this respected jewellery chain), and *Great Pretenders* (charming fake jewels).

Oakridge has masses of free indoor and outdoor parking, a children's play area, a swanky *Safeway* (with easy access from parking) and a number of fine first-run cinemas. *To get there by public transit take the #15 bus south on Burrard.* Open Monday, Tuesday and Saturday 9:30 to 5:30; Wednesday to Friday 9:30 to 9; and Sunday noon to 5. Safeway, however, keeps its "normal" hours of 8 to midnight, seven days.

Pacific Centre:
(688-7236)
Anchors at this splendid downtown mall at 700 West Georgia Street

are *Eatons*, and the very posh *Holt Renfrew*. Among the 200 stores and services in the cool underground corridors of the centre are *Galloway's Specialty Foods, The Sock Drawer, Ports International, Pennington's* (large sizes for women), *Shoppers Drug Mart. Baskin-Robbins* and the world-famous *Eddie Bauer Outdoor Outfitters. Most downtown public transit runs right by the doors of Pacific Centre (the SkyTrain stop is Granville Station), since it's located at the major crossroads of Georgia and Granville Streets — the heart of Vancouver, and you might prefer to arrive by bus* since underground parking is rather expensive. Hours are Monday to Wednesday 9:30 to 6; Thursday and Friday 9:30 to 9; Saturday 9:30 to 5:30; and Sunday noon to 5.

<u>Park Royal Shopping Centre:</u>
(922-3211)
This toney shopping centre is on both the north and south sides of Marine Drive in West Van, just west of Taylor Way. Anchors are *Eatons, Woodward's* and *The Bay*. Other discoveries include the *Book Company* (an upmarket branch of Coles with a great specialty book-ordering service), *Gulliver's The Travel Accessory Store* (one of our favourites), *Bowrings, Birks, The Bombay Company, W.H. Smith books, Shoppers Drug Mart* and the wonderfully-fragrant *Murchies Tea & Coffee* (ship to your friends worldwide).

You can reach Park Royal by crossing the Lion's Gate Bridge from Vancouver and heading into West Van (careful: it's a quick right turn after Taylor Way), or by taking TransCanada 1 across the Second Narrows Bridge and continuing on the highway until the Taylor Way exit. By public transit you take the #250 ot #257 bus on Georgia St. Open Monday to Wednesday 10 to 6; Thursday and Friday 10 to 9; Saturday 9:30 to 5:30; and Sunday noon to 5. Please note that Woodward's closes at 5:30 Monday to Wednesday.

<u>Park & Tilford Centre:</u>
(984-8200)
This cosy mall at 333 Brooksbank North Van features cinemas, *Save-on Foods, Save-on Framing & Art, Save-on Cuts, Woodwynn* and *Oscarsson's Bakery. To get there by transit, take the SeaBus to Lonsdale Quay and transfer to the #239 bus.* Hours: Monday to Wednesday and Saturday 10 to 6; Thursday and Friday 10 to 9; and Sunday 11 to 5.

<u>Richmond Centre:</u>
(273-4828)
Among the delights in the newly-renovated glass and marble wonder are locations of *The Gap, Goodies for your Bath & Kitchen, Gullivers The Travel Accessory Shop, Laura Secord, Murchie's Tea & Coffee, People's Jewellers, Shoppers Drug Mart, W.H. Smith, Zellers* and

Sears. There are also movie theatres and over 230 shops and services, all at 6551 No. 3 Road. *By public transit, take the #401, #403 or #406 on Howe St.* Open Monday and Tuesday 10 to 6; Wednesday to Friday 10 to 9; Saturday 9:30 to 5:30; and Sunday noon to 5.

Robson Street:

(Robson Street Business Assn. 669-0181)

Maybe we should have given the colourful and touristy area localled dubbed "Robsonstrasse" its own section, but this year we've noticed so many places dropping in and out of the high rents that we decided instead to include it here. It's kind of a mall anyway, isn't it?

To get there by transit, take the #3 bus on Robson or south on Granville Mall.

Among the treats are: *The Underground* (ask any 14 year old where the best place to shop is) at 710 Robson (681-8732); *Duthie Books* main branch at 919 Robson (684-4496). *Bread Garden; Margareta* (fabulous women's fashions) at 948 Robson (681-6612); *Cotton Ginny* at 990 Robson (685-5759); *La Vie En Rose* (luxurious lingerie) at 1001 Robson (684-6612); *Rocky Mountain Chocolate Factory* at 1017 Robson (688-4100).

Courreges is at 1025 Robson (681-1671); *Kettle Creek Canvas Company* is at 1046 Robson (669-4306); and we love the clutter and wonderful gifties at *Chatchkas* at 1070 Robson (688-6417).

You won't want to miss *Angel Handpainted Fashions* at 1082 Robson (681-0947); *Galloways Specialty Foods* (the only place we know you can get Mexican vanilla extract) at 1084 Robson (685-7927); *Manhattan Books* at 1089 Robson (681-9074); *Brussels Chocolates* (frequently voted the region's best) at 1092 Robson (681-5971); *Olympia Oyster & Fish Company* at 1094 Robson (685-0716); and what Anne's daughter refers to as "The 3-D *House of Clogs*" at 1102 Robson (685-8710).

Hansen Art Supplies is a bit of time-travel at 1130 Robson (684-4015); *Pegabo Shoes* at 1137 Robson (688-7877) is unique; and don't overlook the *Alfred Sung Boutique* at 1143 Robson (687- 2153).

The Book Warehouse has a branch at 1150 Robson (685-5711) and *Dr. Martens* (for "the original", trendy Dr. Martens shoes and boots) is usually our last stop at 1208 Robson (689-4998).

Royal Centre Mall:

(689-1711)

Among the 55 shops and services at 1055 West Georgia are the *Royal*

Bank Foreign Exchange, Cineplex theatres, Victoria Chinese Restaurant, Giorgio's Men's Wear, Les Bijoux and *Purdy's Chocolates. Reach it by transit from the Burrard SkyTrain station.* Open Monday to Thursday 9:30 to 5:30; Friday 9:30 to 7; Saturday 9 to 5; and closed Sunday.

Royal Square Mall:
(526-1516)
This neighbourhood mall in New West is at 800 McBride and includes a *Peoples Drug Mart* and *Triangle Toys, Games & Hobbies. By transit, take the SkyTrain to Columbia station and transfer to the #102 or #108 bus.* Hours are Monday to Thursday and Saturday 9:30 to 6; and Friday 9:30 to 7.

Scottsdale Mall: (596-4811) This one has 55 varied stores right on the Surrey-Delta border at 7031 120th St. at 72nd Ave. This mall includes *Black Bond Books, Zellers, Just Kid'n Children's Wear* and *Suzanne's.* A number of Scottsdale stores are described in our Surrey-Delta tour. *To get there by public transit, follow the SkyTrain to its end at Scott Road Station, then transfer to bus #391 which goes directly to the mall.* Hours of operation are Monday, Tuesday and Saturday 9:30 to 5; Wednesday to Friday 9:30 to 9:30; and Sunday noon to 5.

Seven Oaks:
(853-7153)
The main anchor here is *Woodward's*. Location is 32900 South Fraser Way, Abbotsford. Abbotsford is near the Sumas border crossing. Mall hours are Monday to Wednesday and Saturday 9:30 to 5:30; Thursday and Friday 9:30 to 9; and Sunday noon to 5.

Sinclair Centre:
(666-4483)
Four heritage buildings linked by glass atriums over complex passageways and entryways make it easy to get lost in here, but you won't mind a bit! The main anchor is an opulent store, whose name has become synonymous with "luxury" in Vancouver: *Leone.* Yes, prices are very dear, but their sales are sensational. Other delights include *Miriam's Ice Cream* and *Gullivers The Travel Accessory Store.* Sinclair Centre is at 757 Hastings (at Howe) and *within easy walking distance from any of the major downtown hotels and the Vancouver Visitors and Convention Bureau.* Hours of operation are quite simply Monday to Saturday 10 to 5:30; closed Sunday.

Station Square, Metrotown:
(433-8438)
Fifty shops and services and 12 theatres are found here, at 6200 McKay

Ave., Burnaby. There's also *Egghead Software, Starbucks, Consumers Distributing, Save-on Foods, the Future Shop,* and a favourite of ours: *Discount Shoes & Boots. The SkyTrain runs right there (Metrotown Station, of course).* Hours are Monday to Wednesday and Saturday 10 to 6; Thursday and Friday 10 to 9; and Sunday noon to 5.

Surrey Place Shopping Centre:
(588-6431)
Main anchors are *The Bay, Zellers* and *Fairweather,* and there are also outlets for *Shoppers Drug Mart, Stitches* and *I'm Impressed* (a great source of unique rubber stamps). The mall is located at 102nd Ave. & King George Hwy; open Monday, Tuesday and Saturday 9:30 to 5:30; Wednesday to Friday 9:30 to 9; and Sunday noon to 5. *By transit, take The SkyTrain to Scott Road station and transfer to the #320 or #321 bus.*

Trenant Park Square Shopping Centre:
This recent addition to the lower mainland malls is at 5200 Ladner Trunk Road, Ladner, and includes *Bi-Way, Woodwynn* and *Workwear World* branches. Open Monday to Wednesday 9 to 6; Thursday and Friday 9 to 8; and Saturday 9:30 to 5:30. *By transit, take the #601 bus south on Howe St.*

Vancouver Centre:
(684-7537)
Twenty unique shops and upmarket boutiques are located in this branch of Pacific Centre at 650 West Georgia. Hours are Monday to Wednesday 9:30 to 6; Thursday and Friday 9:30 to 9; Saturday 9:30 to 5:30; and Sunday noon to 5. *Closest transit route is the SkyTrain Granville station.*

Westminster Mall:
(525-8866)
Highlights at this mall at 555 6th St., New West, include a *Shoppers Drug Mart, Fields, Fancy Brass & Gifts, Black Bond Books, Royal City Bingo* and the bargain-priced *New West Cinema III* where all seats for current movies are $1.50! *To reach the mall by transit, take the SkyTrain to Columbia Station and transfer to Bus #108 or 106 (catch the latter on Agnes St.).* Hours are Monday to Wednesday and Saturday 9:30 to 5:30; Thursday and Friday 9:30 to 9; and Sunday noon to 5.

Westminster Quay Public Market:
(520-3881)
Specialty shops and produce-mongers combine at 180 Quayside, New West, including shops such as *Cody books, Kidsland, Nancy's Pots & Pans, Farm Cottage Bakery,* and *Joan's Gems & Minerals.* There are a couple of fine dining spots, including *Fins Waterfront Restaurant.*

Take the SkyTrain to Columbia Station, right to its door. Open Saturday to Thursday 9:30 to 6:30; and Friday 9:30 to 8.

Westwood Mall:
(464-5215)
This enclosed shopping centre with discount fashions as well as traditional stores is near Coquitlam Town Centre at 3000 Lougheed Hwy., Coquitlam. Stores include *K-Mart, The Brick, Cody Books, The Local Craft Nook* (that's its name, folks!), and *Shoe Warehouse. To reach it by transit from downtown Vancouver, take the #160 bus on Burrard St.* Hours of operation are Monday and Tuesday 10 to 6 (a few stores are open till 9:30); Wednesday to Friday 10 to 9:30; Saturday 10 to 6:30; and Sunday 11 to 5..

White Rock Semiahmoo Centre:
(531-4543)
This nice mall at 1701 152nd St. in White Rock is anchored by *K-Mart* and *Overwaitea.* Hours are Monday, Tuesday and Saturday 9:30 to 5; Wednesday to Friday 9:30 to 9; and Sunday noon to 5. *By public transit, either take the SkyTrain to 22nd St. station and transfer to the #353 bus, or just take the #351 bus south on Howe St.*

Willowbrook Shopping Centre:
(530-2115)
Just expanded to include a location of *The Bay,* this mall also includes a *Woodwynn, Shoppers Drug Mart, The Sony Store* and *K-Mart.* There's also a location of *Toys'R'Us,* a rarity in this area, plus other points of interest like *Willowbrook Bakery, Just Petites, Bata Shoes* and *Toys & Wheels.* Find it at 19705 Fraser Hwy. in Langley *(better drive there).* Open Monday to Tuesday and Saturday 9:30 to 6; Wednesday to Friday 9:30 to 9; and Sunday 11 to 5.

Windsor Square Shopping Centre:
(531-3112)
This is the best of "South Surrey", what we would normally call "White Rock". There's a *Technokids* (science-oriented toys and kits), a *Mary Rose* (a great clothing outlet for women — the only one of its kind in B.C.), the very upscale *Margareta, Boutique Elegante Shoes,* and more, all at 1959 152nd St., Surrey. *It's a heck of a long transit ride to the area, so this one may be better to drive.* Hours vary, but on average, mall shops are open Monday to Thursday and Saturday 10 to 5:30; and Friday 10 to 8.

For more details on Farmers' Markets, please see our section on Fruit and Fruit Stands, page 201.

Maps

Categories Index

Anne Garber is Vancouver's foremost bargain sleuth, and author of The Vancouver Super Shopper (discounts), Shopping the World (global mail order), and Cheap Eats (Vancouver's diners, cafes, cafeterias - in short, cheap eats). Garber's expertise spans writing, film, art, marketing, broadcasting and advertising, but she is probably best known for her unflagging research. Currently, she works in radio and television and writes three different columns for The Province, and periodic columns for B.C. Home Digest, TV Week and Equity magazine. She has two children.

Lorraine Gannon is a professional teacher-librarian who is herself the mother of two. Gannon regularly teaches consumer education classes and lectures on bargain shopping. She has run the innovative "Deals on Wheels" shopping tours and knows the lower mainland like the back of her hand!

Serious Publishing grew out of the Garber-Gannon kitchen-table collaboration on The Vancouver Super Shopper into an earlier publishing venture, namely Cheap Eats. The Serious Shopper's Guide is their second project.

Copies of either **Cheap Eats** or **The Serious Shopper's Guide to Vancouver and Beyond** are available direct from the publisher at a cost of $12, which includes tax, postage and handling. Please specify which book (and how many of each) you wish to order and enclose your cheque or money order (U.S. residents should remit $12 in U.S. currency) ***payable to Serious Publishing, Vancouver.*** Mail your request, together with the appropriate remittance to: Serious Publishing, 7249 Waverley Ave. Burnaby, B.C. V5J 4A7. Please do not send cash through the mail.

Please be sure to enclose your complete address, including postal or zip code and print your name to avoid lost books. If you wish to correspond with us by facsimile, our fax number is (604) 875-0007.